Teaching Listening
in the Elementary School:
Readings

compiled by
SAM DUKER

The Scarecrow Press, Inc.
Metuchen, N.J.   1971

Copyright 1971 by Sam Duker

ISBN 0-8108-0428-X

Library of Congress Catalog Card Number 75-168604

Other Scarecrow books by Sam Duker:

Listening: Readings. 1966.
Individualized Reading: An Annotated Bibliography. 1968.
Individualized Reading: Readings. 1969.
Listening: Bibliography. 2d ed. 1968.
Listening: Readings, Vol. 2. 1971.

To

my beloved sister

Katie Leilani

with much aloha

Table of Contents

vi

vii

Preface and Acknowledgments

A book of this kind is made possible only through the
generosity of the authors of the items that are included. In
a sense, the formal acknowledgments which follow serve as
an expression of appreciation but in reality additional mention
must be made of my gratitude for the spirit in which the
permissions were so readily and willingly given. Hopefully,
these authors will find their ideas properly placed in per-
spective both in terms of the selection of excerpts used and
of the placement of the articles in the general scheme of this
book.

In addition to the authors of articles included here, it
is fitting to mention those whose pioneer work in listening
made possible my own research in this field and consequently the selection and arrangement of the material in this book.
Preeminent in the development of listening as a recognized
discipline is Ralph G. Nichols of the University of Minnesota
whose constant and unfailing encouragement and help is grate-
fully acknowledged. Many of the major figures in the development of listening as part of the elementary school curriculum
have permitted me to include materials they have written in
this book of readings. Among these are Althea Beery, long
time Director of Curriculum for the Cincinnati, Ohio schools;
Donald D. Durrell of Boston University; and Margaret J.
Early of Syracuse University. Others to whom I am particularly indebted for ideas on the listening process are
Margaret B. Parke of Brooklyn College who first called my
attention to the parallels between reading and listening; the
late Donald E. Bird of Stephens College; James I. Brown
who pioneered in the testing of listening; and Charles R.
Petrie, Chairman of the Speech Department of New York
State University Center at Buffalo, whose scholarly skepticism tends to make all of us more discriminating in our acceptance of research findings.

The wide reading of the literature in a field which
must necessarily precede the selection of material for a
book such as this one is made possible only through the cooperation of many librarians. My first work on listening

11

was done at Iowa State Teachers College (now University of Northern Iowa) Library at Cedar Falls. Later on I used the extensive resources of the library at Teachers College, Columbia University. My greatest debt is, of course, to the Brooklyn College Library and to its Head Librarian, Humphrey G. Bousfield, and to his very capable and co-operative staff.

Finally, before listing formal acknowledgments for the material appearing in this book, thanks are expressed to the authors of material not included, for the guidance furnished, the information absorbed, and the lessons taught me by the material they wrote.

Excerpts from the article, "Developing Listening Ability in Children," by Walter B. Barbe and Robert M. Myers which appeared in the February 1954 issue of Elementary English are used with the kind permission of the senior author and of the National Council of Teachers of English, publishers of Elementary English.

The excerpts from two articles, "Listening Activities in the Elementary School" and "Experiences in Listening," which appeared in the February 1946 issue of Elementary English Review and the March 1951 issue of Elementary English respectively, are used with the kind permission of the author, Althea Beery, and of the National Council of Teachers of English, publishers of Elementary English Review and of Elementary English.

Dr. Mary Butler Brassard of Tufts University generously permitted the use of several lengthy excerpts from her 1968 Boston University doctoral thesis, Listening and Reading Comprehension in the Intermediate Grades.

Permission was kindly given by Dr. Kenneth L. Brown for the use of the substantial excerpts from his doctoral thesis, An Analysis of the Speech and Listening Content of Selected Pupil Textbooks in the Language Arts for the Elementary Schools, Grades Three through Six, which he completed at Northwestern University in 1965.

Excerpts of the article, "Learn to Listen," from the March, 1955 issue of Grade Teacher magazine, are used with the kind permission of the senior author, Professor Cedric L. Crink, and of the publisher. This article is copyrighted © 1955 by CCM Professional Magazines, Inc.

Professor George Robert Canfield of New York State University College at Oswego graciously granted permission for the use of excerpts from his article, "Approaches to Listening Improvement," which appeared in 1958 in Elementary English. Permission was also given by the National Council of Teachers of English, publishers of Elementary English. In addition Professor Canfield also was so kind as to grant permission to use an excerpt from his 1960 Syracuse University doctoral dissertation entitled A Study of the Effects of Two Types of Instruction on the Listening Comprehension of Fifth Grade Children.

The material from "Channel L-i-s-t-e-n" is reprinted from the September 1961 issue of Education. Copyright 1961 by The Bobbs-Merrill Company, Inc, Indianapolis; used with the kind permission of the author, Mildred Berwick Cashman, and the Bobbs-Merrill Company.

My article, "The Teacher of Elementary Science and Listening," which appeared in the October 1958 issue of Science Education, is used with the kind permission of that journal.

My May 1955 Instructor article, "How Listening Can Be Taught," is used with the permission of the publisher of the Instructor.

Professor Donald D. Durrell of Boston University kindly consented to the use of excerpts of his article, "Listening Comprehension Versus Reading Comprehension," which appeared in the Journal of Reading in March 1969. Permission was also given by the International Reading Association, publisher of that journal.

Permission was given by Professor Margaret J. Early of Syracuse University and by the Syracuse University Press to use "Developing Listening Skills" which originally appeared in Frontiers of Elementary Education in 1958.

The short passage from Dr. Eldonna L. Evertts' 1961 Indiana University doctoral dissertation, An Investigation of the Structure of Children's Oral Language Compared with Silent Reading, Oral Reading, and Listening Comprehension is used with the kind permission of the author.

Dr. Vern L. Farrow graciously granted permission for the use of an excerpt from An Experimental Study of Listen-

13

ing Attention at the Fourth, Fifth and Sixth Grade which he wrote as a doctoral thesis at the University of Oregon in 1964.

The passage from the 1963 University of Pittsburgh doctoral dissertation, The Effect of Training in Listening Skill upon the Listening Skills of Intermediate Grade Children, is used with the kind permission of the author, Dr. Annabel E. Fawcett Bower.

Professor Edna Lue Furness kindly permitted the use of a portion of her article, "Proportion, Purpose and Process in Listening," which appeared in the July 1958 issue of Educational Administration and Supervision.

Excerpts from The Teaching of Listening Skills Through Music Lessons in Fourth and Fifth Grade Classrooms by Justyn L. Graham is used with the kind permission of the author who wrote this as his doctoral thesis at Colorado State College in 1966.

Permission was kindly granted by Dr. Richard S. Hampleman to use excerpts from his 1955 Indiana University doctoral thesis, Comparison of Listening and Reading Comprehension Ability of Fourth and Sixth Grade Pupils.

Excerpts from Dr. Jewell H. T. Hancock's 1960 University of Colorado dissertation, The Effect of Listening and Discussion of Social Values Held by Sixth-Grade Children, are used with the kind permission of the author.

John C. Harvey kindly gave permission for the use of excerpts from his 1961 Sacramento State College master's thesis, Study of the Durrell-Sullivan Reading Capacity Test as a Measure of Intelligence.

Professor Paul M. Hollingsworth granted permission for the use of a major portion of his article, "So They Listened: The Effects of a Listening Program," which first appeared in the March 1965 Journal of Communication.

Excerpts from An Investigation of the Relationship Between Listening and Selected Variables in Grades Four, Five, and Six, a 1966 Arizona State University doctoral thesis, are used with the kind permission of Dr. Ann Elizabeth Jackson.

Dr. Marie-Jeanne Laurent gave her permission to use

14

substantial excerpts from her doctoral dissertation, The
Construction and Evaluation of a Listening Curriculum for
Grades 5 and 6, which she completed at Boston University in
1963.

Portions of an article, "Age Trends in Selective
Listening" by Eleanor E. Maccoby and Karl W. Conrad,
which originally appeared in the May 1966 issue of the
Journal of Experimental Child Psychology are included in this
book through the kind permission of the senior author and of
the Academic Press, Inc., publisher of that journal.

Miss Doris Niles gave her kind permission to use
portions of her article, "Teaching Listening in the Fundamentals Course." Permission was also granted by the
Speech Association of America, publisher of Speech Teacher
in which this article first appeared in November 1957.

Professor Charles. F. Reasoner graciously permitted
the use of a very long passage from his 1961 Teachers College, Columbia University, doctoral dissertation, The Development of a Series of Television Scripts Dealing with the
Language Arts Practices in Elementary School Classrooms.

Dr. Quentin Stodola, the senior author, kindly gave
permission for the use of excerpts from a 1962 Office of
Education Research Report entitled, Administering a Listening Comprehension Test Through Use of Teacher-Readers,
Sound Film, and Tape Recorders, which he and his co-
authors, Donald F. Schwartz and Ralph H. Kelstoe, wrote
at North Dakota State University in 1962.

Substantial excerpts from an article by Dr. Edwin E.
Vineyard and Robert B. Bailey, "Interrelationships of Reading
Ability, Listening Skill, Intelligence, and Scholastic Achievement" are used with the permission of the senior author and
of the International Reading Association, publisher of the
Journal of Developmental Reading in which this article first
appeared in 1960.

With the kind permission of Professor Richard Wynn
and the New York State Teachers Association, publishers of
New York State Education, substantial portions of an article
which appeared in that journal in February 1954, copyright
1954 by the New York State Teachers Association, are used
in this book.

Excerpts from the Beloit, Wisconsin Public Schools'

15

curricular publication, Bulletin No. 157, Language Arts, English Encountered, Elementary Program are used with the kind permission of Joseph W. Rhodes, Assistant Superintendent of Schools.

Assistant Superintendent-Curriculum Development, Herman F. Benthul graciously consented to the use of material from the Dallas, Texas, Independent School District's bulletin, Speech Arts Activities, A Curriculum Guide for Elementary Schools, 1964.

Excerpts from curriculum bulletin Number 354.1 of the Fort Worth, Texas, Public Schools, English, Communication Skills, Grade 10 are used through the kind permission of Dr. Dewey W. Mays, Jr. Assistant Director of Curriculum.

Permission was granted for the use of an excerpt from the Long Beach, California, Unified School District's publication, Handbook in English for Senior High School Students, 1969, by Mrs. Bessie R. Hoge, Editorial Assistant, Curriculum and Instruction.

Use is made of excerpts from a Los Angeles City Unified School District's curricular publication No. X-60, 1967, English for Low-Index Classes in Junior High Schools. A Course of Study, through the kind permission of Mildred Naslund, Associate Superintendent, Division of Instructional Planning and Services.

Material from Bulletin No. 32, 1967 of the Meridan, Mississippi Public Schools, English, Revised Curriculum Guide, Grades 7-12 is used with the kind permission of that school system.

Montgomery County, Maryland Public Schools through Katherine B. Greaney, Supervisor of English Language Arts, kindly permitted the use of material from And All This Is Reading. English Language Arts Primary Reading Handbook. Bulletin No. 203, Rockville, Maryland, 1967.

W.W. Lyon, Director of Instruction of the Muncie, Indiana Community Schools graciously gave permission for the inclusion in this book of readings of excerpts from that school system's publication, Language Arts: Listening and Reading, Spelling, Writing, Language Study, Literature.

An excerpt from the Nederland, Texas Independent

16

School District's publication, An Approach to Individualization of Instruction in Elementary Language Arts is used with the kind permission of Mrs. Karen Sue Allen, Coordinator of Curriculum.

Material from Handbook for Language Arts, Pre-K, Kindergarten, Grades One and Two, Bulletin No. 8, 1965-66 Series is used by permission of the Board of Education of the City of New York through the kind cooperation of Dr. David A. Abramson, Acting Director of the Bureau of Curriculum Development.

Mr. Donald Baago, Curriculum Director of the Richfield, Minnesota Public Schools kindly permitted the use in this book of excerpts from Guide for a Summer School Remedial Program in Language Arts.

Excerpts from three curricular publications of the San Diego, California City Schools, Language and Spelling, Grade 6 and Combination Room 5-6, 1968; Language and Spelling, Grade Three, 1968 are used with the kind permission of Dwight Lee, Supervisor of Curriculum Production.

Assistant Superintendent B. Watson of the San Jose, California Unified School District kindly granted permission to use material from Guide to Language Arts Experiences, Kindergarten Through the Sixth Grade: Curriculum Monograph, No. 26.

Excerpts from a curricular publication of the Valley Stream, New York Union Free School District, No. 24 entitled English Curriculum Guide, Kindergarten Through Grade 3, 1968 are used with the kind permission of Selma Stahl, Curriculum Coordinator.

Chapter I

INTRODUCTION

It is doubtful that there is a single elementary school teacher in existence who has not at one time or another expressed the wish that pupils would listen better. At this point similarity ceases. What teachers do to convert this wish into fact varies widely, for there are a number of choices. One choice frequently exercised is to do nothing-- which as any experienced teacher knows will not be effective. Another choice, which is perhaps the one most frequently opted for, is to tell the class to "sit up straight," "pay attention," and "listen." This is quite often reinforced by a chart on one of the class bulletin boards headed: "How to Listen." The most common items found listed on such charts are admonitions to "pay attention" and to "sit up straight." A common companion to these two admonitions is a direction to "clear" the pupil's desk.

While there may well be certain definite advantages inherent in good posture and in the habit of clearing one's workspace, it is extremely unlikely that either of these activities tends to improve the quality of listening on the part of elementary school pupils at any level. The request or command to "pay attention" is most often equally futile because while attention or concentration is an important factor in good listening, this demand is seldom accompanied by any help or even suggestions concerning ways in which attention is most effectively paid or given. There is of course another alternative that can be used by the teacher and that is to deliberately and systematically teach the skills of good listening. It is the hopeful purpose of this book to make it possible for an increasing number of elementary school teachers to select this alternative. The fact is that while there has been a considerable degree of improvement in this regard, many if not most elementary school teachers are still rather ineffective teachers of the skills of effective listening.

Until two decades or so ago the situation just described was quite understandable. Listening as a "subject" or "skill"

19

that should be taught was regarded with a considerable degree
of suspicion. In fact, those who advocated the teaching of
listening were regarded as being somewhat on the zany side
or else as ambitious empire builders. It is somewhat sur-
prising that such was the situation as late as 1950 because
Dr. Paul Rankin, now retired as Chief Deputy Superintendent of Schools of Detroit, had begun the scientific investigation of listening in a University of Michigan doctoral thesis
in 1926. Rankin's work is most often quoted or rather mis-
quoted in connection with a very minor point in his thesis
concerning the amount or proportion of time spent daily in
listening activities by the average person. His estimates
were based on the observations of a very small sample for
a short period of time. Strangely and, under the circum-
stances coincidentally, his estimate was a very good one and
has been verified by several research studies since that
time.

In 1948 Ralph G. Nichols, now Head of the Department of Rhetoric on the St. Paul campus of the University
of Minnesota, completed his doctorate at the University of
Iowa. The growing recognition of the importance of teaching listening and of the necessity of teaching the skills involved, stem largely from Nichols' far ranging and pene-
trating doctoral thesis, "Factors Accounting for Differences
in Comprehension of Materials Presented Orally in the
Classroom." In his investigation of good and poor listeners
among a group of college freshmen, Nichols isolated certain
good, as well as certain bad, listening habits. His findings
were greeted with great interest and resulted in a very
rapid growth in the recognition of listening as a teachable
skill. Some measure of this growth is given by the fact
that Professor Harold A. Anderson's 1949 bibliography on
listening contained about thirty items, while the 1968 second
edition of my published bibliography on listening contains
1332 items. Since the publication of the latter book at
least 250 new items on listening have appeared.

Much of the earlier research and writing on listening
was concerned with the teaching of this skill at the college
level and with the importance of effective listening in business and industrial milieus. Most of those interested were
concerned in one way or another with the field of speech.
By and large those engaged in education were not as quick
to investigate the listening area. In 1949 Professor Miriam
Wilt, now of Temple University, made the first major investigation of listening at the elementary school level in her

Pennsylvania State College thesis. She discovered that the
amount of listening called for in the average elementary
school classroom was far greater than was estimated by
the teachers in these classrooms. Incidentally she also reported that most of the listening was by the children to the
teacher and very little by the teacher to the children. The
quality of the extensive amount of listening demanded in these
classrooms was not the subject of Dr. Wilt's study but it
has to be apparent that the amount of listening demanded of
these young children was far in excess of the amount that
could realistically be expected to be efficient or effective.

Wilt's thesis was followed by a dramatic increase of
material on listening in journals that ordinarily reach classroom teachers, such as Elementary English, Grade Teacher,
and the Instructor. Curriculum bulletins, which had seldom
mentioned listening in the 1940's, for a period of time
stressed the importance of listening but failed to go beyond
this admonition. Gradually the amount of thought being
given to ways of improving listening was reflected in substantial allotments of space in many curriculum bulletins,
most textbooks on methods of teaching the language arts, as
well as in books on methods of teaching reading and speech.
A constantly increasing amount of space concerning the
importance of listening and ways in which its effectiveness
may be increased is also given in books used as textbooks
by elementary school children. One of the articles in this
book reports the 1965 findings of Dr. Kenneth L. Brown
concerning the proportion of space given to listening in elementary school language arts textbooks for the intermediate
grades. It can be seen from the material presented there
that listening still had not reached a status comparable to
that of reading, writing, or even speech. A definite trend
is, however, ascertainable. This book, for example, is
the first that is exclusively concerned with the teaching of
listening at the elementary school level.

By this time a considerable body of research findings
concerning the teaching of listening in the elementary school
has come into being. The unfortunate fact, however, is that
this research has been almost completely uncoordinated.
The result has been an undue amount of duplication rather
than replication. An outstanding exception to this has been
the work done under the direction of Professor Donald D.
Durrell of Boston University. Here we find a discernible
continuity which is reflected in the material presented in
Chapter XI of this book. Substantial contributions to the

area of the testing of listening has resulted from this coordinated approach. Other tests, such as the listening
tests in the Sequential Tests of Educational Progress (STEP)
and the Cooperative Primary Tests - Listening, have been
developed by the Educational Testing Service of Princeton,
N.J., but not in the same developmental manner that the
Durrell tests were prepared.

As David H. Russell pointed out in one of his last
articles shortly before his untimely death, there is a wealth
of material on various phases of listening, specifically in
the matter of testing, that could be retrieved from unpublished theses. Regrettably and also somewhat surprisingly,
this plea for the retrieval and use of this material has not
been heeded although some seven years have gone by since
the suggestion was made.

The increased use of audio materials in the classroom together with the growing amount of literature on
listening has quite naturally led to a greater emphasis on
the teaching of listening skills in the elementary classroom.
In 1965 Van Wingerden made a survey of the practices of
teachers in regard to time they spent teaching listening in
the intermediate grades in four Washington counties including the county Seattle is in. His findings are astounding
and, to some readers, almost unbelievable. The study is
nevertheless very important as it shows that, even if the
teachers responding to the questionnaire were somewhat
liberal in estimating the time they spent on listening skills
in their classrooms, they indicated by their estimates that
they felt that such an amount of time should properly be
spent on this skill. Previous surveys have shown a much
smaller amount of time being devoted to the teaching of listening. It would be most desirable, if we had a coordinated
system of research, that studies of the Van Wingerden type
be replicated at set time intervals.

It is the purpose of this book of readings to fill a
gap by making readily available some of the best materials
on the teaching of listening in the elementary school classroom. Not all the articles included were written within the
last decade as I have chosen to include what I considered
the most helpful rather than the most recent. The fifty
items in this book were taken from journals, unpublished
masters' and doctoral theses, and from a number of curriculum bulletins of various school systems, small and
large, throughout the United States. With the exception

of journal articles, this is the kind of material that is not
widely circulated.

Of necessity, a number of interesting areas related
to listening could not be included in this book because of
lack of space. It would, for example, have been useful to
include material having to do with the teaching of listening
at levels other than the elementary school. Many relevant
ideas and materials have also been developed in business
and industry for management training. The comparative
neglect of listening at the secondary school level and the
constant but slow increase of listening courses at both the
undergraduate and graduate levels in various colleges and
universities could also be examined with profit.

The role of listening in teaching those children who
have trouble with reading is a topic to which a great deal of
space might be devoted. The fact appears to be that the
so-called "disadvantaged child" is handicapped in total
language development rather than only in reading and this
points up the absurdity of assuming that aural instruction
will ipso facto solve the problem of this group.

The use and, for that matter, the misuse of aural
materials such as tapes, recordings, caliphones, radio, and
so forth in the elementary school classroom could also have
been examined at length if space permitted.

One of the intriguing aspects of listening which had
to be omitted in this book of readings is the subject of
rapid listening or compressed speech. It is possible, due
to the extensive amount of redundancy in the English
language, to compress recorded speech by omitting, at random, microscopic portions without destroying intelligibility.
There are a number of as yet not adequately developed
electronic devices on the market which will compress speech
in this manner. The possibilities of educational uses of
compressed speech appear to be limitless and to open up many
possibilities for more efficient and thus improved instruction.

The items listed above are only a few of the more
outstanding ones but could be supplemented by a much longer list of new developments in the field of listening which
had to be omitted in the present work because of space
limitations.

Chapter II

GENERAL CONCEPTS ABOUT LISTENING

It is generally agreed that the one most effective
way to teach listening to children is to first set an example
by listening to them. An excellent discussion of the importance of a genuinely listening teacher is presented in the
first excerpt of this chapter. It was written by Professor
Richard Wynn of the University of Pittsburgh and first appeared in 1954 in New York State Education. In addition to
its worthwhile content, the inclusion of this selection is justified as an illustration of the fact that not every worthwhile
idea must be presented during the current decade. We can
often learn as profitably from the past as from the present.

The second article by Walter B. Barbe and Robert
M. Myers was also written in 1954. Basic principles concerning the teaching of listening are presented here. Dr.
Barbe, now associated with the publication of Highlights for
Children, needs no introduction to elementary school people
as he has made many and varied contributions in this area
for a number of years through his many books, his numer-
ous journal articles, and his active participation in the activities of professional organizations.

Professor Margaret J. Early of Syracuse University
has made substantial contributions to knowledge of and thinking about the subject of listening. Her published work on
this subject began in 1954 in connection with the Warren
English Project carried on at Boston University. The material excerpted as the third selection in this chapter first
appeared in the 1958 issue of Frontiers of Elementary Education, published by the Syracuse University Press. This
valuable series which summarized the proceedings of annual
conferences on elementary education held at Syracuse University is unfortunately out of print although much of the
contents (as in the case of the article excerpted here) is far
from being outdated.

Althea Beery, now retired, was for many years

24

Director of Curriculum for the Cincinnati, Ohio schools.   It
was through her efforts that the first adequate treatment of
the teaching of listening in the elementary schools is found
in the Cincinnati Manual, justly one of the few nationally
used and known curricular publications.   The excerpt in this
chapter from her 1951 Elementary English article shows
insight into the issues posed in improving the effectiveness
of listening.   Another article by Miss Beery on specific
teaching suggestions is excerpted in the next chapter.

        The next article in this chapter is by Professor Ced-
ric L. Crink of Southwestern State College (Oklahoma) and
Arline Buntley.   It first appeared in Grade Teacher in 1955.
The significance of the material presented here is found
principally in the recognition that "listening" is not a unitary
skill but a combination of a large number of specific and
different skills.   In this passage the characteristics of nine
different kinds of listening are analyzed.

        A 1961 article in Education written by Mildred Ber-
wick Cashman, which is the next item in this chapter,
logically follows the Crink article.   While recognizing that
there are different kinds of listening, the author here calls
attention to the fact that there are also levels of difficulty
in each of these kinds of listening.

        The two preceding articles lead up to the article by
Professor Edna Lue Furness of Nebraska State College and
formerly of the University of Wyoming.   Professor Furness
who has made a number of very valuable contributions to
the development of ways of thinking about listening and
about the ways of teaching the skills involved, points out
that the purpose of a particular listening situation is the
determinant of the level as well as of the kind of listening
that is needed.   This material originally appeared in Educational Administration and Supervision in 1958.

CHILDREN SHOULD BE SEEN AND NOT HEARD

Richard Wynn

        A huge truck was stuck when its roof failed by a
few inches to clear an underpass.   The distraught driver,

unable to move the truck in either direction, stepped from
his cab and surveyed the scene. Traffic was tied up. A
crowd gathered. Everyone was annoyed and perplexed. A
boy stepped from the crowd and suggested to the driver,
"Why don't you let a little air out of the tires?" The driver
pondered the suggestion for a moment, slapped the boy on
the back, and acted on his suggestion. In a few minutes the
truck was moving easily under the bridge on its partially
deflated tires. A problem that had stumped scores of adults
was solved easily by a youngster. A child had an idea.
Someone listened to it.

Do teachers know how to listen to youngsters for good
ideas? How can we understand children better by listening
to them? Are special skills involved in good listening? Let
us explore these questions.

There are four basic communication skills--reading,
writing, speaking, and listening. From first grade through
the university, schools seek to improve students' competency with the first three. Despite the fact that the average
adult spends 45 percent of his communication time in listening, we haven't done much to train him for it. It is singu-
larly noteworthy that this most important communication art
from the standpoint of human understanding is the most neglected one. How, then can the social effectiveness of the
teacher be improved through skilled listening?

Listening facilitates understanding of children.

Quite unaware of my presence, my daughter was
playing house with her little friends. She was the mother.

"You mustn't climb over the chairs that way." (How
often had we admonished her the same way.) "They might
look like a jungle gym but they aren't."

Aha! So that was it! I had never thought of a chair
as a jungle gym before. I had the prosaic notion that a
chair was something to sit on. That is about what a child
would expect an adult to think. Now I was beginning to see
how a chair challenged a child to high adventure. Now I
could understand my daughter's delight in climbing up the
back of a chair and sliding into the seat with a jolt. I
could even understand the thrill of seeing how far one could
tilt in a chair before it upset. I decided to talk with my
daughter about chairs and jungle gyms at the first opportunity.

Yes, they had a jungle gym at school. Sure, she thought that climbing it looked like a lot of fun but she seldom tried it. She was embarrassed because she couldn't climb as well as the other youngsters who like to play tag on the jungle gym. Oh yes, she'd love to have a jungle gym of her own so she could learn to climb better. Sure, she'd help me build it.

Now she doesn't climb all over our chairs any more. She gets enough climbing while playing tag on the jungle gym at school. Thus we got a lead on a problem of some importance while listening to our daughter at play.

Listen While They Play

The attitudes and feelings that youngsters express in their play can be very revealing. The ways in which dolls and pets are scolded often help parents and teachers perceive how they sound to children. A child's perception of his teacher can often be revealed by having him play school. A child playing with dolls or puppets may demonstrate subconscious feelings that may be apparent in no other way. Thus skilled listening to youngsters' play not only offers an opportunity for the teacher to understand the child better but through play therapy skilled teachers can actually help children resolve their conflicts and develop a wholesome outlook.

Some teachers learn to understand students better by asking them to write or talk about "What I Would Do If I Were a Teacher (or Mother)," "What I Like to Do Most," "The Things That I'm Afraid Of." Their responses to such topics are frequently very revealing.

Sympathetic listening helps people resolve their problems.

A teenager came to the principal's office much disturbed about a conflict he had with his teacher. The principal listened intently to his description of the problem. He encouraged him to get the whole problem out by asking several questions. As the principal was about to deliver his advice, the youngster jumped up abruptly, thanked the principal for his help, and left. The principal hadn't moralized or criticized. He had simply listened carefully and asked a few questions. This had helped the lad to release his tensions, clarify his own thinking, resolve his own dilemmas, and chart a course of action. This was all that he needed.   This was indirect counseling at its best.

Psychiatrists and counselors are aware of the thera-
peutic value to the speaker when he finds a patient listener.
It helps us to "talk out" our problems once in a while.

For Security, Importance, Adjustment
Listening to children gives them a sense of security.

If students can feel free to come to teachers who will
hear them and counsel them on their problems, a sense of
security and self-confidence is gained.   These are prerequi-
site to learning.   How reassuring it is to have a confidant
who will share one's anxieties and problems.   Parents sometimes fail to fill this role well.   In such cases it is important that the teacher fulfill this need.

Listening to children helps them feel important and accepted.

One of the basic human urges is the desire for acceptance and approval.   We all want to be liked.   Many behavior
problems stem from a desire for attention.   By encouraging
children to talk to us, we give them attention.   We make
them feel important.   Thus we take away some of their drive
to seek recognition in unacceptable ways.   We help to make
them happy and adjusted people.

Listening to children helps them release or adjust to
fears.

An adolescent student asked his teacher to walk home
from school with him.   The teacher was about to decline
when he noted considerable concern on the lad's face.   Thinking better, the teacher agreed to go along.   After some pro-
crastination, the boy got to his problem.   He was afraid he
had a venereal disease.   The teacher hid his shock and sur-
prise and encouraged him to go on.   He was afraid to discuss the problem with his parents but felt free to discuss it
with the teacher as soon as he was sure that the teacher
could accept the problem without condemning him.   After further discussion, it became obvious that the lad wasn't really
ill.   He had simply been the victim of some misinformation
from his immature friends.

Had the teacher not been available to him at the moment, had the teacher laughed off his concern, had the tea-

cher become pedantic, the boy would have been forced to live
with his unresolved fear and confusion. If he had been ill,
he would still have needed desperately an understanding listener who could hear his problem unemotionally and suggest
a constructive course of action.

Thus it is imperative that young people drain their
fears either by discussing them directly or by talking them
out through make-believe stories, poems, and role-plays.
By verbalizing anxieties, one can dissipate or adjust to them
rather than have them recur with greater intensity.

Releasing Aggression
Listening to young people helps them release aggres-
sion.

Teachers can help students bring out angry feelings
that may cause behavior problems if suppressed. "Why
don't we talk about the angry feelings we all have sometimes? I'm sure you feel cross at people sometimes. I
know I get angry at times. Let's talk about the reasons we
get angry. Maybe we ought to draw a picture of a boy who
is very angry at his teacher. Maybe you'd like to write a
story about him." Children can also be encouraged to "play
out" their feelings. These devices encourage the release of
aggressive urges into constructive channels. Thus we reduce
the tendency to release negative feelings in socially unacceptable ways.

(Teachers--and administrators--should also be encouraged to listen to the community. Unfortunately, too much
emphasis has been given to communication in the other direction. Many of the great insights and contributions to education have come from laymen like Ben Franklin, Thomas
Jefferson, Horace Mann, and Martha Beery. Many educational practices have been developed from the ideas of laymen; witness the visiting teacher, the nursery school, and
others. Forward-looking educators should organize channels
of communication that will enable schools to listen to the
ideas of laymen. Intelligent listening by teachers in the community can also help forestall many problems.)

Listening Techniques
What are some of the techniques of good listening?
The following list is neither exhaustive nor mystic. It in-
volves little more than common sense and good manners.

Be easily available and approachable for listening purposes. While there are limits to the time that a teacher can spend in talking with youngsters, able teachers will recognize that this is one of their important functions and will devote as much time as possible in counseling with students.

Relax and make the conversation unhurried. There is no better way to stop him cold than to look at your watch or open your mail. The problem may be more important than his first words would indicate.

If possible, select an informal setting. The cafeteria, for example, may inhibit him less than an office. In any event, avoid talking across a desk.

Get him to talk freely without interrupting him. Distraught people are like alarm clocks. They have high potential energy and pose a real threat as long as they are wound up. They can be stopped arbitrarily but that doesn't relieve the tension. One can deal effectively with them only after they are run down.

Encourage him to be himself. Be prepared to accept calmly anything that he may have to say.

Demonstrate real interest in him and his problem. Talk with him at his own level. Do not be patronizing.

Attempt to orient his remarks to their proper context. It is quite important to know what he is really concerned about before trying to help him. Listen not only to what he says but also to what he doesn't say. His real sentiments may hinge around an unpleasant experience that he hesitates to mention. Thus, if a student wants to drop algebra because he "doesn't like it," he may really mean that he doesn't like the teacher. Transferring him to a section with another teacher may be the real solution.

Refrain from hasty disapprobation. Try not to argue or exhort. The success of the interview will probably depend upon his not your, recognition of the need for changed behavior or attitude.

Express appreciation for his bringing the problem to you. It is completely disarming to be thanked for presenting a criticism or a problem. It establishes wholesome rapport for future conversations and lets the person depart with a constructive attitude.

Study your counseling technique self-consciously. Keep
trying to improve.   Role-play or rehearse difficult interviews
whenever possible.   Don't let your own mistakes get you down.

Your big problem may be in gaining the confidence of
students. It's like getting olives out of a bottle (or kissing a
girl). The first one is hard to get but the rest come easy.

DEVELOPING LISTENING ABILITY IN CHILDREN

Walter B. Barbe
and
Robert M. Myers

Listening is the process of reacting to, interpreting,
and relating the spoken language in terms of past experiences
and future courses of action.   Viewed in this manner, it becomes more than passive participation, more than just hearing.   Even though hearing implies a reaction, it does not
necessarily mean that any interpretation is made.   Listening
is really an individual creative act.   Each listener brings to
the listening situation his experiences, personality, mental
set, and manner of thinking.   Every interpretation is the result of processes that are peculiar to one individual.   We
may all listen to the same thing, but each interpretation will
be different.

Just as a car cannot run on three wheels, neither can
an individual deal effectively with his environment unless the
four facets of communication, listening, speaking, reading,
and writing, are developed to the greatest extent.   Failure
in any one of these abilities hinders an individual's potential
to understand and be understood.

Of the four facets of communication, speaking is most
closely allied to listening.   We speak to be heard, and we
listen in order to respond.   Speaking is to listening as writing is to reading.   It is logical, therefore, that a person's
ability to express himself governs, to a great extent, his
listening capacity.

Basic Concepts

Some of the more important concepts of listening are:

Listening is an effective way of learning.

Listening ability is governed by the physical, mental, and emotional status of the individual.

Listening is an acquired skill, and growth advances in an orderly fashion through developmental levels.

Listening is said to be of three kinds: appreciative, critical, and discriminative.

There must be a purpose for listening, and this purpose governs how we listen.

Listening and speaking are closely related.

It is certain that the majority of people never attain the status of mature listeners. There is every reason to believe that listening can be improved through instruction. The latter stages of development, however, require conscious study and effort for improvement.

Since listening is an acquired skill, it is learned, partially, through imitation. This shows the importance of the role of the teacher. He, too, must be a good listener and possess a pleasant, well-modulated voice.

There are different kinds of listening. We enjoy hearing a symphony, a chorus, or a Charles Laughton interpretation. There is appreciative listening that is gratifying to the whole being. There are also times when we listen to political speakers, sales persons, and others to weigh their arguments and evidence. This is critical listening to persuasive discourse for the purpose of evaluation.

Radio and television have made another type of listening of importance to every person. We listen and watch to gain information, just as a student does in an instructional situation. In this case, we listen discriminately to grasp the organization of the materials presented and the significant points made. Granted that these types of listening are used in everyday living, no school program can be complete without having provisions for each. This will usually involve teacher-pupil planning and evaluating.

It logically follows that if there are different kinds of listening, there must be a purpose for each type, and the kind of listening we do depends upon our purpose. The reason for much of what teachers identify as lack of ability and inattention in children is really failure upon the part of both the child and the teacher to identify this purpose. Purposeful listening should be part of all classroom experiences.

Listening and speaking certainly go together. Contrary to the opinions of many, listening comprises probably 50 percent of classroom time. In too many schools this process is a one-way affair; the teacher talks and the pupils listen. Grown-ups consider a person who talks without listening a bore. Is it any wonder that students in such schools hear only a small percentage of what the teacher says and digest even a smaller amount? Listening instruction implies that more time must be spent in group discussion and problem solving. Children should do more talking and listening to each other instead of to the teacher.

Diagnosing Listening Ability

Growth in listening ability comes about in a logical manner. One thing builds upon another and this progression is in order. Although children vary in the rate of growth, each step is present. It is important then to determine the immediate level of the children we teach in order to help them attain maximum development.

At the same time that we determine the immediate level of the child we gain information pertaining to his strengths and weaknesses. With this knowledge we will be able to build instruction around individual needs.

Emotional status will greatly affect the listening ability. Information regarding the child's relationships with the home, community, and school is important.

In determining the level of listening ability, it will be important to discover the child's immediate level in the other facets of communication. What is his reading level? What is the extent of his vocabulary development? How well does he express himself? How does performance in each of these areas compare with listening ability?

DEVELOPING EFFECTIVE LISTENING SKILLS

Margaret J. Early

Ability to use language is a major component of intelligence. Since listening and reading (like speaking and writing) are forms of this ability, we are not surprised to find positive correlations among listening, reading, and intelligence. To the extent that listening and reading are thinking processes, we would expect that factors influencing one must also influence the other. Relationships among these factors may be shown diagrammatically (see Figure 1).

Figure 1

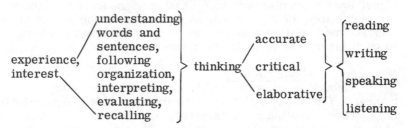

As modes of communication, listening and reading each completes a process. The act of speaking is incomplete without a listener. Writing is noncommunicative without a reader. Yet it is inaccurate to suggest that either "completes" a process, for, as we define reading and listening, each includes interpreting or reacting verbally. For the teacher, at least, evaluation of reading and listening is based on pupils' verbal responses. The communication arts are so interrelated that it is virtually impossible to teach any one of them in isolation, and as a result, teaching and learning are facilitated. The parallels between listening and reading, for example, make it easier for teachers to develop their pupils' skills in each--but only when they teach both.

Listening is Different from Reading

The parallel acts of receiving oral and written messages require different skills and habits. While these differences are fairly obvious, they are worth exploring because they offer clues as to what constitutes listening instruction.

In reading, the printed word alone is the agent for transmitting meaning from writer to reader. The listener, however, responds not only to the verbal symbol, but also to the inflection, pitch, timbre, rhythm, rate of delivery, and peculiarities of pronunciation of the speaker. If the speaker is seen as well as heard, the listener is also affected by his manner, gestures, facial expressions, appearance, indeed, by the whole stage setting.

The listener is at the mercy of the speaker to a much greater degree than the reader is of the writer. The reader can maintain his independence. The author can't stop him from beginning at the end and reading backwards if he so chooses. The reader can set his own pace, review, skip, skim, stop reading when he chooses and begin again without losing the author's message. None of these diversions is open to the listener, unless he has his speaker captive on tape.

More often than not, the writer meets each reader alone. More often than not, listening takes place in a social setting. Attitudes and reactions are frequently influenced by other listeners as well as by the speaker. Witness the effect of mass listening on the studio audience, the political convention, the dictators' rallies.

Listening and reading differ in rate of intake. The listener's rate of intake is set by the speaker's rate of delivery. The reader can speed up his rate of intake to correspond more nearly to his rate of thinking. Not so the listener. How he takes up the slack between the speaker's rate of delivery and his rate of comprehension has a lot to do with his attention, which in turn affects his comprehension. A break in attention in listening is much more damaging than in reading, of course, since the listener may lose the thread of the discourse.

For still another reason, concentration may be more difficult in listening than in reading. Because our ears are subjected to so much that we do not want to listen to, we have learned to "tune out" and "tune in" at will. Children of the television age are expert in this on-again, off-again listening. The weapon in the counterattack is repetition. To catch the inattentive listener when he is "tuned in," the man with a message repeats and repeats. The need to listen weakens. If you did not get the name of the cigarette that tastes good, never mind; you will. If you did not catch the number of the page the first time, she'll say it again.

Listening Skills Deteriorate

Children learn to speak through imitating others.
Through listening, they learn thousands of words--and ideas--
and they do so without formal instruction. Why then should
there be any need to teach listening? Does something happen to this "natural" ability to listen as children mature and
their uses of language become more complex?

In the early grades, pupils continue to acquire more
information through listening than through reading. They
comprehend spoken language at a much higher level than
written language because their meaning vocabularies are far
more advanced than their work recognition skills. For most
children, the time arrives when their reading vocabulary
catches up with their listening vocabulary. At this point they
are able to comprehend language as well through one meduim
as through the other. From this point on, however, their
skill in one may exceed the other, depending upon the amount
and kind of training, their needs, and preferences.

Research seems to indicate that, as an individual's
reading skills improve, listening skills tend to deteriorate.
Better readers are often poorer listeners. Ironically, as
the amount of time spent in listening increases, the need to
listen well declines. Pupils are "talked at" more and more
as they continue in school and college, but the information
imparted by the teacher is almost always available in printed sources.

What happens to children who do not achieve enough
facility in reading to learn through this medium? Research
shows that poor readers are frequently better listeners. Ap-
parently because they continue to depend on oral sources of
information, poor readers maintain and improve their listening skills. For these children, who may be either slow
learners or retarded readers, teachers can use listening as
a substitute for a broken tool.

Four reasons plead the cause for teaching listening:
1) the large proportion of time pupils spend in listening in
school and outside; 2) the increasing influence of oral communication in adult life; 3) the need for training the ear as
well as the eye, since listening and reading require different,
as well as similar, skills; and 4) the importance of listening
as a substitute for reading, especially when the latter ability

is impaired.

In the elementary school we need to use listening less
and teach it more. If this seems paradoxical, it's because
we haven't distinguished between use (of which there is plenty) and instruction (of which there is too little). The essential difference between using listening and teaching it is that
in merely requiring children to use listening we neglect to:
1) find out how well they use it; 2) look for means of improving weaknesses; and 3) check to see if these means have
proved successful. Put another way, we teach listening most
directly when we test pupils' comprehension of the spoken
word. Because many classroom listening situations can be
turned to instructional purposes, teaching listening requires
little additional time in the school curriculum.

Kindergarten and first-grade teachers expect the young
child to be self-centered in social situations. In planning
periods, in dictating experience charts, and in show-and-tell
sessions, the immature pupil is so intent on his own contribution that he fails to listen attentively to what others are
saying. When his turn comes, he is likely to speak as an
individual rather than as a member of a group. The understanding teacher guides young pupils to a better realization
of their responsibilities to the group by directing their attention to other children's comments. She does this by setting
an example of responsive listening herself, by making pertinent comments, by asking questions, complimenting pupils
who make relevant contributions and discouraging irrelevant
comments.

(The reader will recognize that this lesson in responsive listening in a social setting is needed long after the primary grades. Adults, too, in conversations and discussions,
often wait their turn to speak, failing to listen sympathetical-
ly or attentively to others' points of view.)

As primary-grade children continue to practice good
listening habits, they can begin to verbalize their understanding of the process. They can make charts listing such characteristics as: looking at the speaker to show your interest,
listening quietly, listening the first time, responding to what
the speaker says, thinking before asking or answering questions, paying close attention to directions and trying to remember them.

In the middle and upper grades, teachers enlarge upon children's understanding of the listening process. In one fourth grade pupils held a listening campaign. First they listed different kinds of listening situations in school and outside. They selected those which called especially for accurate listening and discussed why we often listen carelessly. They considered what makes a good "listening climate," including not only physical conditions such as absence of distracting noises, but also such psychological factors as the listeners' attitudes and the speaker's personality. They made posters to remind themselves of how they could improve the listening climate of their classroom. They checked each other's everyday listening, counting the number of times directions had to be repeated because of poor listening and questions were misunderstood because of lack of attention.

Another class focused on listening habits that improve the quality of discussions and reports. Their rules for good listening in such situations were:

1. Show interest in the speaker.

2. Ask questions which help the speaker to say what he means clearly.

3. Be courteous in disagreeing with the speaker.

4. Watch for bias.

5. Find out the source of information given.

6. Watch for phrases that help you to follow the speaker's organization.

7. Hold the main points of the discussion in mind and try to stick to them.

8. Distinguish between fact and opinion.

9. Take notes; be able to write a brief summary of a report or discussion.

In another intermediate class, the teacher started her pupils thinking about the importance of listening by giving a standardized test. Pupils were interested in comparing their scores with national norms. Then they wanted to find out whether they listened better than they read. They compared

their scores on comprehension checks after listening and after reading, using passages from basal texts and the Weekly
Reader tests.   They experimented to find out whether distractions affected listening more than reading.

Another teacher improves listening habits by refusing
to capitulate to the on- again, off- again listeners.   First, he
talks with his fifth graders about radio and television commercials and the devices that advertisers use to attract attention and to hammer their message home.   His pupils do
most of the talking; they know all the slogans and appeals.
Do they always listen to commercials?   Can they "tune out"
mentally?   Do they tune out other messages, too--their parents' do's and don't's, their teacher's dullness?   They discuss the need for repetition and the waste of time it entails.
The teacher makes a pact: he will not repeat directions and
will make no allowances for failures to attend.   On the other
hand, he will welcome worthwhile questions, since he wants
responsive, not passive, listening.

We Stress Purpose In Listening
          As in reading, children need to have their attention
focused specifically until purposeful listening becomes a habit and they can set their purposes themselves.   The directed listening lesson is one way of doing this.   It follows the
same pattern as· a directed reading lesson, for the same reasons and with the same results.

Before listening, children need help on words: a new
word that sounds like a familiar one; a familiar word used
in an unusual sense or spoken in an unfamiliar accent; technical words; words not explained in context; figurative expressions; words that appeal to the senses.   When such words
are written on the blackboard and explained, children have a
better chance of catching the meaning, not only of the specific word, but of the whole selection.

The next step in a guided listening lesson is to discuss the type of selection to be heard.   We have different
purposes and use different skills in listening to an informative report, a tall tale, or a historical drama.   Children
should discuss ways in which they will listen.   Will they take
notes?   Will they picture the characters?   Should they listen
for main ideas?   Should they compare two speakers' voices
and diction?   The teacher also directs pupils' thinking to the
content of the selection.   If they we're to listen to an excerpt
from Copper- Toed Boots (on a recording by Sound Book Press

Society), they might think about why boys in a small town sixty years ago traded for what they wanted. They might be told to: "Listen for two 'trades' that Shad's mother approved of." Attentive listening, like silent reading, should be followed by discussion and by a check on comprehension, orally or in writing. Often it will be necessary to replay or reread parts of the selection, as children seek to prove points or illustrate meanings.

Purposeful listening can be promoted incidentally in many school activities as well as in direct teaching lessons. At the same time, care should be taken to eliminate practices which foster inattention or passive listening. Teachers wash the purpose out of listening when they encourage or allow: 1) reading from the printed page while another pupil reads aloud; 2) class "discussions" in which direction of communication is pupil- to- teacher, seldom pupil- to- pupil; 3) irrelevant questions and requests for repeating information that has been clearly stated.

We Can Teach Specific Skills
        In addition to developing habits and attitudes, we can teach specific skills. Accurate listening can be developed in lessons such as these:

        A.   Following Directions.   Have pupils: 1) draw designs from oral directions; 2) write simple directions to be carried out with pencil and paper and read them aloud for others to follow; 3) trace routes on map outlines, according to oral directions; 4) make up directions for several acts that can be performed in the classroom after pupil has listened to all the orders; 5) make a collection of directions, such as how to use dial telephoning, operate an elevator, or reach a certain destination. Directions are read aloud once, and then reproduced in writing. Pupils discuss emergencies where need for following spoken directions accurately is especially serious.

        B.   Spotting Absurdities.   1) Make up a series of absurd or contradictory statements and ask pupils to point out words that do not make sense, such as: "Mr. Burton will show slides on Mexico to illustrate his lecture on 'Europe Today!'" 2) Give oral true- false tests in which recognition of absurdity depends upon accurate listening, such as: "Bring the water to a broil." 3) Make up directions or explanations from which essential information is omitted. Able pupils will enjoy making up these types of exercises themselves.

C. Listening for Main Ideas. Select paragraphs to
be read orally from graded reading skills texts, pupil newspapers like the Weekly Reader and Current Events, and textbooks in content subjects. Pupils respond by 1) selecting a
title for paragraph from several written on board or on exercise sheet; 2) selecting topic sentences from several given;
3) writing titles themselves. 4) Later, pupils summarize a
paragraph after listening by writing headlines, news flashes,
S.O.S. messages, telegrams, and so forth, when comment
is appropriate. 5) Pupils listen to several paragraphs on
same topic. Teachers tell them to "listen for three main
points," which they will later reproduce.

D. Listening for Information. Give practice in obtaining information through listening by 1) reading aloud informational articles; 2) using tape recordings of pupils' reports or "live" reports; 3) showing informational films. Set
purposes for listening and follow presentation by having pupils take comprehension checks or write a brief summary.
In upper grades, note-taking and simple outlining of oral material should be taught at the same time that these skills are
being taught in reading. Because of the greater difficulty of
following organization of speeches, pupils should be given
partial outlines to be completed while listening. Pupils should
learn to take notes on unstructured talks.

We Can Teach Critical Thinking Through Listening
Helping children to react thoughtfully to the spoken
word is one of the most important goals of all teaching. We
are making progress toward this goal when we help children
to understand the listening process, and to develop habits and
skills of accurate listening. All these aspects of listening instruction contribute to an ability to think critically. In addition to these, there are specific aspects of critical thinking
which should receive direct attention in aural situations.

Teachers sometimes imply that instruction in critical
thinking should be reserved for gifted pupils only. But in
adult life, no one takes an I.Q. test before assuming his
right to vote, serve on a jury, or purchase a dishwasher.
Slow learners need direction in thinking critically, too.
Brighter pupils may respond more quickly to questions that
probe into speakers' purposes, use of language, and right to
speak as authorities. But slower pupils also can learn to
ask: "Who said what?" "To whom?" "In what way?" "For
what purpose?" To improve the critical thinking of average-
to-slow pupils, teachers need more patience, more examples

from pupils' own experiences, and a better understanding of
how much, or how little, improvement can be effected. Slow
and rapid learners can profit, though in different degrees, of
course, from situations which demand critical or evaluative
thinking.

From the many activities that teachers use, we have
selected a few samples:

1) In the primary grades, children can learn to distinguish the real from the fanciful if their thinking is directed by questions: "Could this really happen?" "What parts of
the story might have happened to you?" "Why or why not?"

2) In the middle or upper grades, children may distinguish between fact and opinion as they listen to (a) each
other's statements in discussions; (b) pupils' reports; (c) assembly speakers; (d) tape recordings of radio and television
commercials, news reports and commentaries. A few educational films teach this aspect of critical thinking. Such a
film as How to Judge Facts (Coronet) might be used with upper grade pupils.

Opportunities abound for incidental teaching of the differences between fact and opinion. Direct teaching is also
necessary. Teachers may read single statements of fact and
of opinion which pupils must identify. (Models may be found
in reading workbooks. Since pupils are not asked to read
these statements themselves, teachers can adapt examples
from higher level texts.) Later, they will ask pupils to listen for opinions that appear in longer selections.

3) Awareness of tricks of language--snarl and purr
words, shifts in meaning, connotations and denotations--can
be introduced to upper grade children. Appeals in advertising offer the most readily available materials, close to children's experiences, but other oral uses can be studied as
well. Recordings of many kinds give pupils the chance to
reflect on how we are influenced by tone of voice and sound
of words, often to the neglect of meaning. Pupils can study,
too, the effects upon listeners' emotions of music, background sounds, and repetition.

Shifts in meaning are traps for the unwary listener.
Nine- and ten-year-olds are not too young to become aware
of these traps. Teachers can introduce shifts in meaning
with puns and jokes in which humor depends on misinterpre-

tations of multiple-meaning words. Sometimes teachers give
the opening line of a joke and pupils supply the punch line,
showing their understanding of words of more than one meaning. A more serious type of lesson can make use of brief
dialogues that contain words which have varying connotations
for different people. For example, pupils listened to the
following dialogue: Salesman, "With Gleemo you can polish
your furniture without rubbing." Mrs. Jones: "I tried
Gleemo and it left a film that I had to rub off." The pupils
pointed out that to the salesman "rubbing" meant "scrubbing
vigorously," but to Mrs. Jones the same word meant "wip-
ing off." Such simple exercises prepare children to react
critically later on to speakers who, deliberately or uninten-
tionally, shift meanings of words like education, freedom,
democracy, loyalty, and the like.

4) Propaganda devices and fallacies in thinking may
also be studied. Again, radio and television provide plenti-
ful examples of the bandwagon appeal, glittering generalities,
the folksy approach, false analogies, black or white reasoning, false assumptions, and spread-eagle oratory. Children
can listen for examples in their own reports and discussions.
They can note phrases like it is believed, according to well-
informed observers, reliable sources report, and they say,
which conceal the absence of real authority and make opinions appear to be factual statements.

5) Stereotypes are familiar to young television fans.
They can point to the characteristics of the television cow-
boy, Mexican badman, and "savage" Indian, or the typical
father or juvenile. In some respects, this type of discussion is an extension of earlier experiences in distinguishing
between fact and fancy.

6) Critical thinking means reacting to what the speaker does not say as well as to what he says. Children should
be encouraged to think beyond the speaker's words by such
directions as: "As you listen, jot down questions you would
like to ask the speaker." "What other information on this
topic would you like to hear?" "Why does the speaker mention only three uses of atomic energy?"

Always, in teaching critical thinking, we must use experiences with which children are familiar. Otherwise, we
promote superficial arguments, misconceptions, and verbalizing.

We Need to Know More About Listening

Research in listening is still meager. A few factual statements can be made about the subject, but much that is said for or against the teaching of listening is hypothetical. We need many careful studies, especially at the elementary level, that will:

identify types of listening ability;

define the role of attention;

investigate the influences of reading on listening, and vice versa;

measure the effectiveness of recommended practices;

compare oral and written communication as means of changing attitudes and values;

construct measures of "listenability" comparable to readability formulae;

study such aspects of listening as rate of comprehension, personal and recorded communication, delayed and immediate recall, and the values of note-taking..

The classroom teacher does not have to wait upon the results of research, however, to introduce listening instruction. He can experiment with his own ideas and can test recommended practices. Not all the answers can be determined by carefully controlled research, at least not at our present level of sophistication in measuring so complex an aspect of human behavior.

EXPERIENCES IN LISTENING

Althea Beery

"They have eyes and see not; ears have they, yet they hear not."

What have been your own recent adventures in listening? Were they exalting, sobering, instructive, or were they adventures in understanding? Assuming that you really heard

in a language sense, i.e., took in and understood the ideas
expressed, why did you listen? What purposes did you have?
Did the purposes influence or control your "listening level"?
What proof have you that you received the speaker's message? As you compared notes with a fellow listener, you
may have been struck with the fact that in effect the two of
you had listened to quite different speeches.

What "got in the way" of the speaker's attempt to
communicate with you? Perhaps it was lack of background
on your part, or you yourself with the worry and tensions of
every day living, perhaps your attitudes and mind set. Which
were communicated more faithfully, the facts presented or
the general point of view? What effect on your listening had
the environment--the temperature of the room, the comfort
of the chair, the tightness of your shoes, your feeling of rapport with speaker and the audience? Possibly discussing the
shared experience clarified it for you. Did you listen more
profitably in situations in which you had a chance to exchange
ideas with the speaker?

These queries suggest that you may get some insight
into procedures for your classroom as you analyze the factors which condition the effectiveness of your own listening.

How aware as a teacher are you of the listening habits of your children? How much of the time in school is
spent in listening? Perhaps that last question should be re-
phrased--how much of the school day are children supposed
to be listening? We can control how children sit and what
they look at in the classroom more easily than what they
hear, for listening is essentially an intellectual pursuit.

A moment's consideration of language arts as communication, as a powerful means of developing citizens willing
to face facts and act upon them, ready to work together in a
common cause, will convince thoughtful teachers that more of
children's listening time should be spent listening to their
peers. This is especially true in the elementary school
where learning to get along with each other is an important
developmental task.

May we be forgiven, but if we are honest, we must
admit that in all too many classrooms, for all too much of
their time, children listen all too often to a teacher who
speaks with the voice of authority in a way that stifles in-
quiry and investigation. If the teacher in the next classroom

counters the suggestion that children spend more time listening to their peers with the remark, "But children's reports are so boring," you may assure her that the remedy is not to be found in the teacher's report but in the relevance of the child's report to the group's purposes.

If it is fruitful for a teacher to analyze her own listening and the listening habits of her children, might it not also be profitable for children to analyze their own listening habits?

LEARN TO LISTEN

Cedric L. Crink
and
Arline Buntley

Listening is the first and maybe the most important of the four areas of communication, since the child listens for some time before he matures enough to speak, read or write.

In spite of the rather obvious fact that listening, starting as early in life as it does, is an important factor in man's living, it seems that the conscious teaching of listening has lagged far behind the other communication skills.

Listening is a specific skill, a skill that is seldom passive and must be taught just as surely and with as careful planning as any other language skill. Listening can be improved through instruction with the conscious planning of the teacher and the conscious effort of the child, for while hearing is a natural phenomenon, listening is an acquired skill which comes partially by imitation.

The educational values of listening in school are obvious. Most of the motivation, directions and explanations are oral and require a listening class. It would be hard to think of a subject that could be taught, even for a few minutes, without oral communication. In the primary grades much more learning is received by listening than by reading, but, as learning intake from reading increases in the intermediate and upper grades, the necessity for careful, discriminating listening also increases. Therefore, while there is less quantity of listening, the demands for quality in listening are greater.

From listening in his home the child establishes his moral standards. His speech patterns are formed in like manner. Perhaps his out-of-school listening has as many educational values as that done in the classroom. If we learn so much by listening, how much more could be learned by trained, purposeful listening.

Listening is the best way of getting information for slow readers. Like primary children who learn much more by listening than by reading, the retarded reader of any grade level receives most of his learning by listening. The more retarded the child is, the greater advantage listening has over reading.

The reading readiness program depends heavily upon listening. The beginning reading vocabulary is limited to words in the listening and speaking vocabulary.

Reading and listening are both means of getting information second hand, yet both are active processes and require effort. Reading may be done as slowly as desired while listening is done at the rate set by the speaker, which may make it difficult for a slow thinker to follow. Further, the speaker may use dramatic delivery, voice inflections and the like to influence his hearers, which makes listening a more critical or discriminatory process than reading.

Speech training depends upon listening. The two are closely related and usually poor auditory discrimination and poor speech go hand in hand. Likewise listening capacity and ability to express oneself are closely related. Weakness in auditory discrimination and in reading ability usually go together.

Any young girl can tell you that the way to win admiration is to listen. Most of us like to talk so much that we immediately like anyone who listens to us in an interested fashion. Business deals, national affairs and even international relationships often hang in the balance of courteous, discriminating, critical listening. Not only the attitude of his listening but the amount of learning gained from it would seem to depend upon how well the listener has been trained in this very important skill.

Motivation is a powerful tool in any teaching situation and it is a necessity in developing listening power. To develop a specific type of listening, the child should understand what he is to listen for and why it is important that he gain this listening skill. Children should understand the purpose of their listening and be assured that they will receive meaning whenever they listen. Listening will be enjoyable if the children are led to anticipate enjoyment and feel a sense of achievement when they discover the thing for which they are listening. Experience of the children, their previous learning and general background should be considered in planning listening situations. Much care should be taken in order that planned listening is really planned and that the methods and materials suit the type of listening intended, fill the needs, and are suited to the experiential background and listening level of the children.

In preparing children for listening they should be helped to understand what kind of listening is expected of them. Perhaps much inattention is due to the teacher's failure to make listening purposeful. Listening activities should be a part of every classroom experience.

Interest appeal must be high and listening sessions brief. One writer says, "The mind is a funny thing. It won't stand still unless held by force." This fact makes it hard to hold attention long enough to thoroughly impart new ideas or information. It is a real problem of education, this getting and holding of attention so as to make learning possible.

Since listening is the chief means of knowledge intake in the lower grades, some specific situations for helping children to achieve better listening are suggested.

1. Casual listening-- needs no developing as it is the chief kind of listening used by untrained, small listeners

2. Conversational listening

        a. Telephoning
        b. Introductions (courtesy training)
        c. Show and tell
        d. Parties
        e. Discussions in planning activities

3. Background listening--likely of little value except
to the extent that background music stimulates feelings that
make the primary listening more meaningful.

      a. Radio background music in plays and the like
      b. Television and sound film background music
         or sound effects

4. Appreciative listening

      a. Short excursions to enjoy sounds in nature
      b. Listening for bird songs
      c. Listening for word pictures in poetry or prose
      d. Listening for certain sounds in music as the
         slow tramp of elephants or the rippling sound
         of a brook
      e. Choral speaking
      f. Listening to recordings of fine music or
         speech selections
      g. Sharing orally bits of poetry and prose en-
         joyed in silent reading
      h. Storytelling and dramatization

5. Creative listening--this sort of listening causes
the listener to become a part of what he hears. It causes
new ideas and thoughts and imaginings.

      a. Walk in park
      b. Read good literature to children, especially
         that which creates moods; is highly dramatic
      c. Recordings
      d. Shared favorite bits of beautiful or interest-
         ing poetry or prose
      e. Dramatizations

6. Exploratory listening

      a. Listen for new sounds and discover what
         makes them
      b. Listen for things that will arouse new inter-
         ests or more completely develop old ones
      c. Field trips
      d. Excursions to industrial points of interest

7. Interrogative listening

      a. Question and answer period during "Show and

Tell"
b. Quiz games
c. Radio and television programs given to ques-
    tions and answers

8. Concentrative listening

    a. Reports on unit activities
    b. Announcements
    c. Directions and instructions
    d. Programs and assemblies
    e. Discussions requiring listener to respond
        orally
    f. Speeches or other such programs on "School
        of the Air"

9. Critical listening

    a. Discussions between children who express di-
        vergent opinions
    b. Listening to any speech to see if the speaker
        tried to change the listeners' hearing by the
        way he spoke
    c. Making lists of words that cause a feeling of
        displeasure or disgust such as: slimy,
        treacherous, crawling
    d. Watch for words that cause a happy feeling:
        mother, freedom, skipping

Probably one of the best ways of getting children to
listen carefully is to listen carefully to them.   Teachers who
listen to unburdening of the hearts of youngsters with half
an ear can hardly expect courteous, thoughtful listening from
them.

CHANNEL   L - I - S - T - E - N

Mildred Berwick Cashman

My work as a reading supervisor gives me the opportunity to visit many classrooms, and I am amazed how widely children differ in their ability to listen.   Some pupils follow directions very well, while others have the teachers re-

51

peat the directives as frequently as the children ask for
them.   Many able readers get only two or three questions
out of ten on a listening test correct, others get almost a
perfect score.

        Poor listening is not limited to children, but the same
pattern follows through college when we check recall on material that is presented in a lecture.   Some students glean
pearls of wisdom; others collect only chaff for their efforts.
No wonder we hear teachers from kindergarten through college make these complaints: "If they would only listen,"
"Everything goes in one ear and out the other," and "It seems
that children have tin ears."

        Many people do not listen well day after day. Unless
they are spurred on to listen intently by some strong force,
they do it only sporadically.   How then, can we establish habits of good listening?   Make listening habits as unbreakable
as ivory rather than as fragile as china or glass.

        This may be accomplished in several ways.   In
school it must begin with the teacher.   Teachers should have
clear concepts of all the listening elements, and know how to
train pupils in becoming efficient listeners.   Some teachers
have a fallacious idea that children do not have to be taught
to listen.

        Another concept for teachers to acquire is that lis-
tening instruction is an integral part of the total school program.   It is not a separate subject to be taught in ten or
fifteen minute periods, and then to be forgotten for the rest
of the day.   Opportunities for teaching this estranged language skill are whirling around all day long.

        First, there are as many levels of listening as there
are in reading so that we can begin by setting up listening
levels of instruction.   Hence, teachers will then have instructional materials to use with pupils with varying listening proficiencies in the same classroom.

        Suggested levels are:

First Level--includes specific concepts without details for
                the poor listeners.

        For example:
                The boy went fishing.
                He caught one fish.

The teacher reads the story to the pupils, and asks these questions:

> Who went fishing?
> How many fish did he catch?

The next level of difficulty which would be effective in increasing listening efficiency is:

Second Level--specific concepts with some detail.

> For example:
> My father and I went fishing.
> We rowed to the middle of the lake.
> Suddenly my line jerked.
> I pulled in a large, striped bass.

After the reading, the teacher would ask these questions:

> 1. Who went fishing?
> 2. In what part of the lake did they fish?
> 3. How many fish did he catch?
> 4. What kind of fish did he catch?

Advancing listening skills which will add further competency to the pupils who have already attained mastery of the first two levels include:

Third Level--several concepts with many details.

> For example:
> On Monday afternoon my father and I and one of his friends drove twenty miles to a beautiful lake in the mountains where the fishing was said to be good. When we got to the lake we stopped at the wharf and hired a motor boat. My father started the motor and quickly brought the boat to his favorite fishing spot. We baited our lines and almost instantly my father's friend caught a pickerel about fifteen inches long. Father kept catching fish so small that he had to throw them back in the water. The largest fish I caught was seven inches long.

After the reading, the teacher would ask these questions:

> 1. Who went fishing?

2. Where did they go fishing?
3. How far was the lake?
4. Where did they hire the boat?
5. How long was the pickerel?
6. How big were the fish Father caught?
7. What was the size of the largest fish that the boy caught?

In a somewhat similar manner levels of difficulty could be developed on all succeeding levels, and in the several kinds of listening areas as critical listening; following directions; discriminative, informative, appreciative, abstract, and sequential listening. Thus, teachers would then have programmed instructional materials for pupils with different kinds of ability in this language art.

Conclusions
There are many problems in the field of listening instruction. It is dependent upon many factors such as memory, attention, imagery, which are difficult to probe. However, if we can give teachers information about the importance of listening instruction, we will find our first inroads for teaching sound and effective listening skills.

It is the author's opinion that we should teach children to depend more upon what they hear per se, than to give them props. Many times children are given pictures or words on the board, either before or immediately after material has been read to them, so that they do not have to exert themselves to listen because they can lean on all the visual crutches. This leads to passive listening with too much reliance on visual aids.

If we made an analogy of teaching listening with the methods of teaching music appreciation, then we would find that the desire to hear actively would come from within a child rather than from external stimuli.

PROPORTION, PURPOSE, AND PROCESS IN LISTENING

Edna Lue Furness

Listening is an important mode of learning. A high proportion of instruction is addressed to the ear whether in lectures at the college level or in student reports and discussions in the elementary and secondary schools. In fact, each day in school is a series of adventures in listening.

When children listen for a purpose, they get more out of the experience than when their response is undirected. Children look and listen all day long. They are taught to identify words, birds, insects, and their peers by sight. They might also be taught to identify them by sounds. Children learn to listen better when they establish a purpose for listening in an atmosphere conducive to listening. If students are to listen effectively, they must have something worthwhile to which to listen, a reason for listening, someone to whom they care to listen, and facility for listening.

As our division of work- reading into subtypes is based upon the reader's purposes, so our division of work- listening into subtypes must be based upon the listener's purposes. Thus we distinguish between listening for directions and listening for news of an election or of a sport event. The following purposes have been indicated [Citation 4, p. 554--see end of this section]:

1. Listening for the answer to a definite question.
2. Listening to a question, with the intention to answer.
3. Listening to form an opinion on a controversial question.
4. Listening for news--no particular news.
5. Listening to an argument in order to answer it.
6. Listening to directions which one expects to follow.
7. Listening for unspecified information on a topic one is interested in.

According to a statement by Althea Beery [Citation 1, p. 78], who is, as we said, one of the pioneers in this phase of communication, the purposes of listening are to show courtesy in disagreeing with a speaker; to watch for transitional phrases; to hold the thread of a discussion in mind; to discount bias in a speaker; to listen to content that does not affect the listener directly; to take notes during a speech or report; to write notes or a brief summary of an oral report; to show by remarks that the listener has been considering what has been said; and to reserve judgment in listening to different viewpoints in the discussion.

Purpose is important and so is knowledge of the listening process. Instruction in listening will be more effective when the sequence of its development is better understood. Much critical observation by teachers is needed to determine what constitutes normal progress in intelligent listening, what differentiates one level of listening from another, and what are effective methods of teaching listening.

The following kinds of listening overlap, yet they serve to bring out important differences [Citations 2, p. 120; and 3, p. 139].

(1) Passive, marginal, or secondary listening: listening that is prevalent today as many children study with the radio on. In fact, there is often a deliberate "tuning out" of what is heard with just enough consciousness of the language or sound to bring the child back to attention when a favorite radio personality comes on. Similarly, in classroom or home the tone of voice of teacher or parent may flash the danger signal which alerts the child whose attention has been wandering. The way one listens to background music while reading differs markedly from the type of listening one does when evaluating critically a proposed plan for action which affects one personally or professionally.

(2) Conversational and courteous listening: listening in social situations in which people chat about matters of mutual interest and listen to one another in order to make appropriate responses.

(3) Exploratory listening: listening in which the mind is alerted to find matters of new interest, additional information on a topic, or perhaps a juicy bit of gossip.

(4) Appreciative listening: listening to poetry or other literature for enjoyment or appreciation.

(5) Creative listening: listening which results in a child's reconstructing imaginatively the pleasures of sound, vision, and kinesthetic feelings suggested by what he is hearing. The act of entering imaginatively into the experiences, the setting, and the feelings of the characters in a story, which is being told orally or produced on screen or stage.

(6) Attentive or discriminating listening: listening needed in situations in which accuracy of comprehension is involved, as in directions, announcements, and introductions.

Probably there is a different mind set in situations in which
the hearer participates, such as in conversation and discussion; this might be called responsive listening.

(7) Concentrative or directed listening: listening in
which there is definite purpose to elicit items of information,
to attain understanding, to follow carefully the sequence of
ideas, to perceive the speaker's organization of ideas, and
to settle on his main premise.

(8) Analytical listening: the listening that takes place,
for example, when the listener weighs what is heard against
personal experience and is alert to attempts by the speaker
to sway his opinion by the devices of propaganda. This kind
of listening must be developed by older elementary and high
school pupils in order that they may evaluate what they hear.

Efforts have been made to determine specific factors
operative in the listening process. Nichols [Citation 5] reports that in addition to intelligence and reading comprehension, the factors influencing listening most significantly include recognition of correct English usage, size of the listener's vocabulary (number of words understood when heard),
listening for main ideas as opposed to specific facts, use of
specific techniques while listening to improve concentration,
ability to see significance in the subject discussed, interest
in and emotional attitude toward the topic, and audibility of
the speaker. Like reading, listening depends upon analytical
and critical ability; and it is at its best when "the listener
understands and weighs what he hears, adds to it from personal experience, ponders it in his heart, and does something about it if a problem is involved."

As we well know, the teacher's job is to teach children to listen. It seems altogether reasonable to assume
that the teacher who is aware of the proportion of times
spent in listening, who is informed of purpose and process
in listening, will do a better job of teaching, whatever the
subject, whatever the level of teaching.

Citations

Abbreviated references 1-5 in preceding text are citations to
works below.   Numbers underlined below refer to entry numbers in Sam Duker's Listening Bibliography 2nd Ed. (Scarecrow, 1968) where the full citation may be found.

1.   Beery, Althea, 68.
2.   Dawson, Mildred, 269.
3.   Dow, Clyde W. and Charles Irvin, 308.
4.   Hatfield, W. Wilbur, 532.
5.   Nichols, Ralph G., 873.

Chapter III

THE TEACHING OF LISTENING
I. GENERAL CONSIDERATIONS

The first selection of this chapter, which serves as a
general introduction to the teaching of listening at the elementary school level, is by Althea Beery who was identified in
the introduction to the previous chapter. It first appeared
25 years ago in the Elementary English Review and might
well have been written today as the ideas and reasoning have
in no way been weakened during the intervening period.

Eight specific aids to the development of listening
skills are presented in the second passage which is taken
from a handbook for senior high school students, prepared
by the Office of Curriculum Instruction of the Long Beach,
California schools. This is the first of a number of instances where material prepared for the high school level has
been included because the content seemed equally applicable
to the elementary school level.

The third selection in this chapter is a description of
the teaching of listening in elementary classrooms by students in one of my graduate classes at Brooklyn College. It
first appeared in the Instructor in 1955.

The next excerpt is from Speech Art Activities: A
Curriculum Guide for Elementary Schools, part of the Curriculum Bulletin Series of the Dallas, Texas school system.
A useful description of the scope of listening instruction is
followed by a list of expected outcomes and a number of suggested learning experiences. Any moderately creative teacher should be able to extract many viable ideas from this
short selection.

In 1963 Marie-Jeanne Laurent wrote The Construction
and Evaluation of a Listening Curriculum for Grades 5 and 6
as her doctoral thesis at Boston University. The fifth selection in this chapter is an excerpt from that thesis. It is in-

cluded in the hope that noting the flavor of this outstanding thesis will induce some readers to obtain the thesis itself as it has many valuable ideas and suggestions to offer. Either a photocopy or, at much lower cost, a microfilm of this thesis can be purchased from University Microfilms of Ann Arbor, Michigan. Professor Laurent is presently associated with the Education Department at Central Connecticut State College.

The passage by Professor Robert Canfield of the New York State University College at Oswego first appeared in Elementary English in 1950. Two years later Dr. Canfield completed a doctoral thesis at Syracuse University in which he compared the effects of direct and indirect teaching of listening. An excerpt from that thesis appears immediately following the journal article. In addition to a discussion of some of the general aspects of the teaching of listening, the excerpts used in this chapter give very specific suggestions for ways of building a listening vocabulary and for securing children's attention during listening experiences.

A tabulation of a suggested sequence for teaching listening skills in the first five elementary school grades taken from a curriculum bulletin of the Nederland, Texas schools is the next passage in this chapter.

The ninth passage is taken from the 1963 University of Oregon doctoral thesis of Dr. Vern L. Farrow who is presently Dean of the School of Liberal Arts and Sciences, Ambassador College in Pasadena, California. It presents some thought provoking facts about his research concerning attention in listening. This passage is followed by an excerpt from a Beloit, Wisconsin curriculum bulletin concerning the role of listening centers and of tape recorders in the elementary school classroom.

The last passage is one that I wrote for Science Education in 1958. There I try to make the point that teaching of listening is every teacher's responsibility and should not be compartmentalized into a language arts period and then forgotten for the rest of the school day.

LISTENING ACTIVITIES IN THE ELEMENTARY SCHOOL

Althea Beery

How can we as elementary teachers improve the listening of children? There are at least six ways:

By sensing the relationships of listening to other
    phases of communication;
By understanding the psychological process of listen-
    ing;
By providing general conditions conducive to listening;
By utilizing opportunities for children to listen;
By understanding the developmental levels of listen-
    ing--the goals toward which teachers and pupils
    should work; and
By keeping alert to new inventions and equipment
    which will aid the program.

Speaking and listening, writing and reading--these are reciprocal processes of communication. Why speak if no one is to listen? Why write if no one is to read? Listening and reading are similar processes psychologically. Each involves the perceiving of ideas from others, but each demands more than passive reception. What principles that have proved beneficial in reading may we tentatively apply to listening?

Some of these are:

1. Pupils read better when they have a purpose.
    Surely pupils will listen better when they expect
    to use what they hear.
2. Reading results in greater learning when it is
    combined with other modes of learning; listening,
    too, needs to be reinforced by other forms of
    experience.
3. Reading readiness is essential to successful at-
    tainment in reading; listening readiness should be
    similarly explored.
4. Comprehension improves when pupils are encour-
    aged to check themselves on the ideas gained
    from reading; listening probably needs similar
    checks.

For primary children, studies indicate that the use of the spoken word, including the give-and-take of spirited discussion, is a more effective way of learning than the use of the written word. Without questioning the important place which reading must occupy in education, it would seem reasonable that the substantial control over the mother tongue which a child brings with him to school should be widely used to facilitate his learning during those years in which he is acquiring control over the tool of reading.

At the same time, attention to the limitations of listening is in order. There is some evidence that people are more easily misled by the spoken than by the written word. Children can reread if they have missed a point, but in listening this is not possible; frequently the speaker goes on unaware of the learners' confusion. Reading can be individualized much more readily than listening. As teachers we need to help children decide when to seek information from the spoken word, and when to turn to books for guidance. The child must use both repeatedly.

Improvement of Listening
The following general suggestions for the improvement of listening may be helpful:

>Choose appropriate opportunities for listening in terms of pupils' interest and needs and commensurate with their ability to understand.

>Provide an atmosphere conducive to listening; seat young children close to the speaker.

>Discuss with pupils the factors that make a good listener; encourage them to set appropriate standards for listening.

>Help children learn when to listen, what to listen to, and how to listen.

>Utilize everyday class activities to develop more alert listening.

>Place emphasis upon what is said rather than upon errors in usage.

>Encourage pupils to demand meaning in what they hear; urge them to ask for explanations when they do not understand.

Provide, when appropriate, for interaction of the speaker and group during the listening period.

As a teacher, exemplify good listening habits yourself.

Be consistent in the formation of listening habits.

Listening has always been an inseparable part of oral language and has never been completely ignored. If we examine the standards toward which we have worked in story telling, discussion, dramatization, and other activities of oral language, we can usually find tucked away some place a reminder to the pupils that they must be polite and keep quiet when others are performing; but alas, most of us have been satisfied with the outward evidence of reception. The speaker expects a certain modicum of politeness and appropriate posture but is frequently surprised when listeners react with questions or challenging statements.

Situations Involving Listening

Brief consideration will be given to typical oral situations with emphasis on the listening skills involved.

1.   Conversation and Telephoning

Fortunate are the children who have had opportunity at home to listen to and participate in sparkling conversation. Polite response to the contribution of others, as the conversational ball is tossed from one to the other, is dependent upon attentiveness as others speak. The teacher must be alert to the needs of two types of children; first, pampered, only children who demand exclusive attention and, at the other extreme, children who listen passively to others, but take no part in the conversation.

For young children natural experience in learning to listen to conversation is afforded by the informal give-and-take of ideas as the group meets in the morning, as they move about during work period, and as they visit during the mid-morning lunch. With older children, it is profitable to discuss what listening well in conversation means and to use occasionally the device of a group conversing while the rest of the class listens, especially if this is followed by an analysis of the conversation for evidences in the dialogue that the participants had listened carefully to each other.

Telephone conversations call for unusually intent listening not only to the words, but to the overtones in the verbal responses of the person at the other end of the line. By later elementary grades, pupils should not limit telephone conversations to close friends since listening to older people and strangers places a greater burden on listening. Dramatization of imaginary conversations in the classroom is healthful, but genuine needs for telephoning should be utilized, whenever possible.

2. Discussion

Improvement in listening during discussion will come as children sense the purpose of the discussion and are allowed due freedom in reaching conclusions, and as they learn to feel responsible for seeing that their personal contributions do not duplicate points already made. Occasional summarization is helpful. There is a place, too, for older children to listen to planned discussion in which a committee that has done preliminary investigation on some problem leads the class in considering the facts and basing discussion upon them.

3. Directions and Announcements

Frequently young children have difficulty with directions because, in pre-school experience, directions and requests were addressed to them as individuals, whereas in school they need to give attention when remarks are addressed to the group. Children's attention should be called to the importance of sequence in directions. The typical seven-year-old can be expected to remember three simple commands long enough to execute them in sequence. The proof of listening to directions is, of course, correct execution.

In connection with science, arithmetic, written work, and hand work of all kinds, the teacher has a responsibility for improving children's listening to explanations.

In announcements they make, children learn to include what, when, and where. They should listen for the same points in the announcements they hear.

4. Listening to Music

Music comes to us only through our ears, so listening is basic to this field. Background music is useful for

relaxation in connection with rest periods. Enjoyment of
good music is so dependent upon familiarity that it is essential that time within the school day be provided for children
to hear over and over appropriate good music. Pupil recordings and the microphone enable the group to hear themselves
more objectively. Music teachers tell us that records which
supply the missing parts or reinforce the singing of the bud-
ding tenor or bass are of great benefit during the seventh
and eighth grades when boys' voices are changing. Rhythmic
and graphic interpretation of music builds listening habits in
children.

5. Creative Listening

Those of us who believe that creative expression re-
leases and develops a child need to examine the possibilities
of creative listening. Children should be encouraged to gain
sensory impressions from what they hear. They can learn
to see pictures, smell scents, and feel textures as they listen creatively. Music and poetry, as well as direct experience, may be the impetus to creative expression. Each
sense stimulates and supports the others. Topics for children's writing can well come from the listening they do in
and out of school.

6. Sounds Around Us

Children need only encouragement to sensitize themselves to the sounds in nature and in the man-made world
around them. During a two-hour period in a nursery school,
a master teacher, interested in music, picked out on the
piano a tune which a child made upon the spot as he worked,
repeated with a youngster the rhythmic pattern he had
pounded out with blocks, stopped with a group to note the
deep sound and repeated pattern of a fog-horn, and encouraged five or six other explorations in sound which I have
since forgotten. In no case was the teacher imposing attention to sound; she merely gave value by her attention to
what the child had already noted.

The preceding illustrations do not in any sense exhaust the possibilities for listening inherent in everyday living in schools. Perhaps they will serve to suggest to teachers other situations in which the listening of children can
be improved, and additional values to be obtained from the
situations discussed.

The teacher who would improve the listening habits of children must have clearly in mind the abilities that are essential to listening, the sequential order in which these normally develop, and the situations in which growth in these habits and attitudes may be naturally developed. In addition he must interpret the listening behavior of each child in the light of his total development.

EIGHT SUGGESTIONS FOR BETTER LISTENING

From a Curriculum Bulletin of the
Long Beach (California) Unified School District

Listen carefully and thoughtfully if you want to learn, interpret, appreciate, and enjoy what you hear.

Some suggestions follow which will help you to develop this important skill:

1. Determine your purpose for listening.

2. Find out all you can about a speaker's qualifications for speaking on his topic.

3. Identify the speaker's purpose by listening carefully to his introductory remarks. Also, listen for cues to the structure of his speech.

4. Listen for transition words which show the relationship of the speaker's ideas.

5. Try to pick out the main ideas that the speaker presents. Write these as notes, if you wish. (Try to number the main ideas so that your notes show logical progression from one point to another.)

6. Weigh carefully what the speaker says and how he says it.

   a. Decide whether he is using facts as well as opinions to achieve his purpose.

b. Determine whether he gives sufficient specific
    details to make his point.
c. Determine to what extent the speaker appeals
    to the listeners' emotion through voice, ges-
    ture, vocabulary.
d. Try to decide what the speaker chose to tell
    and what he chose to omit.
e. Compare what the speaker says with other in-
    formation you have on the subject.

7. If there is a question period, ask about any part
    of the presentation that you did not understand.

8. Discuss with someone else what you heard so that
    you will remember what was said, and so that you
    can test your reactions to the speech against some-
    one else's.

HOW LISTENING CAN BE TAUGHT

Sam Duker

Teaching children to listen effectively has become an
important part of elementary school language arts instruction
at all levels. The conscious teaching of this skill is a com-
paratively recent development, and so far most articles on
listening have dealt with the importance of teaching it rather
than with ways of doing it.

Recently a Brooklyn College graduate class spent an
entire semester studying ways of teaching listening. Seven
of the students were teaching elementary classes in Brooklyn
public schools and thus were able to apply the principles discussed in this course to their own classroom practices. Here
are some of the devices that they found worked well.

GRADE 5

Miss Elaine Fettman taught two fifth-grade social-
studies classes. In one of these classes no particular emphasis was placed on listening. In the other, there were
class discussions about the following aspects of listening:

1.   Listening for main ideas.
2.   Listening for key ideas.
3.   Paying attention to the topic rather than to varied objects and persons in the room.
4.   Keeping one's mind on the subject being discussed in order to keep in the spirit of the idea.
5.   Taking notes to aid in remembering.

Identical social-studies lessons were taught to both classes over a period of ten weeks.   Both classes were given the same biweekly tests.   A significantly greater improvement in test results was observed in the class in which good listening was being emphasized.   When these test results were discussed with the control group at the end of the ten-week period, the pupils in that class expressed eagerness to also learn about listening.   Thus two classes became diligent students and practitioners of ways in which to become good listeners.

GRADE 4

Miss Phyllis Weinberg found the opaque projector a great aid in teaching listening skills in her fourth-grade classroom.   A noticeably greater amount of interest was shown by her children as a result of the planned use of this device as an aid to careful listening.

GRADE 3

Miss Lois Herschkowitz found the following techniques helpful in increasing skills in critical listening among pupils in a third-grade class:

1.   The children closed their eyes and after a short period told about the various sounds they heard during that time.

2.   After a lesson the children were asked what extraneous sounds they had heard while the lesson was going on.   Using this list as a springboard for discussion, the children made up this set of rules for good listening:

Listen carefully.
Pay attention.
Be wide awake.
Look at the speaker.
Don't listen to noises.

Listen so you can answer questions.
Listen so you can learn.

3. In arithmetic the child called on to answer a problem clapped her hands the required number of times; the other pupils listened carefully to check the answer.

4. Radio programs, Show and Tell periods, and the oral reading of original compositions were discussed by pupils not only as to content but also as to quality of presentation.

Miss Annabelle Bernard, in another third grade, found that a discussion with the children in her class on the differences between merely hearing something and really listening to it substantially improved the degree of attention paid to, and the comprehension of, school radio programs.

GRADE 2

Miss Barbara Darvin used several methods to develop good listening habits in her second-graders.

1. She took the children for a walk around the block and on their return asked them to name the various sounds they had heard on their walk. After this list had been put on the chalkboard there was a discussion of ways in which more sounds might have been heard. In a few days another walk was taken. On their return the children listed 35 more sounds than they had on the first occasion.

2. Children closed their eyes and attempted to identify various sounds such as the crumpling of paper, and the closing of a door.

3. Miss Darvin found that asking questions before reading a long paragraph aloud to the children enabled the pupils to give many details contained in such a paragraph that they ordinarily would not have spotted. She asked the children to listen to a selection for the purpose of picking out the most appropriate title for that selection from several titles suggested before the reading. Over a period of two months these exercises were continually varied.

A considerable increase in both interest and comprehension was noted as a result of this emphasis on efficient listening.

Miss Mary Jane Shea and six other second-grade teachers had found that tuning in on school radio programs was rather impractical because the children appeared to lack both interest and the ability to pay attention. Miss Shea developed a series of lessons as introductions to these programs emphasizing ways of listening well. All seven teachers taught these lessons preceding the use of the radio programs over a period of months and found that without exception the attitude of the pupils was completely changed. Radio program time became a delightful experience commanding a maximum degree of attention and anticipation. Comprehension of the programs, which consisted largely of fairy tales, was considerably improved. It was clear to all concerned that a listening experience is of greater value when children are adequately prepared for it and are motivated to have interest in and curiosity about the content of the program they are to hear.

GRADE 1

The most extensive program in the teaching of listening was carried on by Miss Elsie Digons with her class of 39 beginning first-graders. Miss Digons found that most of the objectives of a beginners' program can be carried out through a planned emphasis on listening. Here are some of the things she did.

1. Using the common device of having children close their eyes and listen for sounds, she first asked for all sounds heard. Then she asked children for sounds made by human beings, such as the teacher walking, a monitor opening the door, a child sighing.

On a stormy day the children were asked to listen for sounds of nature. They heard the wind howling and banging, the rain sweeping against the windows, and even a bird bumping against the window. On another occasion, children were alerted to listen for mechanical sounds, which resulted in reports of airplanes buzzing by, a truck roaring uphill, an automobile trying to get started, an automobile horn blowing, and so forth. At another time the boys and girls were given practice in identifying a particular sound purposely produced. The advantages of such practice in attentive, selective listening and in vocabulary development seem quite obvious.

2.   Musical records were played after a carefully prepared list of motivating questions had been asked.

3.   Practice was given in following a gradually length-
ening series of oral directions in the form of a game.   For
example, one child was told to: "Go to the door, turn the
knob, take the ruler from my desk, and bring it to your
seat."   Other children watched to see if the directions were
properly carried out in the right order.

4.   Listening for various kinds of sounds on walks
around the neighborhood was substantially improved by discussions of possible sounds before taking the walks.

5.   Listening games, some old, some new, were frequently played.   Among them were:

Beast, Bird, or Fish.-- The player who is "it" points
to a child and calls out either "bird," "beast," or "fish."
Then that child must name one of whatever he was asked to
name before "it" can count to ten.   He then becomes "it,"
and so on.

Whispering Game.-- The pupils form a circle.   The
first player whispers a sentence to his neighbor who in turn
whispers it to the child next to him, and so on.   The child
farthest away from "it" who can correctly repeat the sentence becomes the new "it."

6.   Miss Digons presented a film strip, showing children drawing pictures.   The teacher in the strip tells the
children to put their drawings on her desk and get their out-
er clothing.   All the children except Jimmy follow instructions.   Jimmy's drawing blows onto the floor and is trampled.
An enlivened discussion of the importance of attentive listening to directions was the outcome of this showing.

7.   Children made up class charts on listening; for
example:

Why Should We Listen?

We want to learn our lessons.
We want to hear directions.
We want to hear what others have to say.
We want to be polite.
We want others to listen to us when we speak.

What Makes Us Want to Listen?

We listen if the speaker talks loud and clearly.
We listen when the talk isn't too long.
We listen when the speaker is nice.
We listen when the talk is interesting.

Frequent use was made of these charts on appropriate occasions to emphasize the need for good listening. Miss Digons says of these charts: "The rule, 'We want others to listen to us when we speak,' made the most lasting impression on the children. Many times when the children are listening to their peers, I hear a child say: 'Shhh!' I hear others say, 'Be quiet so the children will listen to you when you have something to tell'."

As a result of this emphasis on listening the children did not lose ground in developing readiness for other skill subjects. The effect of the practice of good listening habits on discipline was marked. Class discussions were improved. It was obvious that the children found satisfaction and security in mastering a skill for which they had full readiness and in the exercise of which they could meet with success.

There are many ways of teaching listening and the teaching devices these seven teachers tried represent only a very small number of the many possible approaches. They did accomplish the purpose of increasing pupils' awareness of and interest in the importance of listening. Why not try some of them in your class?

LISTENING

From a Curriculum Bulletin of the
Dallas, Texas Independent School District

Scope

In speech arts, the pupil learns that one listens with the mind, not with the ears alone, since the ears are merely agents through which the sounds that one hears travel to the brain. There are many types of listening. One listens to the radio, television, records, debates, panel discussions, everyday conversation, instructions, and directions. One listens to gain facts, to respond creatively, to hear particular sounds, and to gratify many other needs and pleasures. Since there are many types of listening and ways to listen, a continuing effort is made to help pupils learn how to relate listening to its various purposes, what to listen for, and how to respect the rights of other persons who want to listen.

Expected Outcomes
       As a result of instruction in the types and purposes of listening the pupil:

> Realizes that listening involves thinking and is as important to communication as speaking;
>
> Realizes that one forms concepts, images, and ideas from the sounds he hears, combined with thought processes and experiences;
>
> Recognizes that oral communication is real only when the speaker is heard correctly and when it relays thought that has meaning to the listener;
>
> Learns the processes of hearing;
>
> Learns that there are many types of listening depending upon purpose;
>
> Learns appreciative listening to sounds of nature, music, and voices;
>
> Learns that one is engaged in exploratory listening when listening to sounds never heard before;
>
> Learns creative listening by adding what he has experienced, felt, heard, seen, touched, smelled, and read to what is heard;
>
> Listens carefully to grow in word power;
>
> Listens actively to understand relationships of ideas, follow sequences, and comprehend details;
>
> Learns the importance of courteous listening;
>
> Learns to evaluate by listening; and
>
> Respects the listening rights of others.

Learning Experiences
                  The primary pupil develops good listening habits
through:

> Listening to distinguish between sounds, to follow in-
>   structions, and for various other purposes to be-
>   come aware of different types of listening;
>
> Practicing ways of listening with the mind;
>
> Re-telling simple stories that have been read or told;
>
> Practicing words on different pitch levels (for ear
>   training);
>
> Listening for simple facts;
>
> Listening for rhyme and rhythm;
>
> Listening for comparisons;
>
> Counting from 1 to 8, using C scale;
>
> Listening for color words;
>
> Listening for specific sounds;
>
> Listening for pure enjoyment;
>
> Listening for a specific sound, idea, or other element,
>   as the need arises, after being prepared and mo-
>   tivated by the teacher to listen; and
>
> Discussing what makes listening a cooperative process.

The middle-grade pupil grows in ability to listen well
through:

> Participating in group discussions on how to listen;
>
> Writing a short résumé of a story read or told to the
>   class;
>
> Telling the meaning of a poem which was just heard;
>
> Repeating a short, unfamiliar jingle after hearing it
>   once;

Naming as many different types of listening as possible
and practicing for skill in each type;

Listening for specific facts;

Listening creatively;

Listening for a certain sound, idea, or other element,
motivated by the teacher;

Listening to sounds in nature; and

Listening to music for appreciation, interpretation,
evaluation, structure, composer's methods, or
just enjoyment.

A PLAN FOR TEACHING LISTENING

Marie-Jeanne Laurent

Description of Materials
Discriminative listening.--The first ten lessons of the
instructional plan dealt with discriminative listening. Many
of the skills here were similar to those developed in a reading program; for this reason primarily it was decided to
commence with what seemed to be relatively familiar ground.

There were five separate skills areas within this section, and two lessons were devoted to each of these special
subdivisions. These were as follows:

1. Listening to hear details,
2. Listening for sequence or order of events,
3. Listening to grasp the main idea,
4. Listening to follow directions, and
5. Listening to distinguish the relevant from the irrelevant.

The materials used for analysis and practice included
poems, stories (among these a Greek myth), paragraphs
from essays, and team games. The subject matter contained in these was varied so as to appeal to as wide a range of
interests as was possible.

Because this section introduced the students to the study of listening, they were asked to think about and discuss such questions as:

Why is listening difficult sometimes?
In what ways is it like reading?
In what ways can we improve our listening ability?
What part does attitude, or frame of mind, play in
    listening?

Critical listening.---The second section of the listening program was concerned with critical listening, without doubt the most complex to teach, to learn, and even for which to build lessons. If discriminative listening is largely a question of listening attentively to recall facts or ideas, critical listening is a more intricate and mature activity: it requires recall and retention, with the added responsibility of evaluating what is heard. It is this evaluation or reflection about what is listened to that is crucial and intricate.

Again, it was decided to divide the general section into five sub-skills areas and two lessons given over to each of these:

1.   Listening to detect bias or slant,
2.   Listening to differentiate fact from opinion,
3.   Listening to detect poor logic, unreasonable argument,
4.   Listening to discover poor organization and presentation, and
5.   Listening in order to make judgments and inferences.

Materials used in this section were largely of three types: paragraphs from essays, newspaper articles (including editorials), and short biographical sketches. Some of the activities the students were asked to participate in were: finding, bringing to class, and discussing news articles and editorials; listing types of writing or speaking which are factual as opposed to opinionated; writing well-organized arguments for holding a given opinion; outlining material listened to; and defending orally the conclusions drawn from certain selections heard.

Discussions in this part of the program were concerned with the nature and purpose of propaganda, the difference between factual reporting and editorializing, the definition and exploration of what is meant by "expert opinion," the nature of gullibility and skepticism, and those factors necessary to the formulation of value judgments, conclusions, and inferences.

Appreciative listening.--The third large area of concentration in the listening training was appreciative listening. This section was shorter than the first two and contained only five lessons. Both poetry and prose selections were utilized. The main points developed were: the power and beauty of well-chosen words in describing people, places, and feelings; the color or mood of language; and the musical or rhythmical aspects of written and spoken symbols. Some attention was given also to the infinite variety in vocabulary and the resultant possibility with regard to individualism and exactness in speaking and writing.

Correlated listening.--The last section, also shorter than the first two, was called correlated listening, and presented social studies types of materials dealing with three different geographical areas and one historical figure. The students were asked, with regard to these articles, to listen and be aware of:

1. Recalling details and main ideas,
2. Observing sequence or pattern of organization,
3. Noticing objectivity (or lack of it) in presentation, and
4. Thinking so as to be able to draw conclusions and inferences from the material.

It was hoped that these selections, and the ensuing class discussions, would serve as a review and synthesis of the several skills and attitudes stressed throughout the instruction period.

Sample lessons, one from each of the four areas just described, follow.

I. A Lesson in Discriminative Listening

The aim of lessons, always stated at the beginning of lessons, may be made clear to students in any way the instructor feels is appropriate to his special class. Materials to be used will be attached to lessons.

AIM: To practice listening for <u>detail</u> and <u>emotional</u> slant.

PROCEDURE:
1.   Teacher will read aloud the poem "A Summer Morning" by Rachel Field.   Before reading, the students should be asked to listen for:

      a.   The things mentioned in nature that indicate it is summer.
      b.   The words that might indicate how the poet feels about her subject.

2.   After completing the reading, these questions will be written on the board:

      a.   What time of day is it in the poem?
      b.   What kind of birds are seen?
      c.   What did the ocean do?
      d.   What type of tree was mentioned?
      e.   Whom did the poet hear and what did he say?

Students should check their own papers, grading them on the basis of 20 points for each correct answer.

3.   Follow-up discussion with students:

      a.   For what two reasons were we listening to the poem?
          To recall details re summer.
          To note poet's feeling, or bias, or slant.

      b.   Why did we forget certain things?
          Inattention?
          Only one reading?
          Too many details?

      c.   How can we know the poet's feelings?
          Words she associates with summer are
            pleasant.
          Pictures she presents are agreeable, happy.

      d.   Does the reader or speaker help or hinder listening?
          Good reading can make it interesting, mean-
            ingful.
          Good reader holds listeners' attention.
          Poor reader makes listening difficult.

> e. How can you be a better listener?
>   Give reader strict attention.
>   Concentrate, think while listening.

Materials for This Lesson

"A Summer Morning" by Rachel Field

I saw dawn creep across the sky
And all the gulls go flying by.
I saw the sea put on its dress
Of blue mid-summer loveliness,
And heard the trees begin to stir
Green arms of pine and juniper.
I heard the wind call out and say:
"Get up, my dear, it is today."

II. A Lesson in Critical Listening

AIM: Listen to detect bias, emotional slant, lack of objectivity.

PROCEDURE: Discussion:

1. What is bias?
    Prejudice; to incline to one side.
    To present only one side of question.
    Could explain where meaning comes from (to cut material on bias, across the grain, not with line of material).

2. What is slant?
    Not straight, on an angle.
    Inclined--again to one side.

3. What is objectivity, subjectivity in writing or speaking?
    One is physical, actual facts or realities reported.
    Other deals with emotional, mental attitudes of writer.

4. In what kind of material would you find each kind of writing?
    Objective: texts and scientific or medical journals.

Subjective: fiction, poetry, drama, editorials.

5. In what areas of life is this difference important?
Where should we be aware of it?
Politics-- study of history?
Religion?
Art, music, literature?

Read the selections on attached sheet, asking class to
see if these are evident: bias, slant, etc.

After each reading, discuss _how_ they detected it, _why_
it is important.

Follow- up assignment: Ask students to bring in an
article showing either bias or the lack of it, and be ready to
discuss these questions.

Materials for This Lesson

SELECTION 1: What sickening details in the daily journals!
Even the family newspapers, like the Herald Tribune and the
London Times record freshly the horror of crimes committed
daily.   Politics were never more corrupt and brutal; government is riddled with small, materialistic minds.   The arts--
our novels, plays, and music-- are shocking and deal with the
undignified and degraded.   Our painters are obsessed with un-
lofty thoughts; our sculptors represent the trivial and the un-
important.   Businessmen are shameful, greedy, and interested only in profit and material gain.   Our culture is immoral,
tragic, and selfish in every corner; beyond repair and beyond
hope.

SELECTION 2: We had a funeral today in this town, and the
longest funeral procession in the memory of these hills.   A
good man has gone away-- and yet remains.   In the short
time I have been here, I never came to know him personally,
though I saw him often in the country roads, a ruddy old
gentleman with thick, iron- gray hair, somewhat stern of
countenance, shabby of attire, sitting as erect as a trooper
in his open buggy, one muscular hand resting on his knee,
the other holding the reins.   No one who knows this community can help knowing Dr. John North.   I never so desired
the gift of moving expression as I do now, that I might give
the faintest idea of what a good man means to a place like
this and how vividly and long his memory will live here
among us.

SELECTION 3: Our Europe cannot perish; she will certainly remain. Her religion has in it those victorious energies of defence which are the basic condition of establishment. Europe, though she may repel attacks from within and without, is always secure. The soul of her is a certain spirit, reasonable and full of chivalry. The gates of hell shall not prevail against her. Her people have merged, her cities fallen, her soldiers believed to have lost all because a battle turned against them. Her colonies have been dangerous, some say on the decline. She has risen from her misfortunes; sne will always rise. She cannot die, but only grow stronger and greater.

SELECTION 4: The Soviet Union's twin cosmonauts both landed by parachute after their epic flight through space. Their ships weighed about five tons each. The closest their ships came to each other during their joint flight was about three miles. They landed six minutes and 125 miles apart in the desert region of remote Kazakstan. They both observed "glowing particles" passing their spaceships during flight. Col. Glenn of the U. S. also had remarked the presence of such particles. Commander Scott Carpenter observed the particles during his later flight as well. "We do not feel we understand the nature of these particles yet; they may be simply exhaust of the rocket motor," one of the Russian spacemen commented.

SELECTION 5: Associate Judge of the Supreme Court Felix Frankfurter today retired, and President Kennedy has appointed Secretary of Labor Arthur Goldberg to replace him. Mr. Justice Frankfurter, Vienna-born, came to the U. S. at the age of 12, not speaking a word of English. At the Law School of Harvard University, he was brilliant and successful. He was the leader in the Supreme Court of the conservative wing. Although Mr. Goldberg is classified as a liberal, and even a radical by some, he may be difficult to classify, as was his predecessor, Mr. Frankfurter.

III.   A Lesson in Appreciative Listening

AIM: To listen to hear rhythm and mood in poetic language.

PROCEDURE: Discussion:

        Is language rhythmical? Yes, especially poetry, often prose.

Is language capable of expressing moods, feelings through sound? Yes.

1. Read Selection #1. Ask class to listen for "mood words."

How do the words here help mood or feeling?
Image of being awake--eternal motion.
Words such as "beauteous" instead of beautiful--softer.
"holy time" suggests peace, quiet
Image of the Nun in adoration--again suggests repose.
"sun sinking"--tranquil scene.
"Heaven is gentle"

2. Read Selection #2

How is mood set here? Is it sad or just quiet?
"tolls and knell"--l's are liquid, soft sounds.
"lowing herd slowly o'er the lea"--more l's.
"glimmering landscape"--soft lights suggested.
"solemn stillness"--l's and s's are soft sounds.

3. Read Selection #3

How did poet achieve mood here?
Short, emphatic phrases.
Hard-sounding words such as mark, bound, mocks, storm.
Image of boundlessness, space in phrases like earth's wide regions, blue above and blue below.

4. Read Selection #4

Why is this so "rhymy"?
A nonsense verse, for amusement, delighting the ear.

5. Read last selection.

How did poet get across mood of courage, manliness, fearlessness?
Short, clipped words:

"black as the Pit from pole to pole"
"bludgeonings"
"bloody but unbowed"

Images are bold, masculine:
"unconquerable soul"
"clutch of circumstance"
"have not winced nor cried aloud"

Materials for This Lesson

SELECTION 1: "It Is a Beauteous Evening"
by William Wordsworth

It is a beauteous evening, calm and free,
The holy time is quiet as a Nun
Breathless with adoration; the broad sun
Is sinking down in its tranquility.
The gentleness of heaven is on the sea.

Listen! the mighty Being is awake
And doth with His eternal motion make
A sound like thunder--everlastingly.

SELECTION 2: "Elegy Written in a Country Churchyard"
by Thomas Gray

The curfew tolls the knell of parting day
The lowing herd winds slowly o'er the lea
The ploughman homeward plods his weary way
And leaves the world to darkness and to me.

Now fades the glimmering landscape on the sight
And all the air a solemn stillness holds,
Save where the beetle wheels his droning flight
And drowsy tinklings lull the distant folds.

SELECTION 3: "The Sea" by Proctor

The sea! The sea! The open sea!
The blue, the fresh, the ever free!
Without a mark, without a bound,
It runneth the earth's wide regions round.
It plays with the clouds, it mocks the skies
Or like a cradled creature lies.

I'm on the sea! I'm on the sea!
I am where I would ever be
With the blue above and the blue below
And silence whereso'er I go.
If a storm should come and awake the deep
What matter--I shall ride and sleep.

SELECTION 4:   "The Owl and the Pussy Cat" by Edward Lear

The Owl and the Pussy-Cat went to sea
In a beautiful pea-green boat
They took some honey and plenty of money
Wrapped up in a five-pound note.

The Owl looked up at the stars above
And sang to a small guitar
"O lovely Pussy, O Pussy my love
What a beautiful Pussy you are.
        You are, you are,
What a beautiful Pussy you are!"

SELECTION 5:   "Invictus" by William Henley

Out of the night that covers me
Black as the Pit from pole to pole.
I thank whatever gods may be
For my unconquerable soul.

In the fell clutch of circumstance
I have not winced nor cried aloud
Under the bludgeonings of chance
My head is bloody but unbowed.

IV.   A Lesson in Correlated Listening

AIM: To present Social Studies material in order to 1. Listen for facts, 2. Listen for bias, and 3. Listen to make judgments.

PROCEDURE:
    1.   Read selection about Japan, asking the students not only to listen to facts but to be ready to make certain judgments about them.

        a.   Ask students after reading to put down at least five facts they heard in the selection.

b.   Ask them to write one fact which seemed un-important to them.

c.   Ask them if the selection revealed any bias, feeling or emotion regarding the facts, that is, if the speaker did anything more than objectively stating the facts.

d.   Ask them how they feel this was done if it was at all.

2.   Discussion:

a.   What do you feel are some of the important facts?

> Size of country
> Products
> Large cities
> Tremendous growth and change since World War II

b.   Do you feel speaker was completely objective?

> No, since many qualifying words were used to describe places and facts, thus hinting that speaker has reacted to these himself.

c.   How do you know there is opinion involved here?

> Use of words such as beautiful, lovely to describe mountains, countryside, women, homes.
> Use of words such as fascinating to explain cities, industries.
> Statements that many Americans reacted favorably to its appeal.

d.   Has opinion any place in this type of material?

> Possibly influences listener to want to find out more about this topic?
> Holds our attention better?
> Makes for more dynamic talk, less dull?

e.   Does it influence our judgment?
> Probably, unconsciously.

Materials for This Lesson

"Mountains in the Ocean"

The island group which makes up what is known as
Japan is in the western part of the Pacific Ocean, close to
the mainland of the continent of Asia.   The largest of these
islands is Honshu; the four islands of the country all together are not as large as California.   Japan is inhabited by [105]
million persons; California has only [19] million.

Japan's seasons resemble ours very much, and its
climate is ideal in many ways.   There is enough rain throughout the year: the spring is green and in autumn many leaves
turn splendidly vivid as they do here.   The countryside is
lovely all year around.

Much of Japan's land is used for raising rice and other vegetables such as peas, beans and sweet potatoes.   The
hillsides are used for planting tea, for which Japan is justly
famous.

Japan is perhaps best known for its silk and the beautiful kimonos, or robes, made from the silk material.   Japan
makes much of the silk used throughout the world.

Because Japan is an island country, the Japanese catch
and eat more fish than any people on earth.   The fishermen
catch tuna, shark and mackerel in the deep ocean waters,
and close to shore in the shallow waters there are fine fishing areas also.

Japanese homes are generally simple and quite lovely--
wooden with thatched roofs, and always with a garden, which
is often a thing of beauty.   The Japanese are artistic in many
areas, and in flower raising and arranging they are world-
famous.

Tokyo, now a very much westernized city of about 8
million people, is in the beautiful Tokyo Bay.   Many modern
buildings have sprung up in Tokyo since the last World War,
and clothing styles, as well as many other older customs,
have become almost completely western.   The influence of
the United States has been great on Japan: its government
has slowly become democratized, its industries have grown
astonishingly rapidly since the war, and its people have pros-
pered with its new liberalism.   Americans in the armed ser-

vices during the war found Japan intriguing, and we continue
to travel there and find it so--with its charming women, its
lovely countryside, famous Mount Fuji, the famed cherry
blossoms, and the new bustling cities. Japan has emerged
as a new and surprisingly complex nation of the 20th century.

APPROACHES TO LISTENING IMPROVEMENT

Robert Canfield

        Ideas for helping children improve their listening abil-
ity are appearing in increasing number. These suggestions
are usually organized according to skills involved in direct,
self-contained lessons or according to the use of activities
associated with an integrated teaching unit. One type of organization suggests listening as improved by direct instruction, the latter by incidental instruction. As information is
assembled relative to these two approaches, a discerning
teacher recognizes the need to provide the type of listening
instruction his class especially needs. When the teacher and
children together see the need for such activities, a lesson
may have as its sole purpose the improvement of a listening
skill. On other occasions the teacher may capitalize on a
unit activity designed to satisfy another goal but which also
provides a splendid opportunity to teach listening skills. In
either case improved auditory comprehension should result.

        A review of the nature of the listening process re-
veals that both of these approaches can help in improving
listening. What most people call "listening" is a complex
of physical and psychological functionings. Hearing, auditory
perception, attention, and refined comprehension skills are
involved. The teacher who would improve listening needs to
look analytically at the process to determine what approach
to instruction to employ. Other things being equal, it is
probably safe to predict that the teacher who is the most
careful in matching instruction to discovered need will be
the most successful listening teacher.

        As a guide in selecting particular listening experiences
a teacher may want to assess the children's ability to attend.
Attention and understanding are factors in the listening process that influence each other. A child who fails to pay at-

tention has little chance to comprehend.   There is little use in providing direct skill practice if a readiness to attend is not first achieved and maintained.

What are the factors encouraging attention that a teacher may provide in his classroom?   Aside from the child with atypical behavior most children attend well when the following conditions are met:

1.   Adequate physical conditions are provided.

a.   Comfort in terms of temperature, lighting conditions, and seating arrangement allows full concentration on the experience at hand.   Fatigued children also tend to be poorer attenders.

b.   The auditory experience is of adequate volume and tonal quality (the teacher's voice is not excluded from this provision).

2.   The experience at hand is adjusted to the general interest and intellectual level of the children.

3.   The purpose of the experience is understood and accepted by the listener.

4.   Opportunities for expressing one's views are interspersed with listening to the contributions of others.

5.   Visual and auditory distractions are minimized.

6.   Good rapport between the speaker and listener is established.

7.   There is abundance and variety in the type of experiences a child is expected to attend to.

Habits of good attention are built on satisfying experiences.   When a child gains enjoyment and satisfaction from listening, the attention factor ceases to be a limitation.

Successful listening not only depends on a willingness and effort to understand but also the tools with which to recognize and interpret spoken words.   Probably the most significant single factor influencing vocabulary is experience. Many opportunities to hear, see, and talk to people in various situations enlarges the reservoir of words recognized

through listening.   Through television and radio many of them
come vicariously.

The teacher who is conscious of vocabulary development does not depend on incidental instruction alone to introduce words.   The following practices allow for growth of listening vocabulary in the classroom:

1.   Judicious use of new words by the teacher in her
everyday conversation with the children.

2.   Intelligent praise for children exploring new words.

3.   Reading good literature to the class.

4.   Noting sound and structure similarities in new
words used in speech.   Becoming new-word conscious.

5.   Use of appropriate recordings, transcriptions,
FM radio programs, and television.

6.   Conversational use of new terms introduced in
content subjects.

7.   Oral vocabulary games where children guess
words on basis of context of structural clues.

The teacher's attempt to help children improve their
listening reaches a critical point when comprehension skills
taught in a "developmental" lesson are applied in a functional listening situation.   The true evaluation of attempts to
teach vocabulary and organization skills directly is in the
children's use of these learnings in social studies, science,
etc.   Listening is peculiarly functional and, while there are
aspects of the skill that benefit from direct instruction, the
bulk of listening improvement comes from skillful guidance
in its use in receiving and evaluating information in other
areas of the curriculum.

It is probably true that, consciously or unconsciously,
good teachers have been teaching listening for several years.
Listening is a way of learning in many instances.   Those
elementary teachers who have allowed for the principles of
learning in teaching children have undoubtedly enriched their
students' skill in auditory understanding.   Quality of listening is quite naturally a function of the satisfaction of children's needs.   A variety of learning activities conducted in

a classroom that provides challenge and success for every
child stimulates communication in a most significant way.
Listening improvement has been newly publicized rather than
discovered or invented. It has always been with us in the
elementary school.

DIRECT AND INDIRECT APPROACHES
TO THE TEACHING OF LISTENING

G. Robert Canfield

The purpose of this study was to obtain information
for elementary teachers seeking ways and means of teaching
listening. More specifically, information was sought on the
effectiveness of two methods of teaching listening at the
fifth-grade level.

A Definition of Listening
The term "listening" as used in this report refers to
the process of attending to, recognizing and interpreting aural language. While other aspects of listening are important
in the elementary school program, this study will be concerned with understanding aural language.

Understanding aural language involves attention and
hearing. Without these processes no understanding could
take place. Auditory perception, interpretation and critical
evaluation are skills basic to the thinking aspects of listening. Skills in recognizing main ideas, transitions and over
all organization are important to listening comprehension.

Language arts teachers recognize the value of direct
teaching of language skills when pupils show a readiness for
such instruction. Through explanations, illustrations, discussions and guided practice, improvement of language skills
takes place. Such lessons have as their explicit purpose the
pupils' understanding and improved use of basic language
skills. In this study, lessons which propose to develop skill
in listening for main ideas and important details are known
as "direct listening instruction."

Experienced teachers will recognize another classroom situation in which improvement of language skills takes

place. The purposeful use of language in the pursuit of understandings in other subject matter areas provides opportunities for the improvement of language skills. Such lessons
have as their purpose the gaining of understandings in the
subject matter being considered. Yet use of language in such
lessons provides natural opportunities for improving language
skills. In this study a series of lessons in which listening
is the major tool for gaining information in the social studies
is known as "indirect listening instruction." Such lessons do
not explicitly refer to listening skills but provide for effective use of these skills in the pursuit of other information.

Statement of The Problem

This study is concerned with the effectiveness of two
types of listening instruction in the fifth grade. Information
on the comparative effectiveness of direct and indirect instructional methods was sought. Relationships between listening and such variables as reading, intelligence and report
card grades were examined. The sample used in this study
was comprised of 149 fifth-grade pupils from two elementary
schools.

Design of The Study

This investigation sought information regarding the effectiveness of direct and indirect instruction through an experiment in teaching, listening to fifth-grade pupils from two
elementary schools. One group received twelve lessons by a
"direct instruction method." Another group received twelve
lessons by an "indirect instruction method." A third group
received no special instruction in listening but rather participated in the usual classroom activities. All three groups
were tested at the beginning and end of a six-week experimental period with the STEP Listening Tests.

Since each school had three sections of fifth grade,
it was possible to establish direct, indirect and control
classes in each of the two schools. The test results of the
"direct instruction" classes from the two schools were combined to form a total direct instruction group of 54 pupils.
The same procedure was used in forming the indirect instruction and control groups. The total indirect group was
composed of 47 pupils while the total control group included
51 pupils. Two pupils from a direct instruction class and
one pupil from a control class were randomly selected to be
excluded from the experiment leaving a total sample of 149
pupils. The exclusion of these three pupils provided three

groups that had the same proportion of pupils from each
school.   Therefore, this design had the advantage of helping
to distribute school differences proportionately among the direct, indirect and control groups.   Combining two classes
from each school to form a group also made it possible to
provide three groups reasonably well matched in mean I.Q.
scores.

Instruments Used in The Study
The Cooperative Test Division of the Educational Testing Service published the Sequential Tests of Educational Progress in 1957.   These tests, commonly known as STEP, are
a series of objective tests in the major academic areas.
Listening is one of the tests developed as part of the communication area.   Forms 4A and 4B of the listening test were
the criterion measure of listening skill used in this study.

Other Instruments Used in The Study
The pupils' I.Q. scores on the California Short- Form
Test of Mental Maturity were available.   The "total mental
factors" I.Q. scores was used as the index of a child's intellectual status.

One week before the start of the experiment, the
Reading Comprehension section of the Iowa Tests of Basic
Skills was administered to all the pupils in the experiment.
Scores on this test were used as an index of the pupils' read-
ing skill.

Subjects
A total of 149 fifth- grade pupils participated in the
experiment.   Seventy- one girls and 79 boys made up the
total group.

Raw scores on the STEP Listening Test were used as
the indexes of the listening skill of pupils in this study.

Instruction in Listening
The direct and indirect instruction in listening began
on the day after the first administration of STEP Listening
Test.   Twelve lessons were taught to the direct group during a six- week period.   Twelve lessons were also taught to
the indirect group during this period.   The direct and indirect lessons ranged from 25 to 35 minutes in length.   Since
this study was aimed at providing information for elementary
teachers, the experiment was conducted in regular classrooms using facilities available to teachers.   The teaching

procedures employed were planned to be practical for classroom use.

All the lessons in this study were taught by the writer.
All the lessons taught in the study were tape recorded.

Direct Instruction

In this study, direct instruction in listening involved
pupils and teacher working together for the single purpose of
developing the pupils' skill in listening. Discussion of the
qualities of a good listener, identification of listening skills,
and practice in using these skills characterized the instruction offered. Listening for main ideas and important details
was emphasized.

A typical lesson included a brief introduction by the
teacher in which the purpose of the lesson was discussed.
Techniques in listening for main ideas and important details
were introduced and explained in this part of the lesson.
Practice in using these techniques followed this introduction.
Discussion of the group's success in applying these techniques when listening to short illustrative exercises helped to
clarify and explain the techniques involved. Opportunity for
individual practice in listening to a longer selection dealing
with the social studies was then provided. After this longer
selection, multiple-choice questions were asked by the teacher. Each pupil recorded his own response to the questions on a prepared answer sheet. The answers were then
given orally and each child scored his own answer sheet.
Discussion of the appropriate answers to the questions followed.

The following skills were introduced in the direct lessons:

1.   Recognizing main ideas when stated as topic or
key sentences.

2.   Inferring main ideas when not stated.

3.   Recognizing main ideas when expressed as a feeling.

4.   Distinguishing between main ideas and important
details.

     5.   Distinguishing between relevant and irrelevant details.

     6.   Recognizing main ideas based on opinions.

     7.   Recognizing transitional phrases.

Indirect Instruction

     Indirect instruction was based on pupils' use of listening in gaining information in the social studies.

     Each of the twelve lessons was developed around a social studies selection to be read orally by the teacher. The selections all dealt with foreign countries. They were the same selections used in the direct group for listening practice. Opening comments by the teacher acted as preparation for the aural selection to follow. Preliminary discussion of the topic and introduction to unusual words in the selection took place during this time. The selection was then read to the pupils. After listening to the selection, the pupils answered multiple-choice questions on the content of the selection. The pupils scored their own answers to these questions. As the answers to the questions were reviewed, further discussion of the content took place.

Summary of the Experiment

     The purpose of this study was to examine the effectiveness of two types of classroom instruction on the listening comprehension of fifth-grade pupils. One hundred forty-nine fifth-grade children from two schools were used as the sample population for the experimental study.

     Three fifth-grade classes from each of the two participating schools were assigned to direct, indirect and control groups. There was no significant difference at the .05 level among the three groups when the mean I.Q. scores of the California Test of Mental Maturity were considered. However, there was a significant difference among the groups' mean scores on the STEP Listening Test administered before instruction began. Significant differences also existed among the groups' mean reading scores as measured by the Iowa Every Pupil Test of Basic Skills. The control group had the highest mean score on both the reading and listening test.

     Twelve direct instruction lessons were taught to two fifth-grade classes, one class from each school. The direct instruction emphasized explanations of listening skills and guided practice in listening for main ideas and important details.

Twelve indirect lessons were taught to two fifth grades, one from each school. The indirect instruction emphasized listening to social studies selections with accompanying comprehension questions but with no direct instruction in how to listen. A control group of two fifth-grade classes, one from each school, did not participate in the planned listening lessons.

Since significant differences existed between the mean scores of the two elementary schools on the pre-test, examination of the mean gains of groups formed by combining classes from the two schools is a debatable procedure. However, results obtained by this procedure indicated that both the direct and indirect instructional groups made statistically significant mean gains in listening at the .01 level of significance. The control group did not make a significant mean gain in listening during the experimental period. The largest gain was made by the direct group.

Since the three groups started the experiment with significantly different mean listening scores it was necessary to examine the gains with the influence of initial listening scores held constant. The examination of the mean gains of the groups, independent of the influence of initial listening differences, resulted in failure to reject the null hypothesis. The effectiveness of direct and indirect listening instruction over no special listening instruction disappeared when initial differences were statistically controlled.

Pupils' initial performances on the STEP Listening Test were shown to be negatively related to the gains made during the experimental period. Poorer listeners tended to make larger gains than the better listeners after the six-week experimental period.

Listening was found to be positively related to intelligence, reading and grade point average. A correlation of .50 was found between listening and intelligence. Reading and listening had a correlation of .64, while listening and grade point average had a correlation of .74.

Conclusions
    1. The listening comprehension of fifth-grade pupils can be improved significantly by instruction that emphasizes

direct instruction and practice in listening for main ideas
and important details.

When the instruction emphasized only two listening
comprehension skills, significant gains were made on overall listening performance as measured by the STEP Test.
Increasing skill in listening for main ideas and important details are important to overall listening improvement.

2.   Significant listening improvement can be made by
fifth-grade children who have regular opportunities to listen
to oral selections dealing with the social studies curriculum.
The children in this group received no direct instruction in
how to listen.   Yet with adequate introduction to the theme
of the selection and careful questioning after the listening
selection, their listening comprehension, as measured by the
STEP Test, made significant gains.   Careful planning of listening experiences can bring about significant listening improvement without direct teaching of listening skills.

The results of this study indicate that listening instruction can be effective in developing better listeners at
the intermediate-grade level.   In the past, listening development has been largely incidental to the organized teaching of
other language skills.   Listening needs separate consideration as an important part of the elementary school curriculum.   Teachers concerned with the improvement of pupils'
listening are justified in developing courses of study providing for instruction in listening.

The present study has suggested that more than one
method can be effective in improving pupils' listening. While
teachers will want to further individualize listening instruction according to pupils' recognized language needs, there is
evidence that the direct and indirect procedures used in this
study can be helpful in a program of listening improvement.

A SEQUENCE FOR TEACHING LISTENING SKILLS

From a Curriculum Bulletin of
the Nederland, Texas Schools

GRADES

SKILLS	1	2	3	4	5
To assimilate directions heard first time	I	D	D	R	M
To carry out given directions	I	D	D	R	M
To correlate directions with materials on hand	I	D	D	DR	DR
To hear sounds	ID	DM	DM	M	M
To listen imaginatively	I	D	D	D	D
Recognize responsibility of listener to speaker and other listeners	I	D	RM	M	M
To hear differences in sounds	ID	D	D	R	M
To ask intelligent questions	I	D	D	DR	DR
To listen for answers to questions	ID	D	D	DR	DR
To recognize sequence	I	D	DR	RM	M
To remember things in sequence	I	D	DR	RM	M
To feel rhythm and charm in poetry	I	D	D	DR	DR
To associate sounds and symbols	ID	D	DR	R	M
To discover new words and ideas	I	DR	DR	DR	DR
To recognize key words and phrases	D	D	D	D	DR

Legend: I - initial experience with skill; D - development of skill; R - reinforcement of skill; and M - maintenance of skill.

ATTENTIVE LISTENING

Vern L. Farrow

The major purpose of this experimental study was to investigate the listening attention of a sample of intermediate-grade pupils. Specific purposes were:

1. To develop apparatus for recording responses to a tape-recorded test of listening attention.

2. To measure the listening attention of fourth-, fifth-, and sixth-grade pupils in terms of: (a) an objective test of listening attention; (b) a subjective teacher ranking of listening attention; and (c) a delayed recall test on the content of the Test of Listening Attention.

3. To determine the ability of a sample of intermediate-grade teachers to rank their pupils with respect to listening attention.

4. To determine the relationship between Test of Listening Attention scores and: Teacher Ranking of listening attention, Delayed Recall Test scores, and Grade Level, IQ, CA, MA, Sex, and Kindergarten Experience.

5. To determine the relationship between Test of Listening Attention scores by five-minute intervals, and Grade Level, IQ, CA, MA, Sex, and Kindergarten Experience.

The sample population was selected from two elementary schools by a Listening Pre-Test, and comprised 101 fourth-, 109 fifth-, and 107 sixth-grade pupils.

The Test of Listening Attention consisted of a 25-minute series of tape recorded stories describing familiar animals. Animal names aperiodically embedded in the stories served as stimulus words. Each subject was asked to respond to the auditory stimuli by pressing an electrical switch. Electro-mechanical apparatus printed the responses on paper tape every ten seconds. The total responses recorded during the test represented the subject's objective listening attention score.

A ten- point rating scale completed by each cooperating teacher provided a subjective listening attention score, and a delayed recall test score was obtained two weeks after the Test of Listening Attention. The Henmon- Nelson Test of Mental Ability provided IQ, CA, and MA for each subject.

Within the limitations of the research instruments and procedures, and with respect to the sample population, the major conclusions of the study were that:

1.   Objective listening attention scores increased significantly with increments in grade level, IQ, CA, and MA, indicating a positive effect of maturation.

2.   Correlations of objective listening attention scores with sex tended to favor girls slightly.

3.   Objective listening attention scores correlated only slightly (.15) with IQ. This suggested little dependence of auditory attentiveness upon IQ and indicated that the experimental apparatus and procedures successfully isolated listening attention from intelligence.

4.   Teacher ranking of listening attention correlated very substantially with IQ (.54), but only slightly with objective listening attention scores (.25), suggesting excessive teacher dependence upon knowledge of IQ in evaluating listening attention.

5.   Correlation of teacher ranking of listening attention with sex tended to favor girls slightly.

6.   Delayed recall scores correlated significantly with only Grade Level (.12), and MA (.17), indicating no influence by IQ; CA; Sex; or Kindergarten Experience.

7.   There was a close similarity in objectively measured listening attention between fifth and sixth grades which was significantly superior to that of the fourth, suggesting that the latter grade is transitional, with special listening needs.

8.   No significant differences within grade levels with respect to objective listening attention scores by five- minute intervals were observed between upper and lower quartiles of IQ, CA, or MA; between boys and girls; or between subjects with or without kindergarten experience. This suggests

no need for differentiation of listening experiences within
grades.

LISTENING CENTERS AND TAPE RECORDERS

From a Curriculum Bulletin of the
Beloit, Wisconsin Public Schools

The Listening Center

A number of teachers stress listening skills as a part
of the language arts curriculum by establishing a listening
center in one corner of the room.   For the center, a tape
recorder and six headphones are usually minimal equipment.
The earphones may be attached to a jackbox in the center of
the table which is in turn connected to the tape recorder.
Other equipment may include a partitioning table and shelves
for storing tape.

An advantage of the listening center is that it encourages independent work by children and frees the teacher to
work with other groups.   It is not difficult to teach children
to use the equipment.   One individual may be chosen to push
the button and to stop it.   Teachers may want to develop
techniques for labeling and storing tapes so that children can
actively select and store lessons.   Full instructions for lessons which require a process of listening, thinking, answering can be given.   After children have followed instructions
and recorded answers, they can listen to the correct answers on the tape, thus encouraging self-checking and evaluation.

The tape recorder, described by one teacher as an
"assistant, " may be useful for the organization of classroom
activity.   One group of children can be engaged in a reading,
arithmetic, or spelling lesson, while the teacher is working
with another group.   Teachers may find it useful to be able
to record lessons in after-school hours or the summer, thus
relieving some of the burden during classroom hours and sav-
ing some classroom time.   In one case a summer curriculum committee made up a series of 22 ten-minute tapes for
teaching phonetic concepts sequentially and the stencils to go
with the lessons.   In this experiment, they found reading instruction definitely improved.

Innumerable uses for the center have been described by teachers who frequently find that once the listening center has been established in the classroom, they continually find new uses which include:

1.   Assistance in teaching primary reading lessons through tapes.

2.   A series of lessons for teaching phonics sequentially.

3.   Lessons for building speed in arithmetic.

4.   Taped spelling lessons enabling children to work and test themselves independently.

5.   Reading lessons in which children are taught certain listening skills such as recalling the sequence of events in a story or poem, answering questions about material read, listening for details or the main idea in a story, following directions.

6.   Individualized reading plans.

7.   Speech and oral interpretation skills in which children can record and listen to their own oral reading, and evaluate their own particular problems.

THE TEACHER OF ELEMENTARY SCIENCE AND LISTENING

Sam Duker

Whatever disagreements there may be among teachers of science in the elementary school, there is agreement on the point that one of the most important aims of such teaching is to develop in the pupils a critical, reasoning, problem-solving set.   This, in general, is also true of secondary school science teachers.   There was a time when science was taught, especially at the secondary level, entirely for the sake of content.   This view has been rather generally discarded.   In stating the newer view Blough, for instance, says that one objective of elementary science teaching is to "help pupils to grow in ability to solve problems effectively."

Craig says: "We can teach objective thinking about many natural and social phenomena" and "We should not depend upon
mere hearsay and gossip; unwarranted prejudices against others should never be allowed to influence our actions."

One of the phases of life in a democracy most in need
of the application by an intelligent citizenry of such critical,
reasoning, and problem-solving attitudes is the process of
communication. All contact between persons involves this
process.

If we compare human communication in pre-literate
days, when all knowledge, tradition, and folklore were
passed on by word of mouth, with our present-day communicative scheme of things we see a remarkable parallel. In both
periods there is to be found an almost implicit faith in the
efficacy and efficiency of the listening process. Today most
of our social, political, recreational, religious, and educational communication is carried on at the aural level. Whether it be the morning conversation at the breakfast table,
the evening television program, a meeting at the United Na-
tions, or a sermon in church or synagogue, we find this un-
reasoning confidence in the effectiveness of this type of communication.

Strangely enough, we have been very much more concerned in our teaching with the less-used communicative
skills. Reading and "Riting" have always been two respec-
table members of the three R's. The receptive portion of
the oral communicative process, listening, has been almost
entirely neglected. It has been assumed that this is some
sort of a natural endowment of all humans. Such an assumption is, of course, completely unfounded for there are many
skills involved in listening which are not provided for by any
of the genes so far known.

It is a false assumption to suppose that listening is
taught by the common admonition to "sit-up and pay attention" or by similar admonitions so often heard in classrooms.
Listening is certainly not so much a function of the body or
even of the ear as it is of the mind. Just as one can see
without reading so one can hear without listening.

If we examine the process of effective listening we
see that it involves the use of just those skills the development of which are mentioned by Blough and Craig as some
of the most desirable outcomes of science instruction in the

elementary school.

A good listener has a purpose, and even more important, is aware of that purpose. This purpose may be to be
entertained, it may be to obtain ideas, it may be to get information, or it may be any one of many others. The kind
of purpose governs the kind of listening that is done.

If one is listening to or for ideas, it becomes of the
greatest importance to identify and follow the structural
framework or outline of what is being listened to.

Effective listening assumes that the listener brings to
bear all that he knows about the subject but also that he is
able to distinguish that which he is listening to from that
which he already knows or already believes. The poor listener has a tendency to hear only the echo of his own ideas.

One of the hallmarks of a good listener is that he is
critical in the sense that he is evaluative. He weighs the
logic used, is perceptive to the use of propaganda devices
and is analytical in his evaluation. This implies that he is
open minded and free from prejudices but not gullible.

Above all else, the good listener must implement that
which he has heard. He must alter or pursue his present
course of conduct on the basis of information received.

If one accepts the above thesis on the nature of an
effective listening process it seems apparent that the responsibility for the preparation of good listeners cannot fall solely to the language arts portion of the curriculum. It is true
that the social studies teacher has a great responsibility in
this direction but no one is in a more powerful position to
make a genuine contribution to the kind of mind-set that will
make a good listener than is the teacher of science.

It is true that at the elementary level the language
arts teacher, the social studies teacher, and the science teacher may be the same person. It is equally true that the
trend toward integration has tended to eradicate sharp lines
between subject matter fields. On the other hand, our psychological knowledge about transfer of training and the necessity of stressing common elements to secure such transfer makes it imperative that we consciously stress the communication skill of listening in our teaching of science as
much if not more than we do in our teaching of the language

arts.

It is in the belief that in order to carry out this function the science teacher needs to know more about the teaching of listening, that the following summary of some of the things we know about the listening process, things we need to know, and ideas for the teaching of listening is presented.

Listening has been the most sadly neglected phase of the communication skills. The art of listening has only been subjected to examination by research to any considerable extent in the last decade and such research is still, unfortunately, at a very superficial level. Unhappily, also, most of such research has been done at the college level rather than at the elementary or secondary levels.

The limited amount of research on the nature of listening and on ways it may be taught has fairly well established the following propositions:

1.   About 60 per cent of the elementary school day is spent in listening of one sort or another. This is far more than was estimated to be the case by elementary school teachers.

2.   There are as yet no adequate instruments for the evaluation and measurement of listening ability but it is possible to arrive at satisfactory approximations of degrees of listening skills by using some reading tests at an oral level.

3.   In the first four grades there seems to be a greater efficiency in listening than in reading; at the fifth- and sixth-grade levels there is no substantial difference between listening and reading skills; thereafter reading skills are more highly developed.

4.   There is no ascertainable correlation between intelligence and listening skills. It seems, however, to be a fact that those of lower intelligence tend to depend more on listening than on reading.

5.   While no one best technique for the teaching of listening has been developed, every available study shows that it is possible to increase listening efficiency by direct instruction.

There are three principal needs in the field of listening which must be met by future research:

1.   An adequate set of tests to measure listening proficiency needs to be developed.

2.   Specifically validated ways of teaching listening need to be developed.

3.   A responsibility for teaching this important communication skill needs to be inculcated in teachers of children.

The fact that such research is needed in no way decreases the opportunity or the responsibility of the science teacher with respect to seizing every possible opportunity to sharpen the listening skills of his pupil. Some of the ways in which this may be done are as follows:

1.   An emphasis on following oral directions accurately.   Science experiments are ideally suited to this purpose. Directions should be given clearly and explicitly.   The suggestion sometimes made that in order to improve listening ability the directions should not be repeated, does not appear to be well taken.   Emphasis should, however, be placed on the desirability and necessity for attempting to understand them on the first occasion on which they are given.

2.   Science lessons are ideally suited to teaching proper techniques of note-taking.   Such note-taking can be a very effective aid to efficient listeners when emphasis is placed on them as a means of following the outline of what is being said.

3.   The application of principles of scientific thinking to the analysis of radio and television speeches and discussion programs for the purpose of detecting propaganda devices and illogical non-sequiturs.

4.   Practice in distinguishing that which one already knows from what is being said.

5.   Practice in listening _for_ ideas as well as _to_ ideas.

6.   Practice in listening to other pupils as well as to the teacher.

First and foremost among all methods of teaching better listening is that of teaching by example. Teachers are too often guilty of being inattentive and even disinterested when pupils are making their contributions.

It seems implicit in any discussion of teaching method that any one topic such as listening cannot be taught in isolation but only in an integrative combination with other skills. Science teaching lends itself ideally to such an approach.

The teacher of science or the teacher teaching science at the pre-college level can certainly enrich his instruction by consideration of the connection between the objectives of such instruction and the art of skillful listening. Not only will the pupils' skill in using communicative processes be enhanced but they will also gain a better understanding of the practical applications of the scientific problem-solving attitude.

Chapter IV

THE TEACHING OF LISTENING
II. TEACHING DIFFERENT KINDS OF LISTENING

In this chapter four selections from curriculum bulletins are included all of which are concerned with the teaching of particular kinds or types of listening skills. The first is taken from a curriculum bulletin of the Muncie, Indiana schools. It is concerned with the teaching of interpretative listening.

The second selection is taken from a San Diego, California curriculum bulletin and is included because of the analysis it presents of teaching suggestions, instructional materials, children's learnings, and children's experiences in connection with the learning of appreciative, attentive, and analytical listening. This selection is followed by excerpts from a San Jose, California curriculum bulletin having to do with teaching the same skills.

The final article in this chapter is taken from a curriculum bulletin of the Beloit, Wisconsin schools. This passage examines the development of a number of listening skills associated with different kinds of listening.

TEACHING INTERPRETATIVE LISTENING

From a Curriculum Bulletin of
the Muncie, Indiana Schools

A great deal of knowledge and enjoyment comes to human beings through the ear. More than half of a person's waking hours are passed in listening to parents, friends, teachers, and to radio and television programs.

Unfortunately too many children are hearing, but are not listening. Listening occurs only when the pupil organizes and remembers what is heard. The major goal of all communication, including listening, is understanding or comprehension. Skill in listening is closely related to proficiency in many academic areas. For some children who are slow learners and for children who are poor readers, listening is the most important skill for achievement.

Children are not equally ready for listening; not all of them will reach the same levels of listening proficiency. The teacher must begin with lower levels of listening skill and gradually lead the students to higher levels. The distinction is commonly made between listening "to" and listening "for." This distinction is important in that it points up the basic skill of anticipatory listening which is a basic communicative skill. The teacher promotes the listening habit mostly by being a good listener himself and by providing the proper psychological climate for listening. He helps to formulate a purpose for listening.

Since listening occupies such a large part of daily life, improvement of listening ability is important. Therefore, it is very necessary to practice good listening habits, so that one can increase his ability to learn and to enjoy.

Skills Required for Interpretative Listening
The Listener Must:

1. Identify the speaker's purpose.
2. Develop empathy with the speaker.
3. Anticipate what is being said.
4. Listen for the main ideas.
5. Listen for the details.
6. Follow oral directions.
7. Remember a sequence of details.
8. Draw inferences and conclusions.
9. Mentally summarize what has been said.
10. Distinguish fact from fiction.
11. Identify transitional elements.
12. Listen in terms of past experiences.
13. Listen for relationships.
14. Listen appreciatively, creatively, and critically.

Teacher-Directed Activities
1. Use quotes pertaining to listening on the bulletin boards or chalk boards.

Examples:

> a.   Give us grace to listen well.--John Keble.
> b.   A bore is a person who talks when we wish he'd listen.--Devil's Dictionary.
> c.   A good listener is not only popular everywhere, but after a while he knows something.--Wilson Mizner.
> d.   While the right to talk may be the beginning of freedom, the necessity of listening is what makes the right important.--Walter Lippmann.
> e.   Nature has given to men one tongue, but two ears, that we may hear from others twice as much as we speak.--Epictetus.

2.   Have students test their listening ability in conversation.   For one day ask them to keep a record of how long they talked and how long they listened.   Keep a record of how many times they caught listeners' "distress signals," include the number seen while the student was doing the talking; also those caught while others were talking.   At the end of the day, sit down and try to recall what can be remembered from having listened throughout the day.

3.   Discuss distractions to good listening and decide how they may be eliminated.

4.   Use group planning, group discussions, and panels to teach listening.

5.   The pupils learn to listen for "language signals" such as "first," "there are several ways," "furthermore," "several suggestions are," or "on the other hand."

6.   Give the class one or more sets of directions. The class will do one or more of the following to help remember them:

> a.   Number the steps of the directions and be able to repeat how many steps were involved and what they were.
> b.   Take some physical action (such as pointing) to help remember the directions while those directions are being stated.
> c.   Follow directions given for a specific activity, such as getting to another room in the building or properly using a pencil sharpener.

7. For attentive listening read a list of ridiculous statements to the class and have them write the answers called for. Example: write 9, no matter what the sum of 5 and 6 is.

8. The teacher reads a short paragraph containing a sentence or two that are not in harmony with the context. He may read materials that omit evidence, that are based on a false premise, or that are not logically organized. The pupil may be asked to discriminate between fact and fiction. He should learn to detect propaganda in advertising, in newspaper accounts, and in essays; and he should learn to listen for implied meanings. Later it is hoped that he will apply these critical listening skills in reading.

9. Give a quiz orally one day and then give it on paper the next to see which test is easier for students.

10. The teacher can administer tests orally:

    a.   for main ideas
    b.   for critical thinking

11. Read a speech to the class. Have them make a detailed outline of the speech illustrating plainly whether chronological, enumerative, or logical organization has been used. (If the latter has not been taught, the outline of the main parts could be used without the analysis.)

12. Select a radio or television commercial to evaluate. Include such items as the uses of the factors of interest, credibility of statements, proof, exaggerations, effect of voice and manner, use of special words and phrases, use of special effects, and whether interest or prejudice results from the commercial.

    a.   Can you tell what a person's mood is by his tone of voice? Write a paper on this.
    b.   Present a list of statements to the class and have them tell if each is fact or opinion.
    c.   Pupils listen to two different broadcasts or recordings on the news content, one giving a factual report, and the other one giving an analysis. Pupils should analyze the two reports, studying the vocabulary used and looking for indications of distortion. This exercise again teaches critical thinking.

        d.   Listen to detect prejudice, half-truths, emotionally loaded words, implied meanings and questionable propaganda in speeches, discussions, commercials, newscasts, literature, and conversations.

     13.   Read aloud a description of a physical scene. Have the listener list the items mentioned and read them aloud. Then sketch the scene as he "sees" it.

     14.   Read a paragraph to a student while several other students are out of the room. See how many facts the student can recall and relate to the next student outside the room.

     15.   Tape the students' speeches or oral book reports (or some other oral activity).

     16.   Tape record book reports and drama, and play them back to listen for usage, enunciation, and sound of voice.

     17.   Listen to poems and stories to determine the main idea, to list the sequence or events, and to anticipate the outcome.

     18.   Read a short, short story. Ask factual questions about the story to test comprehension.

     19.   Giving dictation to the students is a good practice.

Pupil Activities

     1.   Students listen to paragraphs, stories, poems, plays, or speeches for:

        a.   Main ideas (outline of speech).
        b.   Fact versus opinion.
        c.   Enjoyment.

     2.   Manners

        a.   Observe listening manners of others in church, school, movie, or another class.
        b.   Conduct class discussion on listening manners.
        c.   Compile their set of listening manners.

3. Introduction

    a. Let students introduce each other as formal introduction.

    b. Let students list items about themselves (name, nickname, hobby, special interests, books, movies, unusual facts about themselves), shuffle the cards and have another student interview from information on cards.

4. Listen to ways people laugh and relate laugh to physical characteristics.

5. Demonstration

    a. How to accomplish a task.
    b. How to make a simple toy.
    c. Directions for how to get to someplace.
    d. How to use some item (camera, etc.); then test in some way .as to how well the others listened to demonstration.

6. Listen without taking notes to:

    a. Announcements.
    b. Newscasts.
    c. Instructions.

Then quiz as to how well the students retained original subject matter.

7. Listening Game

    Ask the pupils: How well do you understand directions? and How quickly can you follow them?

    a. Write <u>yes</u> no matter with what letter your name begins.
    b. Of the words school and box, write the shorter.
    c. Write <u>no</u> even if you think cows are larger than dogs.
    d. Write the numbers 2, 7, 9, 5, 8, and circle the largest.
    e. If you circled 7, make a square; if not, make a cross.

  f. If birds can fly, complete this sentence correctly. Hens lay_____.
  g. Give the wrong answer to this question: Are
you in the United States?
  h. If Washington were not the first President of
the United States, write the shorter of the words red
and green; if he were, sign your name.

Checklist of Classroom Observations
on Pupil's Listening

Interest
_____Listens attentively.
_____Listens part of time.
_____Easily distracted.
_____Restless and preoccupied.

Comprehension
_____Evident appreciation of story, talks about it.
_____Asks related questions.
_____Responds to humor and excitement.
_____Answers factual questions.
_____Tells main ideas.
_____Tells whole story accurately.
_____Relates ideas to own experiences.

TEACHING APPRECIATIVE, ATTENTIVE AND
ANALYTICAL LISTENING

From a Curriculum Bulletin of the
of the San Diego City Schools

Listening
         The effectiveness of oral communication is dependent
upon the degree of development of listening skills. Pupils'
listening skills are often inefficient, and instruction in the
skill of listening becomes an important part of planned language experiences. Some of the most effective instruction
to develop listening skills occurs when children are guided
to set up standards and give reasons for becoming better listeners in classroom situations. Children should be given a
variety of experiences in listening to many different types of

material.

     In general, the purposes for listening include listening to:

        -- Appreciate and enjoy.
        -- Obtain helpful information.
        -- Make judgments about the validity and value of
           the items presented.

     Listening improvement will result in learning improvement only if children are ready to listen, know why they are to listen, have a purpose for listening, and know how to listen efficiently.

Listening for Appreciation and Enjoyment

     Learning to listen for appreciation and enjoyment will bring personal satisfaction to pupils. It relates closely to oral reading and speaking. Helping a child learn how to listen for these purposes increases creative appreciation and enjoyment.

Points to Remember: Teacher

        -- Establish a physically comfortable and relaxed atmosphere.
        -- Provide an experience within the child's understanding.
        -- Discuss the meanings of only those words that are needed to add to enjoyment and appreciation.
        -- Have pupils recall related experiences.
        -- Reread a portion of a poem or story for greater appreciation.
        -- Adjust the length of listening time to the class level of listening.
        -- Provide an opportunity for a class discussion after each listening experience.
        -- Keep noise at the lowest level possible.
        -- Tie-in listening improvement with everyday learning.
        -- Make sure pupils know why they are to listen, what they are to listen for, and how they are to listen.
        -- Set a good example as a listener.

Points to Remember: Children

        -- Be interested.
        -- Follow the ideas of the speaker and the sequence in which he presents them.
        -- Think about what the speaker is saying.

--"Tune out" distracting noises.

Suggested Activities
   --Read aloud a poem which is likely to evoke emo-
     tion, and then encourage the pupils to discuss their
     feelings.
   --After hearing a song, ask the children to describe
     the story behind the song's words.
   --Listen to sounds and list words that name them to
     see if each was heard.
   --Listen to a poem or example of imaginative writing
     and recall the words that contribute feeling and emo-
     tion.
   --Listen to a tall tale being read. After each page
     is read, ask the pupils to enumerate the exaggera-
     tions.
   --Pantomime, activate puppets, or dramatize spon-
     taneously in response to a story just listened to.
   --Tell chain stories in which each participant carries
     on from where the preceding speaker stopped.
   --Make a tape recording of various pupils' favorite
     stories or poems and let the listeners request a
     personal presentation of the ones that appealed
     most, or have the class discuss the qualities in
     poems and stories that have lasting appeal.
   --Making a personal or class "hit parade" of poems
     or stories heard over a period of two weeks.

Listening for Information and for Special Purposes
   Children need carefully planned instruction to develop
listening skills needed for various purposes. They must be
aware of the importance of being a good listener in the class,
on the playground, and away from school.

   All through the day the teacher will find opportunities
to capitalize upon classroom and auditorium situations to improve pupils' abilities to listen for specific purposes.

Points to Remember: Children
   --Be interested.
   --Follow the ideas of the speaker and the sequence
     in which he presents them.
   --Listening takes effort.
   --Learning while listening is inside action on the part
     of the listener.

Suggested Activities
-- Play games involving the cutting and folding of paper, drawing, or writing according to oral directions.
-- Have students listen to and repeat directions that might be given to a traveler attempting to reach a particular place.
-- Listen to a report made by another child to find the most interesting sentence or phrase.
-- Listen to an announcement, recall the items, then compare them with those of the actual announcement.
-- Listen to a report and prepare a one or two sentence summary.
-- Listen to an invitation to see if the important details of time and place can be recalled.
-- Listen to someone give directions that include a number of steps that must be followed to see if all of the steps can be recalled in proper order.
-- Try to present orally many of the regular tests in all subjects. Read a test's instructions aloud, and also all of the questions, giving pupils time to write each answer.

Critical and Evaluative Listening
Listening requires skill in understanding the meanings of words and ideas. Critical listening skills enable the pupil to:

-- Infer meanings.
-- Analyze information.
-- Arrive at new ideas.

Critical and evaluative listening should be taught whenever appropriate throughout the school day. Occasionally specific lessons should be designed for teaching this type of listening. Children should listen critically when they hear news reporting, social studies or science reports, or student campaign speeches at school.

Points to Remember: Teacher
-- Stress open-mindedness and objectivity.

Points to Remember: Children
-- Be interested.
-- Follow the ideas of the speaker and the sequence in which he presents them.

--Think about what the speaker is saying.
--A critical listener is a careful, accurate, attentive listener.

Suggested Activities
--Read aloud a paragraph in which one sentence does not belong. Ask students to identify the sentence that does not fit with the topic.
--After stating a purpose for an account or description, read the selection, sentence by sentence, and ask the students to accept or reject each sentence on the basis of its relevance to the subject.
--Have students listen to a short selection and suggest a title.
--Read a short poem to the class and ask the pupils to guess the title, or to make up a title. Encourage the children to give reasons for their choices.
--Have students listen to short paragraphs which compare people, places, or events. Ask them to attempt to recall likenesses and differences from memory.

DEVELOPMENT OF SKILLS IN APPRECIATIVE, ATTENTIVE, AND ANALYTICAL LISTENING

From a Curriculum Bulletin of
the San Jose California Schools

Development of Skills in Appreciative Listening

(Definition: appreciative listening is to enjoy and derive real pleasure from the arts to fit various moods, feelings and interests.)

CHILDREN'S LEARNINGS	CHILDREN'S EXPERIENCES
Children learn to listen to poetry	Listen to poems read or told by:
	Teacher
	Child

Objectives: To listen so as to appreciate the works of others.
To listen so as to identify with the experience of others.
To listen so as to establish an emotional outlet.

TEACHING SUGGESTIONS (HOW)	INSTRUCTIONAL MATERIALS
Some teaching suggestions to develop good appreciative listening	Books
Teacher reads poem that stresses particu-	Records

lar mood, etc.

Ask children how they felt.
Was it a picture poem?
Did it make them want to dance?
Did it make them want to laugh?

Teacher reads a poem.
Children listen to the poem and act out.

Teacher reads poem; children discuss it.
Teacher asks children if they thought of something they could do.
Teacher has all children stand.
As poem is re-read, they respond by making motions poem indicates.
Have certain children do a specific part for purpose of evaluation.
Whole group does it again.
Example: "Bear Game."
This could be suited to grade level by increasing difficulty of selection.

CHILDREN'S LEARNINGS

Children learn to listen to stories.

Teacher-collected anthologies

CHILDREN'S EXPERIENCES

Listen to stories read or told by:

Teacher

Children

Listen to dramatizations and plays read by:

Teacher
Children
(from stories in readers)

Listen to music provided through such media as:

Recordings
Broadcastings, etc.

INSTRUCTIONAL MATERIALS

Pictures of Grand Canyon, storms, etc.

Children learn to listen to music.

TEACHING SUGGESTIONS (HOW)

Motivate for listening to story

Ask questions to motivate better listening.
Fold a large paper in half.
Have children draw pictures to show two or
four sequences from a story the teacher
just read.
Set standards with children for appreciative
listening of stories.
Follow with an evaluation.

A sample lesson plan for listening to music.
(Grand Canyon Suite)

Give children something to listen for: rain, gathering storm, thunder, hee-haw of donkey.

Have children listen for specific parts and tell what they think it is describing.

Album of Grand Canyon Suite

Other recordings; maps

Listening to "Rhapsody in Blue"--"American in Paris".

Correlate with study of New York.

Give children red and blue chalk to draw impressions of the music--red for some parts, blue for others.

Create stories to go with the music.

Have the stories read as music is played.

Later tell the children what the composer was trying to tell about "American in Paris."

Pictures of tenement where Gershwin first lived.

Development of Skills in Attentive Listening

(Definition: attentive listening is listening that requires accuracy of comprehension.)

CHILDREN'S LEARNINGS

CHILDREN'S EXPERIENCES

Children learn to listen attentively.

Children listen in:
 Sharing periods
 Evaluation periods

Children learn to listen to directions, instructions and lessons.

Story time
Core subjects as:
    Reading
    Language arts
    Arithmetic
    Science
    Physical education

Objectives: To teach courteous listening.
             To create an attentive attitude.
             To react or respond to listening.

TEACHING SUGGESTIONS (HOW)

Develop standards with children such as:

Sit quietly.
Clear the table (desk).
Look at the speaker.
Take turns.

A suggested lesson.

Listen for one minute to all sounds distinguishable in the building.

INSTRUCTIONAL MATERIALS

Records

Books

Margaret W. Brown: Noisy Books (Country Noisy Book, 1940. Indoor Noisy Book, 1942. Noisy Book (City), 1939. Quiet Noisy Book, 1950. Seashore Noisy Book, 1941. Summer Noisy Book, 1951. Winter Noisy Book, 1947. New York: Harper and Row, 1939-1950.

> "Listening Standards"
>
> Standard Chart
>
> 1. We listen with our eyes, our ears, our bodies.
> 2. We look at the speaker and think with him.
> 3. We have nothing on our desks to distract us.

Enumerate and classify.
Listen for another minute to sounds heard outside the classroom.
Distribute papers.
Label: "Sounds heard by _____"
    Direct children to listen during any period of three-minute duration during the day and to record sounds heard.
Reiterate
Summarize

Motivate children for desirable listening habits.

Guide questions
Facts, observations and deductions
Processes
Rules

The teacher gives directions.
Child repeats the directions.
The teacher demonstrates with instructional material.

CHILDREN'S LEARNINGS

Children learn to listen to reports, sharing current events and announcements.

Children learn to listen to audio-visual material.

TEACHING SUGGESTIONS (HOW)

Suggested teaching technique.

Give a quiz or test after stories, movies, etc.

Encourage note-taking in preparation for tests if class is ready to do so.
(This is a device that can be used to check listening.)

Establish guides for listening such as:

Evaluate and/or state main points.
Listen for new ideas.
Listen for help to solve problems.
Listen in order to contribute additional information.
Think of ways to improve a report.

Set up purpose for listening.

Have children take notes for discussion.
Have children outline the materials, main ideas and significant details.

INSTRUCTIONAL MATERIAL

Attention, Listeners!

1. Was the topic adequately covered?
2. Was the information organized?
3. Was the report interesting?
4. Could you hear?
5. Did the speaker have poise?

Evaluation Sheet

Name _____

Topic _____

	Poor	Fair	Good	Excellent
Material				
Amount				
Organization				
Interest				
Delivery				
Voice				
Pronunciation				
Poise				

Notes:

Questions:

Have follow-up of written work.
Questions to be answered.
Blanks to be filled.
Descriptive paragraph.

Development of Skills in Analytical Listening

(Definition: analytical listening is listening to analyze and evaluate what one hears.)

CHILDREN'S LEARNINGS (WHAT)

Children learn to listen critically.

Objectives: To learn to think systematically.
            To learn to think critically.

TEACHING SUGGESTIONS (HOW)

Encourage children to:
  Have a questioning attitude.
  Analyze purpose of speaker.
  Detect bias, prejudice, or propaganda.
  Separate fact and opinion.
  Recognize emotional appeal.
  Note choice and use of key words.
  Discover organization of subject matter.

Listening to science broadcasts

  Follow up with worksheets, filmstrips, films.

CHILDREN'S EXPERIENCES (WHERE)

Listen to:
  Speakers
    Resource, assembly, peer-group
  Programs
  Core subjects
  Listen and question during interviews
  Listen during evaluations
  Listen to recordings

INSTRUCTIONAL MATERIALS

Tape record:
  Phonograph records
  Television program
  Radio program

Science worksheets, films, filmstrips

Steps to develop analytical listening while recording on tape recorder.

Prepare the article to be recorded.
Record the selections (about 5 at a
    time).
Play it back.
    Note expressions.
    Note enunciation.
    Note speed.
Practice the material.
Record again.
Play back.
Note improvements.
Tape record a short radio newscast
    that presents facts without com-
    mentary.
Also record a news commentator who
    broadcasts his own opinions among
    the facts.
Play the two recordings before class.
Ask the children to point out differences
    between the two recordings.
Learn to separate fact and opinion.

THE TEACHING OF LISTENING

From a Curriculum Bulletin of the
Beloit, Wisconsin Public Schools

What should the elementary teacher teach about listening? Depending on the maturity and needs of the children, he might begin with exercises which increase children's awareness of different natural sounds heard in the school environment. The teaching of letter sounds, phonemes, and morphemes is a part of the reading and spelling program; exercises which strees the audio- recognition of sounds in addition to those which stress audio- visual recognition can be used to extend listening skills. A more complex stage of listening is a more active hearing process involving comprehension, critical and creative thought. Studies in the field indicate that children benefit by direct training in such skills as listening to follow directions, listening for sequence, listening to retain details, and listening for the main idea. In addition to selective listening skills, training should be provided in the elementary grades for critical and aesthetic listening.

One way in which the kindergarten and primary teacher may contribute to a long range program in listening is to make the children conscious of listening as a process, and to sharpen their ability to distinguish between sounds.

1. Listen and discuss natural sounds in the classroom and outside the classroom window.

2. Learn to distinguish between high and low pitch differences, using the rhythm band, records, or the piano.

3. Discriminate between sounds heard nearby and those heard at a distance. Discussion of an approaching and receding siren might serve as a useful illustration.

4. Distinguish between kinds of sounds made by the teacher such as crushing paper, clapping hands, writing on the chalkboard, tapping on such various surfaces as metal, glass, wood.

5. Repeat sounds and rhythms of drum beats. The teacher taps a number or pattern of drum beats, and then the child claps back the same number of pattern.

6.   Listen to sounds taped by the teacher on the tape recorder, such as dripping water, a burning match, a pencil being sharpened, a slamming door.

7.   Listen to sound effects on the radio and guess how they were made.

Following Directions

Beyond distinguishing between environmental sounds and letter-sounds is the listening, understanding and retention of concepts.   So many occasions arise for following directions and completing assignments, that the teacher may want to emphasize listening skills by giving special attention to the listening involved in receiving assignments.   To focus direct attention on listening for directions, the teacher may want to tape a series of directions, which the children follow.   The advantage of the tape is that it does not repeat until all have heard.   Also, the children can check themselves when the tape is replayed.   The primary teacher might distribute paper and colored crayons and have the children follow such directions as: (1) Draw a red line near the top of your page. (2) Draw a blue cat near the middle of your page.   (3) Take the black crayon and draw the first letter of your name.   By replaying the tape children can check to see if they listened carefully.

The teacher might have the children bring to class printed directions for playing games drawn from games at home or game books obtained from the library.   The directions may be discussed, and some of the games may be played.   Or the teacher could provide directions for a new game, select one child to state the directions to the class, then have the children demonstrate their understanding by repeating the directions.

Games for following directions which provide practice in retaining a series of steps might be devised.   For example, have different pupils write a series of directions for acts which might be performed in class.   One author then reads aloud five steps that another is to perform after he has heard all five.   Directions which pupils might think of are: (1) open and shut a window, or (2) take a notice off the bulletin board.

Selective Listening

Listening skills which can be developed are those involving control and choice.   The listener can learn to listen

selectively and to listen for chosen purposes appropriate to
the needs of the situation. Following are some exercises
described by Russell, designed to teach the ability to listen
for details, for sequence, and for main idea.

Listening for Details
   To help children develop the habit of listening carefully for details, the primary teacher might read very short
"stories" and then ask detailed questions: Alertness to details might be developed by dividing children into partners
of two and asking each to prepare a paragraph of two or
three sentences in which one word or idea is obviously ab-
surd. Then have the paragraphs read to the class.

Listening for Sequence
   To draw attention to sequence, cut up a story and
paste the sections on cardboard. Pass out the mixed pieces
to the members of the reading group. The child who thinks
he has the beginning part of the story is to volunteer to read
his sections. Have the others continue until all sections of
the story have been read.

   Predicting what happens next can help children become
aware of sequence. Selecting an unfamiliar story, the teacher may stop at intervals and ask the children to anticipate
what will happen next. Or the teacher might begin a story
and have the children make up the story parts. Each child
stops at an interesting place and then calls on another to
continue the story.

Listening for the Main Idea
   The primary teacher might read to his class short
simple stories and have the children make up a title for
each story. Unfamiliar stories work best for this activity;
teachers may draw on stories not regularly used by the
group.

   It may be helpful to read a story, stop at intervals
and have the children summarize what has happened thus far.
The teacher may then write a summary sentence of the action described. Stories which have a series of a few simple
actions are useful in this exercise.

   Children might be asked to write a short description
of some of the characters in a familiar story and later read
the descriptions aloud. The names should not be given. The
rest of the class should listen to the description and then

take turns in guessing who was described.

One activity common to intermediate grade work is to
have pupils listen for the main idea in paragraphs and other
selections.

Critical Listening

Beyond simple listening and selective auditing is critical auditing which entails analysis and appraisal. To some
extent training can be given for recognition of logical fallacies and emotionally loaded words in intermediate grades.
The primary teacher might help the child by having him ap-
praise his own recorded presentation of a story, a poem, or
a talk.

Short exercises such as the following might be useful
for teaching the logical fallacy of incongruity. The teacher
might read a short six to eight sentence story and interject
an incongruous line, asking the children to listen for it.

> John has a new sled.
> The sled goes fast.
> The sled is painted red.
> Mary likes cookies.
> John wants the snow to come.
> John will ride his sled in the snow.

Listening for Appreciation

1.   Select and discuss descriptive words appearing in
a story or poem.   Examine why the descriptive words enhance the story.

2.   Have the children listen for the purpose of sensing the mood of a story.   Divide the class into small groups
and have one child read aloud.   Have the children listen when
their books are closed and determine whether they have experienced the mood of the story.   Discussion may center a-
round such questions as "Did your feelings change as you
listened?   How did the story make you feel?   Why do you
suppose you felt sleepy (sad, amused, afraid, etc.)?"

3.   Have children listen while others try out for a
part in a play.   How well did the readers capture the feelings of the characters?

4.   Have the children read along with the voice on a
recording of a poem to sense the mood and expression of the
reader.

Chapter V

THE TEACHING OF LISTENING
III. THE PRIMARY GRADES

In this chapter, as in the previous one, all the excerpts are from curriculum bulletins. The first selection is taken from a New York City Bulletin. Here specific ideas are given for development of the listening skills of pre-kindergarten children.

The second article is excerpted from a San Diego, California curriculum bulletin. Here a statement of some general principles is followed by very specific suggestions for the teaching of listening to children in the first grade. This selection is followed by one from a New York City bulletin dealing with the same topic. There are, naturally, similarities between the two presentations but in general the two approaches complement rather than duplicate each other. The excerpts from the Montgomery County, Maryland curriculum bulletin also are concerned with the development of listening skills by first grade pupils. Again there are common elements but this selection provides a number of new ideas which are presented in a novel manner in the form of a classroom dialogue.

The next selection is very brief. Ideas concerning the teaching of listening at the third grade level are excerpted from a San Diego, California publication. The skill development in critical, informational, and appreciative listening are briefly noted in outline form.

The last item in this chapter, excerpted from a Valley Stream, New York curriculum bulletin, lists some very specific and practical ways of developing listening skills at the four levels from kindergarten to third grade.

131

TEACHING LISTENING AT THE
PRE- KINDERGARTEN LEVEL

From a Curriculum Bulletin of
The New York City Schools

Our culture demands the ability to use the spoken and
written word for success in basic social relationships, as
well as for school learning and adult accomplishment. The
pre- kindergarten program aims to help children acquire the
skills of oral communication. The teacher recognizes the
importance of language in helping the child explore his environment, understand his relation to it, and express his
thoughts and feelings about it. Accepting the language the
child brings from home without stifling his initiative and facility is necessary for his self- expression. Those children,
particularly, whose home environment reflects a paucity of
conversation or the use of a foreign language, need a program which fosters verbalization.

As the child responds to his environment, the teacher
guides and assists him by supplying suitable material, responding to his questions, listening to his explanations, stimulating his creative thinking, providing vocabulary and language structure to help him express himself. Through this
guidance, assistance, and support she enriches experiences
for him by helping him to develop and broaden concepts, acquire new insights, and expand his vocabulary. She leads
him to a better understanding of the experience and stimulates him to undertake new experiences. By arranging not
only individual experiences but also small group activities,
the teacher helps the child relate consciously to other children and provides him with a learning situation in which he
might not engage if left to himself.

Getting Ideas: Through Listening
(With Related Verbalization)

The teacher utilizes actual situations in the classroom, school, and community to provide the motivation and
experiences for functional listening. Because many young
children are non- verbal in varying degrees when they enter
the pre- kindergarten, the teacher uses gestures, facial expression, tone of voice, demonstration, etc. to help the
child make the transition from non- verbal to verbal expression and understanding. At the beginning of the term, there-

fore, she often shows as well as tells what to do in the ordinary daily classroom routines.

Functional Listening

THE TEACHER	THE CHILDREN
Uses experience with school bell and gong signals having functional significance, e.g., fire-drill gong.	Learn that school bells and gongs have a meaning. Listen attentively.
Reassures children as to meaning of gongs and bells.	Lose fear of gongs.
Shows and tells children what to do when gong rings for fire drill.	Can identify bells, gongs. Respond in accord with teacher's explanation and demonstration.
Gives direction where immediate response is expected.	Listen attentively.
Gives one direction and demonstrates response expected: Carry your chair this way.	Understand what they are supposed to do. Follow direction and act out as given.
Gives series of simple consecutive directions one at a time and waits for response before giving next direction: Take off your hat and coat. Put your hat in your coat sleeve (demonstrates). Hang your coat on a hook. Awaits children's reaction. Assists if help is needed.	Listen to teacher's words, watch her demonstration and follow the directions.
Takes time to answer questions of individual children.	Wait for answer to own question, e.g., When may I paint?
Answers child's direct question: When Maria has finished, then it will be	Learn that an answer will be forthcoming. Understand and wait turn.

THE TEACHER	THE CHILDREN
your turn.	
Encourage children to listen to other children when they speak:	Become interested in other children's ideas.
You told us about your baby brother. Now let's listen to Mary.	Listen for meaning when another child speaks in a small group situation.
Uses rhythm instruments to develop recognition of difference in sounds of instruments.	Try to identify sound and its source.
Plans experience in listening to street sounds to determine their sources.	Enjoy prospect of listening to sounds in the street.
Takes children outdoors to listen to sounds, e.g., rumble of subway, auto horn, child crying, dog barking, woman calling, construction noises, boat whistles, etc.	Express surprise that there are so many different sounds. Listen to, isolate, and identify individual sounds.
Selects story, e.g., The City Noisy Book, by Margaret Wise Brown. Reads to children, awaiting their response after each question in the story. Relates story to children's experience of listening to street sounds.	Are able to identify sounds in story. Show by their response to the questions in the story their understanding of the source of the sound. Imitate sounds. See relationship between Muffin in the story and themselves in listening to sounds.
Provides experiences in identifying sounds in room, e.g., door slamming, clock ticking, paper rustling, ball bouncing, footsteps, etc.	Make finer distinctions. Identify the objects by the sounds they make.

Appreciative Listening

THE TEACHER	THE CHILDREN
Uses nursery rhymes to develop recognition of rhythm.	Become aware of rhythm in verse.
Emphasizes rhythm in reciting Mother Goose rhymes.	Repeat rhythm with teacher. Suit actions to rhythm of verse.
Guides children to enjoyment of sounds of words.	
Recites a nursery rhyme to develop recognition of rhyming words.	Listen to rhyme. Repeat with teacher.
Leaves out a rhyming word, e.g.: Hickory dickorv dock A mouse ran up the...	Supply rhyming word.
Uses picture of object to identify objects with word, especially with non-English speaking children and children with limited verbal ability.	Develop concepts; acquire related vocabulary.
Tells a story with a repetitive refrain.	Participate by joining in refrain.
Tells a story in which animals or people talk, e.g., The Three Bears.	Develop sensitivity to volume of voice. Distinguish characters in story by tone of voice.
Guides children to love of literature by choosing poems and stories suited to their short attention span and to their interests.	Like stories about: animals, their world; characters with which they can identify.
Selects records suitable to interest level of children.	Are interested in listening even when not being addressed specifically.

THE TEACHER	THE CHILDREN
Chooses a record which requires bodily participation by child, e.g., "A Visit to My Little Friend."	Respond with suitable activity.
Chooses a record which requires verbal participation, e.g., "The Carrot Seed."	Listen with pleasure. Join in the refrain.
Before playing record, uses real or illustrative material for words or concepts unfamiliar to non-English speaking children with limited verbal ability.	Identify illustrative examples with content of record. (Especially non-English speaking children.)
Supplies record which requires no active participation.	Listen quietly. Understand and enjoy the story or music.
Keeps record player and records accessible to the children.	Choose a record and listen to a story, individually or in small group.
Plays tapes of her own voice telling a story familiar to the children. Gives many such experiences before the child records his own voice.	See relationship between story recorded and in book.
Encourages child to record own voice. Encourages small group conversation.	Listen to own voice on tape, to voices of classmates, to content of the conversation.

TEACHING LISTENING IN THE FIRST GRADE

From a Curriculum Bulletin of
The San Diego, California Schools

Children need carefully planned instruction to develop listening skills for various purposes. Throughout the day, the teacher will find opportunities to capitalize on different situations to improve pupils' abilities to listen for specific purposes. When working on these skills, the following points should be observed:

-- Adjust the length of listening time to the class level of listening.
-- Provide an opportunity for a class discussion after each listening experience.
-- Make certain pupils know why they are to listen, what they are to listen for, and how they are to listen.

Suggested Pupil Activities

Critical and Evaluative Listening
State a purpose for an account or description; read the selection, sentence by sentence, and ask the students to accept or reject each sentence on the basis of its relevance to the subject.

Have students listen to short paragraphs which compare people, places, or events. Attempt to recall likenesses and differences from memory.

Read a short story in which events are scrambled and ask students to rearrange the events.

Listening for Information and Special Purposes
Listen to an announcement; then recall the items, and compare them with those of the actual announcement.

Listen to a report and prepare a one- or two-sentence summary.

Listen to someone give directions that include a number of steps that must be followed; see if all the steps can be recalled.

Listening for Appreciation and Enjoyment
        Listen to a poem or example of imaginative writing
and recall words that contribute to feeling and emotion.

        Tell chain stories in which each participant carries on
from where the preceding speaker stopped.

        Make a personal or class "hit parade" of poems or
stories heard over a period of time when children took turns
reading.

        Listen to poetry to understand the meaning of every
word, to build a mental image, and to understand the total
experience the poems attempt to communicate.

        --Relate listening improvement to everyday learning.
        --Make certain pupils know why they are to listen,
          what they are to listen for, and how they are to
          listen.
        --Stress open-mindedness and objectivity.
        --Make a policy of not repeating instructions. If re-
          petition is necessary call on the pupils to repeat
          what was stated.
        --Set a good example as a listener.

                    Listening in the First Grade

        The first-grade child can be taught to listen effective-
ly and purposefully, and as he understands the purpose for
listening, his habits and attitude will improve. The child's
school achievement is often determined by how well he listens and the extent to which he uses what he learns through
listening.

Listening is Important
        Children need carefully planned instruction to develop
listening skills for various purposes. Throughout the day the
teacher will find opportunities to capitalize upon classroom
and auditorium situations to improve pupils' abilities to listen.

Suggested Activities
        In addition to the many excellent experiences suggest-
ed in Ginn Elementary English, here are some additional activities.

        --Develop a chart of listening standards with the children, for example:

> ### A GOOD LISTENER
> A good listener is my friend.
> He likes what I say!
> He sits tall and looks right at me.
> He knows what I have said,
> He is ready to help me when
>   I am finished speaking.
> I wonder if I am a good listener, too.

-- Pantomime, activate puppets, or dramatize spontane-
ously in response to a story or poem just heard.

-- Listen to a message from someone known to the
children or about a subject of interest to the class.
After listening to the tape, children might discuss
what they learned.   Self-evaluation is encouraged as
children discuss how well they have listened.

Points to Remember
-- Establish a physically comfortable and relaxed at-
mosphere.
-- Adjust the length of listening time to the class level
of understanding.
-- Keep distracting noises at the lowest level possible.
-- Provide an opportunity for class discussion after
each listening experience.

LISTENING INSTRUCTION FOR FIRST GRADERS

From a Curriculum Bulletin of
The New York City Schools

The teacher uses the daily experiences of the children to encourage them to continue talking in a natural and
spontaneous way while, at the same time, helping them to
refine and extend their use of language.   They talk about
people, places, things, home and school experiences; look
at demonstrations, pictures, filmstrips, TV programs; listen to explanations and directions, stories and poems.   They
turn to books on their own and become interested in acquir-

ing reading and writing skills. Children learning English as
a second language require special encouragement to speak
and approval of efforts made.

The language arts program in Grade One provides activities and instruction to help all children:

--Develop the habit of using language to inquire about
the world around them, to clarify and organize their
experiences.
--Extend and refine concepts and acquire related vocabulary through experiences in listening, observing,
speaking, reading, and writing.
--Grow in their ability to communicate through increasing control and understanding of language, both
oral and written.
--Acquire specific reading skills of word recognition,
comprehension, and interpretation.
--Develop the habit of reading for pleasure and information.
--Become familiar with children's literature of their
own and other cultures.
--Develop moral and spiritual values and a better understanding of themselves and others through experiences with language and literature.

Language activities are grouped to show the receptive
and expressive aspects of the program. They are arranged
under the headings of:

--Getting Ideas. Listening, observing, and reading
to extend auditory and visual discrimination, comprehension, and literary appreciation.
--Expressing Ideas. Speaking and writing to communicate ideas and feelings.
--Learning About Language. Extending concepts about
English; increasing children's understanding and control of words in context, sentence patterns, and
usage; developing skills of handwriting and speech.

As the teacher plans learning experiences for children, she is aware of the inherent interrelationship of language skills. She knows that, in any one language activity,
listening, observing, speaking, reading, or writing may be
involved. She still finds it necessary, however, to plan activities which focus children's attention directly on one or
the other of the interrelated skills.

Getting Ideas: Through Listening
(With Related Verbalization)

Listening Experiences

Children growing up in a noisy world have learned to
protect themselves by "tuning out." Since listening is an important source of learning, children in schools are taught listening skills and learn when to "tune in."

Listening is hearing with comprehension. The listening experience is affected by each child's personality, emotional stability, and language development. His state of physical well-being at the time, his interest in the subject, his
reason for listening, and the nature of the presentation also
influence his listening. Personal interaction and pupil discussion following a listening activity enhance the pleasure and
learning of the experience and provide a measure of its effectiveness.

Some experiences involve children in the joy of listening to and playing with the sounds of words, phrases, sentences or even nonsense syllables. Children for whom English is a second language need such experiences above and
beyond those provided for native English speakers.

NOTE: In the two-column material which follows, The Teacher column suggests learning experiences which may be
planned by the teacher to implement the program. She need
not use all the activities, nor in exactly the way described.
She selects, adapts, and improvises learning experiences appropriate to her children. The Children column indicates
some of the responses which may be expected, and some of
the ways in which children may participate. Children's ori-
ginality and creativity will frequently result in responses and
reactions quite different from those described. This is to be
encouraged.

Setting the Stage

In every listening activity, no matter what the specific purpose, the teacher and children follow a basic pattern.

THE TEACHER	THE CHILDREN
Seats children suitably (compact group circle can be arranged).	Are comfortable and relaxed.

THE TEACHER	THE CHILDREN
Establishes routines for class and group activities.	Hear and see easily.
Gets children's attention before speaking.	Look at the speaker.
Speaks clearly and naturally. Is an attentive listener and careful observer.	May imitate the teacher's speech and habits of listening and observing.
Establishes a purpose for the activity.	Become interested in participating.
Relates experience to children's previous experiences.	Recall helpful clues learned.
Focuses observation by comment and questions.	Begin to listen without interrupting and to concentrate on content.
Gives simple and clear directions, demonstrations.	Follow directions.
Anticipates vocabulary problems, especially for non-English speaking (N.E.) children.	Repeat new words and begin to use them correctly in a variety of situations.
Keeps activity reasonably short.	Increase span of attention.
Develops standards for pupil participation.	Understand and try to follow rules.
Provides opportunity for sharing reactions or reinforcing learning.	Express reactions through talking freely about the activity, drawing, painting, or carrying out some plan of action.

DEVELOPING SKILLS OF AUDITORY DISCRIMINATION

Listening to Identify and Compare

Provides experiences with many types of sounds: mech-	Sharpen auditory discrimination and identify sources of

THE TEACHER	THE CHILDREN
anical, musical, people, animal, language. (Is aware that sharpening auditory discrimination helps N.E. children with pronunciation.)	sound.
Directs attention to sounds outside of classroom. Encourages thinking about the sounds: Which are loud, soft (louder) (softer)? Which sounds are near to us (far away)? How can we tell from the sounds what is happening on the street?	Listen attentively. Identify sounds of construction, trucks, cars, children playing, vendors calling.
Introduces games to help children identify every-day sounds.	
What Is It? Children close their eyes and identify sounds in the classroom: steam in the radiator, a scraping chair, a cough, the click of a light switch, the whirr of the pencil sharpener; hopping, skipping, marching of other children; knocking at the door; pouring water from one container into another.	Recognize familiar objects, actions, etc., by their sounds. If sounds are not familiar ones, venture a guess.
Who's There? The teacher forms children into a circle; selects one child to be "It" and stand in center of circle with eyes closed, while other children skip or march around him. At a signal from the teacher, "It" extends his arm and points	Are aware of voice differences. Recognize voices of their classmates.

THE TEACHER	THE CHILDREN
to a child, saying: Who's there? The child responds in a set pattern: Hello, John! What's my name? If John guesses wrong, he takes place in circle. If he guesses right, he gets another turn at being "It."	

Uses recorded sounds.

THE TEACHER	THE CHILDREN
Selects a suitable record. Plays the record several times. Discusses sounds; shows pictures, if necessary.	Identify the sounds on the record. Extend vocabulary as they talk about sounds in the home, around the city, or the sounds made by various musical instruments.
Asks children to imitate the sounds. Imitates sounds herself if children can't.	Imitate the sounds.
Records children's voices on a tape recorder. Plays back recorded voices, a few at a time. Allows time for giggling and surprised reaction.	Recite a familiar verse and end with: My name is ... Enjoy listening to own and other children's voices.
Replays tape at another time. Stops tape at: My name is ... Asks children to identify voice.	Try to identify voice.

THE TEACHER	THE CHILDREN
Helps children to recognize the significance of the intonation pattern of language as a clue to meaning.	Learn to distinguish between rising and falling intonation.
Plays Echo in which the teacher selects a child to stand at the rear of the room and repeat a sen-	Imitate teacher's intonation and use as clue to meaning.

THE TEACHER	THE CHILDREN
tence or question exactly as she says it. The class evaluates whether child "echoed" correctly: This is a pencil. Are you going home?	
Guides children to recognize differences in volume (intensity) of speech.	Learn to adapt their voices to size of room and size of audience.
Plays What Did You Hear? Whispers a word, phrase, or sentence. Asks children in various sections of room to repeat what she said. Compares responses of children near and far away.	Repeat the teacher's comments. Realize whispering is not heard at a distance.
Gives other sentences, using conversational tone and classroom speaking voice. Encourages child who is inaudible to use "big" voice in classroom situations.	Reproduce these voices. Gain in self-confidence as they use a quiet, small voice when talking to one person or small group; larger voice when speaking to entire class.
Uses puppet figures to give additional practice in volume control.	Learn to project voices through puppets.
Involves N. E. children.	Find release from shyness in using puppets.
Helps children recognize that voice shows feeling or emotion.	Realize voices reflect and show feeling.
Rereads part of a familiar story or poem in which there is a dialogue. Discusses how tone of voice shows feelings of characters.	Gains sensitivity to use of volume, tone of voice, and facial expression.

THE TEACHER	THE CHILDREN
Calls on volunteers to imitate the conversation of the storybook characters.	Change voice as they imitate characters.
Provides group and individual practice in saying: Happy Birthday! Hooray, it's snowing! I have new shoes. Watch your fingers! Ouch!	Make up other sentences to express surprise, anger, joy, etc.
Encourages children to use words or word sounds that suggest familiar things. Helps N.E. children with these.	Make up other words for sounds.

Develops recognition of rhyming words.

Tells children to listen for words that sound a-like as she recites familiar rhymes or verse.	Sharpen their auditory awareness. Join in the refrain.
Asks for other words that sound like the rhyming words. Gives clues or words if necessary.	Concentrate on sounds of words and identify them. Supply the rhyming words.
Develops the concept that rhyming words sound a-like; uses term.	Understand the expression "rhyming words" and use it spontaneously.
Tells a familiar couplet and stops short of the last word.	Complete the rhyme.
Extends to unfamiliar rhymes and to riddles: I rhyme with hair. You sit on me. What am I?	Solve riddle from rhyming clue.

Guides children to recognize

THE TEACHER	THE CHILDREN

initial sounds of words.

Starts with children's names. Martin supplies a word beginning like his name. All children whose names begin like his, stand and give additional words beginning with M.	Listen carefully to check on words; if word given is incorrect, they raise hands and give correct word.
Extends to other children's names.	
Introduces <u>Name Them,</u> in which she gives a series of three words, one of which begins like the first word named, e.g., <u>mop,</u> toy, <u>mother.</u> Calls on individual children. Increases the number of words in the series up to seven.	Get practice in immediate recall, as they repeat the words
Repeats the activity, using a series not controlled by the first word, e.g., sand, <u>b</u>aby, tall, <u>b</u>asket.	Identify words that begin alike. Compose similar series.
Continues the activity, using pictures of familiar objects, places, or things, whose names begin with same letter. (Arranges pictures on chart rack or on chalk ledge.) If child's response is correct, but does not begin with letter needed, the teacher indicates this and asks for a word beginning like the desired word.	Name pictures.

Grow in ability to associate initial sound with initial letter. |

THE TEACHER	THE CHILDREN
Involves N. E. children in these on-going classroom activities and relates these activities to the sound production in the Language Emphasis Lesson.	Practice sounds of their new language.

HOW LISTENING IS TAUGHT
IN THE THIRD-GRADE CLASSROOM

From a Curriculum Bulletin of
The San Diego, California Schools

Critical and Evaluative Listening
      Read a short poem to the class and ask the pupils to guess the title.   Encourage the children to give reasons for their choices.

      Read a short story in which events are scrambled, and ask students to rearrange the events.

      Read a short story and ask the pupils to tell what happened in a one-sentence summary.

Listening for Information and Special Purposes
      Present activities involving cutting and folding paper, drawing, or writing according to oral directions.

      Listen to and repeat directions that might be given to a traveler attempting to reach a particular place.

      Listen to a report made by another child to find the most interesting sentence or phrase.

Listening for Appreciation and Enjoyment
      Read aloud a poem which is likely to evoke emotion; then encourage the pupils to discuss their feelings.

      Ask the children to describe the story behind a song's words after hearing the lyrics.

Listen to sounds and list words that name them to see if each sound was heard.

TEACHING LISTENING TO YOUNG CHILDREN

From a Curriculum Bulletin of
Montgomery County, Maryland Schools

A child responds to sounds before he gives evidence of seeing. He quickly learns to sort sounds into those categories of pleasant, unpleasant, and frightening.

As a child develops, his listening habits differ in their nature and purpose. In the beginning, listening is simple and more or less incidental and serves as one of the chief means of obtaining experience. At a later stage, listening becomes more pointed, refined, and complex. It becomes a functional means of obtaining information.

The degree of auditory skill and the meaning attachments for words which a child possesses is reflected in his speech patterns and the significances of his thoughts. Sound and meaning tend to merge together.

The child must be so motivated that he has a constructive attitude toward the listening he is to do. The child can be helped in developing this attitude if the teacher joins with him in the effort to establish a clear purpose for listening.

It is also important that a child be cast in the role of both speaker and audience. As a member of the audience, he must experience the need to make those adjustments necessary to listen effectively to a variety of children whose tone, diction, and mannerisms have great variation.

In addition, a child needs to become a critical listener. He needs to evaluate what he hears in light of what he knows. The teacher must help the child develop a rich vocabulary and a rich storehouse of meanings which will enable him to arrive at intelligent decisions.

Listening establishes an important basis for reading, because the attachment of meaning to the spoken word is the same intellectual process as attaching meaning to the written word.

Observing With Our Ears: Creative Listening

In the beginning weeks of school, Miss Babcock had frequently taken her class "exploring" in the music center. The children had experimented with the rhythm instruments·

-- discovering the sounds made by each instrument

-- classifying these sounds as to high, low, loud, soft

-- accompanying a friend's movements with an instrument that interpreted his rhythmic pattern and mood.

The teacher plans to build upon these preparatory activities to ensure continuity of experiences.

On this sunny, autumn day, Miss Babcock and the children had just returned from a walk during which they had been listening for sounds.

Miss Babcock took the children into the music center. She said, "Today, as we explore, see if you can find an instrument that makes a sound like something you heard on our walk."

The children moved among the instruments, experimenting with one and then another. Miss Babcock walked about the room, stopping from time to time to talk to a child.

How does such an activity fit into the total of good listening habits?

"Listen," said William, "this drum sounds like my feet as I walked on the driveway."

"The finger cymbals sort of sound like the birds saying 'tweet'," said Pam.

"I can't find what I want," lamented Ronnie. "I've tried the triangle, the recorder, and lots of other stuff and nothing sounds like the pigeon that said 'peep'."

"You may have to make that sound with your mouth," said Paula.

"Good listening," said Miss Babcock. "It may not be possible to find an instrument that makes a sound like one you heard."

"These sand blocks really sound like my feet walking in the leaves," said James.

Elaine did not have an instrument. "I can use my mouth to make a sound," she announced. "Listen. Sh sh sh sh sh. That's how the wind sounded. If we all do it together, I bet it will sound just right."

What other activities might follow this one?

Now Hear This!: Listening for Differences

The class of 27 children was enthusiastically singing the chorus of a song which accompanies a dramatization of "The Three Billy Goats Gruff."

Although they had seen the play several times with a different cast of characters each time, they watched eagerly as four members of their class performed the favorite story once again.

"It is I, Little Billy Goat," squeaked Alvin as he walked with tiny little steps across the balance-beam-bridge. "You wouldn't want to eat me, ol' Troll. I wouldn't hardly make a mouthful."

The Troll allowed him to pass and crouched in wait for Middle Billy Goat Gruff. But when Middle Billy Goat bleated, "My great big brother will be dee-li-cious! Tasty and really nourishing. Wait for him!" the Troll allowed him to pass.

The children laughed and applauded with delight as Great Big Billy Goat Gruff finally pushed the wicked Troll off the bridge. The

three goats linked arms to sing the
final refrain:

> Alvin: "Little Billy Goat"----
> Lisa: "Mittle Billy Goat"----
> Bill: "Great Big Billy Goat
> Gruff!"

The teacher, Mrs. Motley,
had detected the error in Lisa's pronunciation; and later that afternoon,
as the children were working independently at their desks, she hand-
ed Lisa a slip of paper on which
was written "Little Billy Goat" and
asked her to read it aloud.

Lisa looked surprised but
complied with Mrs. Motley's request.
She looked even more surprised
when Mrs. Motley asked her to
write down the words, "Middle Billy
Goat."

She wrote with no hesitation,
"Mittle Billy Goat."

"What do you think that means,
Lisa?" Mrs. Motley asked.

Lisa shook her head.   "I
don't know what is a 'Mittle Billy
Goat.'   But, that's the way the song
goes."

Mrs. Motley smiled, "Lisa,
describe the position of your desk in
relation to Jan's and Ted's."

"My desk's between their two
desks," Lisa promptly replied.

"Jan is on your right side.
Ted is on your left side.   And
you're smack dab in the _____,"
Mrs. Motley waited expectantly.

"Middle.   My desk's in the
middle," responded Lisa.

Mrs. Motley began, "Little
Billy Goat is first across the bridge
and Great Big Billy Goat is last a-
cross the bridge and _____."

Lisa interrupted, "Middle
Billy Goat goes in between them!
He's the middle one.   I thought he
had a special name, but he's the

The teacher had
learned to listen.

Was this an effective
way of helping Lisa
to arrive at the cor-
rect pronunciation of
the word?

Comprehension clari-
fies what we hear.

middle one!"
        'Now let's see you write
'Middle Billy Goat'," laughed Mrs.
Motley.
        Lisa picked up the pencil,
paused a moment and then asked,
"It's 'd's', not 't's'?"
        Mrs. Motley nodded, and Lisa
wrote "Middle Billy Goat."

The Children Experienced:
        1.   A sharpening of their awareness of sounds around
them.

        2.   The pleasures and difficulties of reproducing fam-
iliar sounds with musical instruments.

The Teacher Thought:
        1.   All of my children seem to be increasing in their
ability to attend to what they hear and to distinguish among
sounds.

        2.   I wonder if they would profit from being intro-
duced to some new musical instruments?   What listening activities will stimulate other levels of creativity?

        3.   Is it possible that those who are not so proficient
at this listening game need more experience in auditory discrimination?

        4.   I am especially interested in Lisa.   Is she poor
at distinguishing among sounds, or are her standards for
doing so even higher than those of other students?

Side Effects: Listening and Remembering
        Michael brought two shells
to a gathering of all first grade
classes.   He was not able to identify the shells by name nor to give
other information.   His teacher suggested that he find pictures of his
shells in a reference book and report to the class the additional information.   Michael did not follow
through with this suggestion.
        The next morning, Katie   When the teacher
brought a shell to the same group.   works with one child,

She had located a picture of it in a reference book and included information in her presentation. She was aided by her teacher who read the name of the shell.

others may be listening.

Riddles and Answers: Listening Comprehension

It was five minutes before lunch time, and the children had just completed their work on a science lesson on animals. "Everyone listen closely," Miss Apteker said. "We're going to play 'What Am I?' I am a large furry animal who walks on four legs. I live in cold lands. I like to swim and I eat fish."

A way to make these "extra" minutes have a purpose.

"I know," said Gwen, "it's a seal."

Harry objected. "No, it isn't, because seals don't have fur."

"Oh, yes, they do," countered Gwen. "My mother has a fur coat and it's made out of seal skin. I've felt it."

"Well, they don't look furry anyway," Harry replied, "because I've seen them at the zoo and they look all smooth in the water."

"Maybe some furs are smooth while others look and feel very shaggy," suggested Miss Apteker. "How about the riddle, then? Is the answer 'a seal'?"

What did the teacher learn about the listening habits of these children?

"No," Mark said quite definitely, "because you said, 'I walk on four legs,' and that couldn't be a seal."

"What then?" Miss Apteker asked.

"A caribou?" Mark questioned. "You said it lives in cold places."

"But caribous don't eat fish," Gwen said disdainfully.

"Oh, yeah," said Mark, "I forgot about that. Maybe you'd bet-

ter repeat the whole riddle, Miss
Apteker, could you?"

    Miss Apteker had barely fin-   What can be done to
ished repeating it when Gwen and   promote progress in
Mark simultaneously shouted, "A po-   listening skills?
lar bear!"

LISTENING K-3

From a Curriculum Bulletin of
The Valley Stream (New York) Schools

Goals for Oral Communication

Listening Skills
1. To listen for enjoyment, appreciation and reflection.
2. To listen for information and for specific purposes.
3. To listen for the purpose of criticizing and evaluating.
4. To listen in order to reproduce sounds and speech patterns correctly.
5. To listen in order to retell and/or dramatize events in sequence.
6. To listen in order to predict outcomes ("curious" listening).
7. To listen courteously.
8. To listen creatively, in order to build imaginatively on what is heard.

Activities

Kindergarten:
1. Listening to stories, poems, records, music.
2. Identifying sounds around us: teacher tapping on window, presenting clock, rhythm instruments, etc.
3. Discriminating between kinds of sounds: near and far, loud and soft, high and low; recognizing voices and objects inside and outside of classroom.
4. Reproducing rhythms: teacher claps a pattern, children imitate singly or in groups.

5. Imitating sounds: animal sounds, story sounds (like a refrain from a well-known story).
6. Following directions: responding to simple verbal instructions, like "Draw a red line at the top of your paper" or "Walk to the board and bring me a piece of chalk."
7. Responding to rhymes: nursery rhymes and jingles.
8. Listening to stories, retelling a story in sequence, finishing a story begun by teacher.

Grade One (in addition to pertinent activities listed previously):
1. Illustrating stories in sequence after they are read aloud, "comic-book" style.
2. Telephone game: a word or message is whispered from child to child and repeated accurately.
3. Listening for beginning sounds, ending sounds and rhyming words.
4. Increasingly complicated rhythm activities (may be correlated with arithmetic, as in clapping out ways to make a number).
5. Telling cumulative stories (adding on to a story): I went to the supermarket to buy a peach; I went to the supermarket to buy a peach and a pear; I went to the supermarket to buy a peach, a pear and an apple, etc.
6. Choral speaking.
7. Listening to short stories for the purpose of answering questions, "Listening Tests."
8. Answering riddles, listening for "clues."
9. Following cumulative directions: Pick up a book, get a piece of chalk, then close the door (with teacher adding to and varying the directions).

Grade Two:
1. Listening to tape-recorded stories read by teacher or pupils for the purpose of obtaining information, hearing oral reading, self-evaluation in oral talks, answering questions, etc.
2. Phonics games.
3. Thinking, planning and telling an original story.

Grade Three:
1. Oral reporting, to disseminate information, correlated with all subject areas.
2. Telephone skills.

3. Conversational skills.
4. Social skills, introductions, courtesies.
5. Listening to music to stimulate creativity, correlated with art work, oral and written work.

Instructional Aids
1. SRA Listening Skill Builder Program.
2. "Mind-Stretchers": class chart of new or unusual words encountered.
3. Teacher-made and pupil-made charts for phonics, rhymes, etc.

Chapter VI

THE TEACHING OF LISTENING
IV. THE INTERMEDIATE GRADES

The first two articles in this chapter were written
with the high school student in mind. It is possible that an
occasional item or example might seem more appropriate to
that level but the reader should not allow this fact to dis-
tract him from the many ideas that are particularly valuable
to the teacher of the elementary grades. The first item is
excerpted from a curriculum bulletin of the Meridan,
Mississippi public school system. After listing the kinds of
skills that a listener should acquire, appropriate activities
for mastering these skills are listed for grades 7 through
12. Most of the skills listed and almost all of the activities
mentioned can be adapted to the needs of the upper elementary grade teacher with only slight modification. The second
article by Miss Doris Niles, who is Chairman of the Department of Speech at Will Rogers High School in Tulsa, Oklahoma, I have long considered one of the best presentations
concerning the teaching of listening, and is certainly valid
for the elementary school intermediate grade teacher. The
fact that this article strongly urges the integration of speech
and listening instruction appears to be of particular value.

The third item in this chapter is an outline of a suggested resource unit on listening which is excerpted from a
curriculum bulletin of the Fort Worth, Texas public school
system. While, no doubt, any teacher would want to modify this outline for use in his own class, the general scheme
is one that should prove useful. The stress on note-taking
is particularly desirable as this is a subject that has been
quite generally neglected especially in the upper elementary
grades.

The last selection is by Annabel E. F. Bower and is
taken from her 1963 University of Pittsburgh doctoral thesis,
The Effect of Training in Listening Upon the Listening Skills
of Intermediate Grade Children. Here is presented a prac-

tical, down-to-earth way of teaching listening which should
provide the reader with good ideas on finding and using suitable materials for the teaching of that skill.

TEACHING LISTENING IN THE FUNDAMENTALS COURSE

Doris Niles

One day last week while I was discussing in one of
my classes the preparation of a new assignment, the better-
than-usual attention one student was giving me impressed me.
I could tell by his eyes that he was listening actively, but I
was puzzled because appreciation (rather than the discrimination for which the content of my explanation called) seemed
to characterize his listening. Later in the period I sat down
to listen to the students speak, and was startled to observe
that the boy who had given me such flattering attention was
wearing a hearing aid.--Or *was* it a hearing aid?

Promptly I broke the first rule of good listening by
writing succinctly to his girl friend sitting next to me,
"Richard! Hearing aid?" to which she replied, just as succinctly, "No! Transistor radio."

In enumerating the fundamentals of speech for my students, I used to include listening among them. Now I'm in-
clined to think my analysis was faulty. Wouldn't it be more
accurate to hyphenate "talking" and "listening" as a descriptive title of speech? It takes two to tango; listening is the
other half of talking. When listening ceases, there is no
point in continuing to talk. The fundamentals of speech, then,
are inherent in both these processes.

Before I learned to hyphenate "talking-listening" in my
thinking, I had difficulties with students who felt that they
were wasting their time in speech class except when they
are speaking. Now, by accompanying many speaking assignments with related listening assignments, I try to teach my
students that they must learn the fundamentals of speech
through listening as well as through talking; that is, they
must develop sensitivity to the audience and grow in their
ability to think critically, to organize material, to use words
with precision, to use the voice and body to communicate--

and even to do research. (Training the auditor to distinguish fact from opinion should motivate learning to search
in every given case for the available means of persuasion.)
Thus, teaching respect for listening as a tool of learning is
one of the first tasks I attempt.

All I have said adds up to the fact that listening is as
broad as the field of speech. I want to discuss a few step-
by-step experiences in listening which I provide for my students in speech.

I believe it is important for students to learn at the
beginning of the course the scope of listening skills as well
as of speaking skills. I impart this learning by direct instruction and by providing a number of activities for the
specific purpose of making them aware of the many knowl-
eges and understandings and step-by-step processes involved
in effective listening.

Understanding the assumptions underlying all the instructional materials I give them makes my students more
amenable to learning. I therefore teach them directly what
research has revealed about listening, the relative amount
of time we spend in listening, the relationship between effective speaking and listening, some of the inaccurate assumptions that make students indifferent to learning the skills involved, such as those that listening ability is largely a matter of intelligence, that there is no need for formal training
in listening because everyone gets so much practice every
day, and that one need only learn to read to learn to listen.

After this direct instruction my next step is to ask
my students to spend two or three days listing the factors
which they believe influence listening effectiveness. We compare these lists with Nichols' [*see end of this section] and
with our composite list as a guide we begin to learn separately the techniques of each factor.

Another method I use to acquaint students with the
scope of listening is to assign a talk about listening. For
individual speeches I have compiled a list of more than 35
suggestions for these talks. These suggestions survey all
kinds of listening and listening processes, and (among others) include the following:

1. A talk showing how Will Rogers' personal qualities were so interwoven through his speech that he induced

greater receptivity to what he had to say.

2. A talk applying Will Roger's famous epigram, "I never met a man I didn't like," to the listening process.

3. A talk showing how orators who are <u>not</u> "good men skilled in speaking" can confuse listeners.

4. A talk showing the responsibility of the speaker to the listener and vice versa.

5. A talk illustrating six ways by which the listener may "take up the slack" between the rate of speaking and the rate of thinking.

6. A talk using a quotation about listening as a point of departure: "A bore is one who is so interested in talking about himself that you don't get a chance to talk about yourself" (Ed Wynn). <u>Or</u>, "An actor is a guy who, if you ain't talking about him, <u>he</u> ain't listening" (Marlon Brando). <u>Or</u>, "Calvin Coolidge was Northampton's favorite listener. He listened his way into every office the town could give him." <u>Or</u> (a paraphrase of Ralph Waldo Emerson's "'Tis a good reader makes a good book"), "'Tis a good audience makes a good speech."

After providing my students with a survey of listening skills by means of these introductory lessons, I try to concentrate on one kind of listening at a time. I question the efficacy of such an assignment as "Listen to a sermon and write a summary or an outline of its content." I'm not sure doing so will improve the student's ability as an auditor to identify the structure of a speech. I believe the best single assignment I have given specifically relevant to this ability is one which also gives the students much practice in listening to difficult exposition. I ask students to find a paragraph (preferably expository) or write one of their own and to prepare to read it to their classmates. They they must construct at least six statements to test how well the class has listened. These statements must include (1) a paraphrase of the topic sentence, (2) a statement neither expressed nor implied in the paragraph, (3) a paraphrase of a detail, (4) a misrepresentation of a meaning in the paragraph, (5) an exact quotation of the topic sentence, and (6) a statement which is partially true and partially false.

At this point the student submits to me his paragraph and the six (or more) statements concerning it. I check the latter for accuracy, and help him revise them to improve them as testing devices.

When I have approved the exercise, the student reads his paragraph to the class and then reads his test statements. He then reads their correct classifications so that the members of the class may check their responses. With only two or three students reading and testing each day, this assignment extends over a period of several weeks. Thus the students have shorter and more frequent practice periods, in conformity with a sound principle of learning.

There is another aspect of listening which I should mention. Should an auditor ever specifically practice concentrating on fragments, rather than on the speech as a whole? Ordinarily, the listener's judgments of voice, diction, and the like should be peripheral judgments, but I believe that in a class in speech the needs of the auditor should determine the specific purpose of his listening. (I am aware that I must guard against my students' becoming hypercritical listeners. I hope, however, that I help many of them to improve faulty techniques by giving them individual assignments to observe good and bad qualities of speakers in the area in which they are having difficulty.)

Surely variety is as essential in the teaching of listening as it is in the teaching of any other skill. Consequently, I make use of some role-playing and parlor games in teaching listening. I give one assignment for which students dramatize various kinds of listening, e.g., attentive, biased, uncomprehending, marginal, selective, critical, and emotional, by interpreting sentences which illustrate these kinds of listening. An example of biased listening might be, "We both listened to the same forum speaker, but you'd never believe it, because Jack heard things I'm sure the speaker never said." Passive: "I have to listen to 'Ding Dong School' every morning when my little sister has it on, but I never hear a word." Selective: "I listened only when the speaker touched on what interested me."

One of the parlor games I utilize is "Conversation." Each member of the class writes on a slip of paper the name of a specific place, and a sentence on another slip. We place these names and sentences in two different "hats." Two opponents (usually a boy and a girl) each draw a sentence from one "hat" and the timekeeper draws a place name from the other. The timekeeper calls "Time!" and names the place where the two converse. The object of the game is for each contestant to listen so well that he can manage to fit his sentence into the conversation without its being detected by either his opponent or the other members of the class.

Another device I can use only when two students get into such a heated argument that they are responding, not to ideas, but to emotion-laden words. (Such arguments erupt now and then in a speech class if the atmosphere is permissive.) I ask these two students to come up before the class and continue their argument--on the condition that Student A does not answer Student B's arguments until the former has stated (to the latter's satisfaction) what the latter has said, and vice versa. There is usually one of two outcomes: either they discover that they have both been arguing on the same side--the problem has been a semantic one; or one changes over to the other's side.

I can't resist closing by telling about a very personal experience I had in teaching listening. Last summer I took an excellent short course at my state university, and while I was there I was inspired to do some research on listening. I left the university determined that when I got back to school in the fall I would do the best job of teaching listening that I had ever done. Although I was mindful that the best teaching is by example and not by precept, until three days before school opened I had no idea just how good an example I would be forced to set: I underwent an emergency laryngeal operation, and I taught for the first eight weeks of the semester without being able to utter a sound.

Paradoxically enough, that physical handicap furnished the necessary rapport for teaching listening, and I am convinced that my disability improved my teaching techniques. During my two months of silence I taught all the introductory listening assignments. I learned that previously I had talked too much, for although that class had more than the usual number of students, we covered the assignments faster than any other class had done before--partly because I wrote out all individual criticisms for each assignment. I also discovered that when I could make no attempt to answer a barrage of questions, early in the course the students formed the habit of listening to my answers the first time I have them. And the atmosphere was relaxed! Because it was impossible to mimeograph all instructions, the class had to be quiet to hear my whispering. Students noted this near-silence, and commented that it was a relief from noise and confusion. Because there was less tension, they took the time to use the tools of thinking while they listened.

So it is possible to teach speech without speaking it:
it can be taught through listening.

[*Note: Ralph G. Nichols and Thomas R. Lewis.   Listening
and Speaking.   Dubuque, Iowa: Wm. C. Brown, 1954. (Com-
piler's note: Since this article was written this book has
been revised: Thomas R. Lewis and Ralph G. Nichols.
Speaking and Listening. Dubuque, Iowa: Wm. C. Brown,
1965.)]

DEVELOPING LISTENING SKILLS

From a Curriculum Bulletin of the
Fort Worth, Texas Public Schools

A.   Motivation
    1.   Quote the old rhyme:

        Old woman, old woman, shall we go shearing?
        Speak a little louder, sir, I am very thick of
            hearing.
        Old woman, old woman, shall I love you dearly?
        Thank you, kind sir, I hear you very clearly.

    2.   Point out that the old woman's response is imme-
diate because she heard what she wanted to hear.

    3.   Discuss the difference between intentional not-
hearing and careless not-hearing.   Mention embarrassments
that may come from careless not-hearing: failing to appear
at a place at the right hour and not being able to introduce
a new classmate because one has listened carelessly to the
name as he was introduced.

    4.   Ask for first-hand experiences of embarrassment
caused by careless listening.

    5.   Point out that failure to listen well to directions
in school often can mean the difference between good and
poor grades.

    6.   Through discussion, point out that in the world
today we depend more upon listening than we do upon read-

ing. We communicate with others through speaking and listening. Most of our directions in class come through listening.

As listeners we are able to think much faster than
the speaker can talk; therefore, we are able to discern certain things as he speaks. We can:

    a. Get his main idea
    b. Notice his feelings about his subject
    c. Notice important details
    d. Notice the important relationships
    e. Evaluate his arguments
    f. Apply his ideas to our own.

    7. Play a tape recording or a record of many dif-
ferent sounds. Ask students to listen and write down the
different sounds they hear. If a recording is not available,
ask students to be perfectly still for two minutes and then
write down the sounds they heard.

B.   Teaching Activities
    1. Ask students to make a Listening Chart for list-
ing their listening experiences for any block of time, perhaps at home as a homework assignment.

LISTENING CHART

Time	Place	Conditions	To Whom Listening	What Was Right or Wrong About My Listening

    2. Place the letters $TQLR_2$ on the chalkboard. Ex-
plain that these letters represent a good formula for listening: Tune-in, Question, Listen, Review, and Recite. Discuss each step in this listening formula with the class.

    3. Begin a discussion of the value of taking good
notes in class.

        a. Make a transparency of the following:

TAKING NOTES IN CLASS

1. Do not attempt to take down everything the teacher says.
2. Look for the cues every teacher gives as to what he considers important.
3. Keep your notes as brief as possible.
4. As soon as possible, go over your notes to impress important things on your mind.

---

    b.   Discuss each point on the transparency using the following information:

    (1) <u>Do not attempt to take down everything the teacher says.</u>
He can speak much more rapidly than you can write. Furthermore, not everything he says is of equal importance. The purpose of notes should be to record the major points presented by the teacher. Make notes, therefore, only on the chief points covered and on the key subpoints.

    (2) <u>Look for the cues every teacher gives as to what he considers important.</u>
Such phrases as "Note that ...," or "The major point is ..." alert you to things you should write down. Also watch for enumeration of details, causes of events, reasons for the truth of a statement, and other such indications of the teacher's organization of his material.

    (3) <u>Keep your notes as brief as possible.</u>
If the teacher is working from a well-planned outline, jot down the headings as closely as you can. Be on the alert for main ideas and key terms, and jot them down. You will find it worthwhile to being developing a system of abbreviations and short cuts that you can use to save writing everything down. Good students use such devices to avoid needless effort.

    (4) <u>As soon as possible go over your notes to impress important things on your mind.</u>

This is an invaluable study procedure. The highest percentage of forgetting takes place in the few hours after you have studied the material. A quick recheck of notes does much to prevent your forgetting what you have just studied.

   c. Read or play a recording of a famous speech (e.g., Lincoln's "Gettysburg Address" or Kennedy's "Inaugural Address") and have the pupils take notes. Or give a short, well-outlined, easy lecture yourself. Evaluate in detail these notes.

4. Continue the study of taking notes.

   a. Review the skills learned about taking notes in class. Emphasize the necessity of listening for. main points.

   b. Show the film "It's Fun to Read Books" [*see end of section]. Ask the pupils to apply the $TQLR_2$ method for listening as they view the film. (If students need additional practice, do the same with another suitable film.)

   c. Motivate the pupils for viewing "It's Fun to Read Books" by asking them to listen in order to answer these questions:

      a. What kind of book did Mary choose? George? Elaine? Fred?
      b. Why did Elaine choose the particular one she did?
      c. Where did Fred find the book he wanted?
      d. What did Fred do on his way home?

5. Evaluation. Prepare the following self-check test. Ask the pupil to read the questions and answer them honestly by writing <u>Always</u>, <u>Sometimes</u>, or <u>Never</u> by each.

   a. Which is more important to me--talking or listening? Should I do more of one than the other?

   b. Do I ever turn a "deaf ear" to the speaker who is not attractive to me?

   c. Should I try to write down every word which the speaker says when I think his message is important?

d. Should I usually try to remember facts in-
    stead of ideas when I listen?
e. Do I find it difficult to listen to a person who
    is expressing opinions contrary to my own?
f. Do I let my thoughts wander when I listen?
g. If I am given clear directions, do I find them
    easy to follow?
h. When I listen, do I make an effort to shut out
    distractions?
i. Am I eager to learn through listening?
j. Can I anticipate what a speaker is going to
    say next?
k. Do I like music?
l. Before accepting an idea I have heard, do I
    attempt to realize its truth and value?

[*Note: "It's Fun to Read Books," 11m. (black and white or
color), 16mm. Chicago: Coronet Films, 1951.]

LISTENING

From a Curriculum Bulletin of the
Meridan, Mississippi Public Schools

Listening Skills
Recognition of:
  Central theme,
  Difference between fact and
    opinion,
  One's own speech defects
    through listening to others,
  Speaker's purpose,
  Comparison or contrast be-
    tween own ideas and
    those of the speaker,
  Language signals announc-
    ing important details and
    materials,
  Meaning from voice in-
    flection, and
  Relationship among ideas.

Adjustment to:
  Rate of speech of commu-
    nication,
  Abnormal listening situation.

Prediction of:
  Next point of the speaker,
  Conclusions.

Proficiency in:
  Taking notes,
  Following directions.

Formation of:
  Answers to questions,
  Critical evaluations,
  Mental pictures,
  Sensory reactions, and
  An appreciation for speech

or oral reading.

Observance of the rules of
courtesy.

Speaking and Listening Activities
Speaking and listening activities are continuing integrated processes, with additional activities stressed at every
grade level, and should be correlated with activities and outcomes of written compositions.

Speaking and listening skills and activities are so
closely related that the following suggested activities are, in
most cases, to be used in both speaking and listening areas.

1	2
Taking part in conversation, Making one-minute talks, Relating brief personal ex- periences, Using the telephone for so- cial and business purposes, Participating in informal discussion (developing re- sponsibility for contribut- ing to group discussion), Asking and answering ques- tions, Making social introductions, Making brief expository speeches based on per- sonal experiences or read- ing, and Following simple parliamen- tary procedure.	Reading aloud prose, poetry, and original compositions, Beginning choral reading, Dramatizing plays based on materials studied or written by class, Giving directions, Making simple explanations and expressing opinions about school and community affairs, Making two- to three-minute reports based on reading from two sources, using notes, Giving character sketches, real or fictional, Reading minutes of class ac- tivities, Reciting short memory selec- tions, and Using parliamentary proce- dure.

3	4
Making announcements, Asking and answering essay- type questions, Pantomiming,	Making impromptu speeches, Summarizing class discus- sions, lectures, assignments, announcements, and reports,

3 (cont.)

Participating in round
 table discussions (learning to organize principal
 ideas),
Introducing a speaker,
Making presentation and acceptance speeches,
Discussing controversial
 issues,
Making talks to sell ideas,
 objects, books, or per-
 sons,
Reading aloud to show in-
 terpretations of various
 literary types,
Interviewing,
Making three- to five-
 minute reports based on
 reading from several
 sources, and
Studying parliamentary procedure.

4 (cont.)

Summarizing from reading or
 listening: radio, television,
 movies, books, magazine
 articles,
Listening to tapes or recordings pertinent to current
 class room study, and
Participating in informal
 debate.

5

Maintaining speaking and
 listening skills developed
 in earlier grades,
Recognizing the varied purposes of speaking: to
 convince, to persuade, to
 inform, to entertain, to
 stimulate,
Using varied forms of speaking to emphasize above-
 mentioned purposes,
Listening with increasing
 emphasis on critical
 evaluation,
Participating in forums and
 symposiums, learning to
 ask relevant key questions
 to further discussions,
Participating in radio and
 television programs,

6

Presiding in varied types of
 situations,
Making speeches of special
 types, such as after- dinner,
 nomination, presentation,
 acceptance,
Speaking extemporaneously,
Conducting employment interviews, and
Participating in formal debate.

5 (cont.)

Participating in assembly
  programs,
Reading minutes,
Using more complex parliamentary procedure,
Expressing carefully ana-
  lyzed opinions on school
  or community situations,
Using support from several
  sources to show opinions
  on important issues,
Giving critical reviews of
  movies, television, radio,
  books, magazine articles,
  and
Quoting meaningful memory
  selections.

TEACHING LISTENING IN THE INTERMEDIATE GRADES

Annabel E. Fawcett Bower

This study [1see end of section] was designed to determine the effectiveness of teaching listening skills to fourth,
fifth, and sixth grade students, and to investigate the relationships of listening ability to selected variables.   The population used in this study was the total enrollment of pupils in
grades four, five, and six of four elementary schools.   A
pre-test of listening ability was administered to determine
initial listening ability prior to any instruction.   The STEP:
Listening, 4A, was utilized for this purpose.   Testing
was done by tape recording utilized for this purpose.   Lessons in listening were administered to the experimental
group for a period of fourteen weeks, three days a week
for twenty-five minutes each day.   The classroom teacher
in each experimental situation taught the two teacher-pre-
sented lessons, while the third lesson was presented by tape
recording, utilizing the experimenter's voice.   The post-test,
STEP: Listening, 4B, was administered after the last
week of instruction had been completed.

An analysis of co-variance and t tests was utilized
to evaluate the effect of listening instruction on the listening
skills of the selected population. Results of the analysis of
co-variance indicated that direct instruction in listening will
significantly influence the results of the post-test of listening
ability. These results correspond with those obtained by
other researchers whose findings are reviewed in this study.

A correlation of .45 between listening and mental age
was obtained. This correlation was significant at the one
per cent level. Other correlations with listening, found to
be significant at the one per cent level, were: language .53,
arithmetic concepts .54, chronological age .28, and school
grade .35.

Correlations ranging from .34 to .46 were found between grades in language arts and arithmetic (both mid-term
and final) and listening ability. These correlations were
significant at the one per cent level.

Sample Lessons

Week 2   Lesson 2   Time: 25 minutes

Today, we are going to continue our work on listening for
important ideas and words. In one of our lessons, we saw
how the main idea is like the top step on a ladder. Many
times, however, as hard as we try to listen, we cannot hear
any one word or sentence that states exactly the main idea.
Many times there is no key statement that tells us this in a
spoken article. When this happens, we must listen to the
whole article before we decide what the main idea is. Listen to these sentences and tell me if any one of them can be
considered the main idea of all the rest of them.

1.   When making a chemical garden, place coal in a
     low dish with a little water.

2.   To make the chemical mixture, combine these
     ingredients in a bowl and mix well:
          6 tablespoons of common salt,
          6 tablespoons of bluing,
          6 tablespoons of water,
          6 tablespoons of ammonia.

3.   Pour this mixture very slowly over the coal.

4. To give your garden some color, borrow some
    food coloring, colored inks, and perhaps some
    fabric dye from mother.   With a medicine drop-
    per, drop the different colors all over the mix-
    ture.

5. In a short time little crystals will begin to form.
    Within a few hours, your chemical garden will
    have odd and interesting shapes. [2]

What are these sentences about?   (Pupil response: Making
a chemical garden.)

What is the main idea of the sentences?   (Pupil response:
How to make a chemical garden.)

Does any one of these sentences, then, give the main idea
of all the rest- - how to make a chemical garden?   (No.)

All of these sentences helped us to tell the main idea by
giving us different steps in making a chemical garden.   Did
one sentence alone, however, tell the main idea?   You then
had to think of all of these sentences together in order to
come up with one main idea, didn't you?   Let us consider
this next article to see if we can find one sentence that contains the main idea.

> The book, Farmer Boy, is one of my favor-
> ites.   It is a true copy of a nine-year-old boy,
> Almanzo who lived on a farm many years ago.
> Laura Ingalls Wilder is the author of the book.
> I enjoyed the book because Almanzo has so
> many exciting and funny experiences right on the
> farm.   His father had given him his two oxen,
> Star and Bright.   Almanzo had to break them to
> wear a yoke.   That wasn't too difficult for him.
> But when he tried to teach them to draw a sled
> over the snow, there was trouble.
> Almanzo liked his oxen, but he could not
> keep away from his father's colts.   That brought
> him more trouble.   How he wins Starlight, his
> father's favorite colt for his very own, is one of
> the most interesting parts of the book. [3]

What is the main idea of the article?   Was there a sentence
in the article that could be the main idea?   (Pupil response:
Yes, Farmer Boy is one of my favorite books; I enjoyed the

book, <u>Farmer Boy.</u>)

Could you see the difference between the two selections I
have just read? The one selection contained a sentence
which <u>gave</u> you the main idea (<u>Farmer Boy</u>), while the other
made you piece together sentences all of which <u>suggested</u> the
main thought, but <u>none</u> of which <u>directly stated or said</u> the
main thought.

Let us listen to this next group of sentences and see if we
can find one sentence that contains the main idea:

1. Be courteous.
2. Be sure to have the right number before you place
   a call.
3. Tell at once who is speaking.
4. Be brief in giving your message or in answering
   a question, but tell enough to make further questions unnecessary.
5. Speak clearly and in a natural tone of voice. [4]

Did you find one sentence that gave you the main idea? (No.)

What are these sentences about? (Pupil response: Telephoning.)

What is the main idea of these sentences? (Pupil response:
The correct way to make a telephone call.)

Now, let's go on to another selection and practice finding the
main idea.

  Weeks ahead of time, a feeling of excitement
began to creep over the town. First, over the
rain-stained election posters and the faded auction
signs there appeared suddenly, as if they had
bloomed overnight, the huge, bright, circus posters. Inhaling the pungent smell of poster paste,
boys and girls stood before them and gawked.
  No color was too bright, no word too big for
the circus: THE MOST STUPENDOUS ... WORLD
FAMOUS ... GREATEST ... BRAVEST ... WILD-
EST .... The posters promised lady acrobats in
pink tights and elephants from the exotic East,
snarling lions from darkest Africa and aerialists
daring beyond belief. Time seemed to stand still,
for, like the Fourth of July or Halloween, Circus

Day drew nearer with agonizing slowness. [5]

Did you find a sentence or phrase that gave you the main idea? (Yes.)

What is the main idea? (Circus days are exciting like a holiday.)

Where did you find the main idea: at the end, beginning, or middle of the selection? (Beginning.)

Who can suggest a good title for the selection? (Circus Days Are Exciting.)

We will listen to another selection and see if there is one sentence containing the main idea.

1. Give the title of the book and the name of the author.
2. Tell what the book is about.
3. Tell only enough of the story to make your listeners wish to read the book.
4. Make your listeners feel that you enjoyed the book. [6]

Did you find one sentence or phrase that gave you the main idea? (No.)

What are these phrases about? (Telling a story or giving a book report.)

What is the main idea of these sentences? (You can make your story interesting by following the rules.)

Can someone suggest a good title for the group of phrases or sentences I have just read? (How to Tell an Interesting Story, or How to Give a Book Report.)

Now I shall read you an article about beavers. After I have finished reading it, I shall ask you some questions, so listen carefully. Listen to see if the main idea is directly stated in the story. Remember, as we have seen, that it may not always be stated in a key sentence:

Beavers are very busy little animals who build their homes of mud and wood and stones. They always build them in a stream. The en-

trances to their houses are under water. They
have very sharp, strong, teeth which they use to
cut down the trees for their houses. They gnaw
around the tree trunk near the ground. Every year
the beavers put a fresh coating of mud upon their
houses. After a few years, the walls become very
thick.

Beavers are friendly and like one another's
company. They build their houses close together,
but there are nver any doors or openings between
them.

Put the proper identification on your paper and number down
the left hand side from one to ten. (Pause for this to be
done.)

1. The main idea of the article is:
    (a) Beavers' homes are built very interestingly.
    (b) Beavers have sharp, strong, cutting teeth.
    (c) Beavers are animals who are very destructive.
    (d) Beavers are friendly, busy animals.

2. These animals build their houses in a:
    (a) swamp
    (b) house
    (c) tree
    (d) stream

3. The person writing this article probably told this to us
    to cause us to:
    (a) enjoy reading about beavers
    (b) buy a beaver as a pet
    (c) want to help build a beaver's home
    (d) appreciate the work of the beaver

4. Beavers gnaw around a tree trunk:
    (a) high up   (b) near the branches
    (c) near the ground   (d) in the middle

5. How often do they put a fresh coat of mud on their
    houses?
    (a) twice a year
    (b) every year
    (c) every two years
    (d) every three years

6. After a few years the walls become:

(a) thin   (b) cracked
(c) crumbly   (d) thick

7. What is used in building the houses besides wood and
    stones?
    (a) leaves   (b) rocks
    (c) bricks   (d) mud

8. How often are there doors between the beavers' houses?
    (a) always   (b) usually
    (c) sometimes   (d) never

9. Beavers prefer to live:
    (a) alone   (b) in company
    (c) on land only   (d) in water only

10. What is <u>suggested</u> in the story, but not actually told?
    (a) Beavers are busy little animals.
    (b) Beavers are friendly animals.
    (c) Beavers' homes may stop the streams.
    (d) The beaver strengthens his home every year. [7]

In our next lesson, we shall continue with our practice of
finding main ideas and important details.

Week 14   Lesson 1   Time: 25 minutes

For the final week of listening lessons, I thought it well that
we deal with a very important subject--the ways young people
can get along well together.   Why is it important that young
people get along well together?   Or is it important?   (Encourage pupil response--accept any reasonable response and
discuss for a while.)

Can you suggest ways that young people can get along well
together? (Pupil response: Encourage the following thoughts
to be expressed: (1) being thoughtful to others, (2) making
friends, (3) sharing ideas, (4) being a good sport, etc. Encourage discussion--can take time for the exchange of
thoughts.)

Today's lesson deals with ways young people can live together happily.   We will consider all the points you mentioned in our discussion.   I shall read several situations
that deal with people's feelings.   After each one, I shall
stop and ask you questions.   Now, I would like you to put
the proper identification on your paper and number from one

to nine down the left hand side of your paper. (Pause.) Now
sit back and relax, while I read you the first incident.

> The invitation to spend a week at camp was
> the most exciting thing that had ever happened to
> Maria Rojas. She could hardly wait to get away
> from the hot tenement where she lived. Away from
> the noisy traffic of the city streets.
>
> Now, at last, Maria was on her way. Her
> nose pressed to the train window, she eagerly
> watched the beautiful farms slip by. Now and then
> she glanced shyly at two girls who were talking
> with Miss Foster, the camp director. How could
> she make friends with them? If only she could
> think of something to say!
>
> Suddenly, she saw wooly animals, which re-
> minded her of some she had seen in the zoo. "Oh,
> look!" she cried, pointing, "Look at the baby
> llamas!"
>
> A burst of laughter came from the girls.
>
> "Miss Foster," one of the girls called, "She
> doesn't know a sheep when she sees one."
>
> Tears came to Maria's eyes. Now she would
> never make friends with the girls at camp.
>
> Miss Foster put her arms around Maria and
> said, "Remember, girls, this is Maria's first trip
> to the country. She hasn't had a chance to learn
> about farm animals. But she can teach us many
> things. When I visited her home, she cooked a
> wonderful Spanish supper all by herself. I hope
> she will cook something for us at camp.
>
> Maria was encouraged by Miss Foster's
> words, but she wondered how she would get along
> with the girls in the week to come.

Question number 1: How did Maria feel on her way to camp?
    a.   happy and contented
    b.   jealous and spiteful
    c.   lonely and ill at ease

Choose the correct answer and place it in the proper place
on your paper.

> That first night in camp was the quietest
> Maria had ever known. It was so still that the
> opening of a soft drink sounded like a gunshot.
> For Maria, who was used to all-night traffic and

street cries, it was too quiet to sleep. The other
girls, tired after their journey, were sleeping
soundly.

Hours passed, and then Maria heard a distant call. "Whoo-O-O!" A whistle answered, high
and clear. Again the call came, and the answer.

"Signals!" Maria thought. "Theives are
breaking into camp! I must tell someone! If only
I had one friend in this frightening place!"

Gathering her courage she awakened Patty,
the girl in the next bed, and told her what she had
heard.

Patty laughed softly, but she was kind. "You
heard only night birds in the woods, Maria. You
have what we call "first-night" ears. All new
campers have them. There is nothing to be afraid
of. Try to get to sleep now.

Question number 2: How did Maria feel on returning to bed?
    a.   tired and hungry
    b.   sleepy and at ease
    c.   mischievous and mean

Choose the correct answer and place it in the proper place
on your paper. The next question is really two, for there
are two answers. Instead of putting both answers after the
number 3, put the first answer that you select after the
number 3, and the second answer that you select after number 4. The question is: What did Patty do that made Maria
feel better?
    a.   Patty laughed.
    b.   Patty realized that the night noises were strange
        to Maria and explained them to her.
    c.   Patty let Maria know that she was not the only
        girl who had ever been frightened during her first
        night at camp.
    d.   Patty told her to go back to sleep.

Now, select the two correct answers. Put one answer after
number 3 on your paper, and the other after number 4.[8]

References

1. A major portion of this dissertation was published under the author's maiden name (Fawcett) and titled
"Training in Listening" in Elementary English 43: 473-76+,
1966.

        2.   Peter John (designer and arranger).   McCalls
Giant Golden Make-It Book.   New York: Simon and Schuster,
1953, p. 124.
        3.   Thomas C. Pollock and Florence Bowden.
"Farmer Boy."   Words Work for You.   New York: Macmillan,
1954, p. 267-68.
        4.   Mildred A. Dawson.   "Guides for Telephoning."
(Grade 5) Language Arts for Daily Use, Yonkers, N. Y.:
World Book Co., 1959, p. 89.
        5.   Freeman Hubbard (narrator).   "Circus Days."
Great Days of the Circus.   New York: American Heritage
Publishing Co., 1062, p. 11.
        6.   M. A. Dawson.   "Guides for Giving a Book Re-
port." (Grade 5) Language Arts for Daily Use.   Yonkers,
N. Y.: World Book Co., 1959, p. 129.
        7.   William McCall and Lelah Mae Crabbs.   Standard
Test Lessons in Reading.   Book B.   New York: Bureau of
Publications Teachers College, Columbia University, 1950.
        8.   Emmett A. Betts and Carolyn M. Welch.   "Living
Together Happily."   Study Books for Adventures Here and
There.   New York: American Book Co., 1963, p. 122.

Chapter VII

THE TEACHING OF LISTENING
V. A TELEVISION SCRIPT

Dr. Charles F. Reasoner, of the Education Department of New York University, wrote his doctoral dissertation at Teachers College, Columbia University in 1961. It is a massive two-volume work which has much to offer the language arts teacher. Two excerpts from this thesis have been combined to form this chapter. The first excerpt forcefully makes the point that there is need for a better way of presenting information concerning public schools of today to the public. Dr. Reasoner feels that one realistic avenue available for this purpose is television.

In the second volume of his work Professor Reasoner presents a series of television scripts concerned with the several language arts which he suggests might be useful in a number of different ways. The second excerpt included in this chapter is the complete text of the script concerning the skill of listening.

This material has been included in this book, first, because a great many important issues concerning the teaching of listening are brought up and discussed here in a rational and interesting manner. Secondly, the idea of a dramatic presentation of a topic such as listening (not necessarily but possibly on television) may offer many ideas to teachers who have been puzzled about effective ways of describing their work to parents, school board members, and to the lay public in general, as well.

A TELEVISION SCRIPT ON TEACHING LISTENING

Charles F. Reasoner

        This document is an attempt to call attention to im-
portant aspects of nine specific elementary-school classroom
experiences in the language arts--speaking, writing, reading,
listening, dramatics, grammar, spelling, vocabulary development, and handwriting--for an audience of television viewers
via scripts for presentation. The problem basic to this
document is one contained in educational television programming for adults: can educational television programs be developed for adults to enable them better to understand what
elementary schools are doing in the area of the language
arts?

        One must recognize, of course, that such television
scripts are not the totality of the medium. There is a limit
to the experimental actions which words alone in a script
can suggest. People, settings, or electronic equipment cannot be reproduced here. What can be done is to present
those materials from which the television program can be
made. In short, it is necessary to provide things for people
to do and say, settings in which people can be placed, and
directions for electronic engineers and uses of equipment so
that points of emphasis--at least so far as the scripts can
do so--may be effectively communicated through the medium
of television.

Need for the Study
        The adult citizens of the United States are sending
more children into their public schools than ever before in
history. Professional educators have long advocated the importance of keeping the lay citizenry informed about school
policies, purposes, and goals, by appropriate means.

        It has been difficult for the layman to reflect or to
act intelligently on questions raised about current and local
issues, policies, and practices in their schools. Various
reasons for this lack of precise understanding can be given.
Perhaps they have not been informed effectively by local
professional leaders. Perhaps the information they have received has been distorted through a lack of clarity and precision in the communication process. Perhaps the messages
sent to the layman have contained too much pedagogical jar-
gon. Perhaps too much of the information comes "second-

hand" to the lay citizen.   Perhaps some instruments of the
communication medium have been employed with lesser effect
than others might have had.   Perhaps the information was not
suited to the interests of the particular group for which it
was intended.

At any rate, today educational theory and practice are
front page news-- evidenced not only by educational writers
and their critics on school issues, but also by interested lay
adults who make efforts to reveal what their concerns are by
way of writing articles for magazines and newspapers.   But
in educational television programming, school issues have not
yet become "front page" concerns.

Educational television has not fulfilled its potential.
Educational television cannot replace what the classroom
teacher can do in parent education about the school.   The
classroom teacher cannot replace television. Each, it would
seem, can complement the other.   Being complementary,
however, does not mean broadcasting stultifying, stereotypic
concepts of school practices.

Experimentation in the uses of educational television
is needed: experimentation in communication with adults
about their schools, about educational practice being used,
about how their children are or might be taught, and the
like.   "The essential thing now," Seldes states, "is that the
road to experiment must remain open .... The arguments
against educational television may all turn out to be valid,
but the argument that it should not be tried is not in keeping
with our tradition" [Gilbert Seldes, The Public Arts. New
York: Simon and Schuster, 1956, p. 276].

NO TUNE FROM THE HICKORY STICK
("The Lost Signal")

WRITER: Charles F. Reasoner

CAST OF CHARACTERS

MRS. WILMA COLLINS (Fourth
    Grade Teacher)
MISS MABLE BIRCH (Principal)
MR. ERIC TILBY (Janitor)
NETSIL (Animated Cartoon Charac-
    ter)
FOURTH GRADE STUDENTS:
    BETTY ANN
    MELVIN
    SUSAN
    BETTY LOU
    SARA
    JANET
    MIKE
    CARL
    KAREN
    WAYNE
    PETER
    STUART
UNDER FIVE:
    RITA ANDREWS (First Grade
        Teacher)
    CANDY (First Grade Student)
    BILLY (First Grade Student)
    MARCIA (First Grade Student)
EXTRAS:
    STUDENTS

MAIN SETS:

1. MAIN HALLWAY,
   FIRST FLOOR,
   ELM HILL
   ELEMENTARY
   SCHOOL
2. FOURTH GRADE
   CLASSROOM

ACT ONE
DISSOLVE FROM
NETWORK TITLE TO
FILM CLIP: SERIES
OF SCHOOL BELLS
RINGING

SUPER TITLES: No
Tune from the Hickory
Stick - "The Lost Sig-
nal."   FADE OUT

SOUND: GRADUALLY OUT ON
BELLS
MUSIC: BRING UP THEME, HOLD
UNDER ANNOUNCER
    ANNOUNCER: (VO)
The language arts . . . people talking, writing, listening, reading, acting. People exchanging ideas and information with each other as they go
about their tasks of daily living. Important tasks . . . like keeping
house, working at a job, helping others . . . relaxing . . . all made
possible through language. A language so important that people send
their children to school to learn it
well . . . from spelling and vocabulary development to listening -
from grammar to phonics - from
speaking to writing - from creative
dramatics to reading. These are
some of the language arts taught in
today's schools, by today's teachers,
to today's children . . . for tomorrow's world. A world that will
scarcely remember the one-room
school and McGuffey's Reader. A
world which will not have been
taught to the Tune of the Hickory
Stick.
MUSIC: BRING UP
    MRS. WILMA COLLINS:
(COMES OUT OF PRINCIPAL'S OF-
FICE. TURNS TO GO UP THE
STAIRS TO HER ROOM BUT STOPS;
WALKS QUIETLY OVER TO OPEN
DOOR OF MRS. ANDREWS' FIRST
GRADE ROOM AND PEEKS IN,
LISTENING)
MUSIC: HOLD UNDER CANDY,
THEN OUT
    CANDY:
And then the third Billy Goat Gruff
came trip-trapping over the bridge
and the mean ol' dole said that
. . . Who is coming trip-trap,
trip-trap, trip-trapping over my

SUPER CHILDREN ON
PLAYGROUND

SUPER SCHOOL BELL
WHICH IS ABOVE
DOOR OF PRINCI-
PAL's OFFICE
GRADUALLY OUT ON
FILM CLIP
PAN DOWN FROM
BELL TO SIGN "PRIN-
CIPAL" ON DOOR
PAN FROM DOOR OF
PRINCIPAL'S OFFICE
TO OPEN DOORWAY
OF FIRST GRADE
ROOM OF RITA
ANDREWS

CUT FROM DOOR-
WAY TO PRINCIPAL'S
OFFICE DOOR WHERE
MRS. WILMA COLLINS
IS EMERGING. PAN
HER TO MRS.
ANDREWS' ROOM

DISSOLVE IN TO
LIMBO: FIRST
GRADE CLASSROOM.
CANDY TELLING
FLANNEL BOARD
STORY OF "THREE
BILLY GOATS
GRUFF"

bridge. Then the third Billy Goat
Gruff said it's me, the third Billy
Goat Gruff and the dole said, Ah ha!
I'm going to eat you up! But the
third Billy Goat Gruff said: No, not
by the hair of my chinny, chin chin!
And he butted him right off the
bridge and the mean ol' dole never
bothered anybody again.
    BILLY:
He didn't say chinny- chin- chin.
That's in the Three Pigs.
    MARCIA:
She can tell it that way if she wants
to.   They don't always have to be
the same.
    MRS. ANDREWS: (VO)
The bell has rung. Suppose we
get our desks ready to go home.
    CLASS:
(NOISILY OBEYS)
    MRS. WILMA COLLINS: (VO)
(REMEMBERS THE TIME, LOOKS
AT HER WATCH, BEGINS TO
HURRY UPSTAIRS. STOPS ON
BOTTOM STEP AND LOOKS BACK:
THINKS ALOUD) How keenly they
were listening! I wonder whatever
happens to them by the time that
they are fourth graders . . . It's
a shame that youngsters have to
lose that gift when learning is just
becoming so important. I wish
. . . if I had one wish, it'd be to
restore that gift of listening to my
fourth graders!
SOUND: TWO TINY RINGS OF
BELL
    NETSIL:
(AN ANIMATED CARTOON CHAR-
ACTER APPEARS STANDING ON
COLLINS' SHOULDER, HANDS ON
HIPS, TUNING FORK IN HAND) So
be it.
    MRS. COLLINS:
What? (LOOKS AROUND QUICK-
LY)

CUT TO GET XCU
MRS. COLLINS,
SMILING UNEASILY
. . . AS IN RELIV-
ING SOMETHING

CUT TO LS
COLLINS

DOLLY IN TO CU

NETSIL:

Oh. Oh. Here they come.

(VANISHES)

SOUND: ONE TINY RING OF BELL

    MRS. COLLINS:

(LOOKS PUZZLED ONLY MOMEN-
TARILY, SHAKES IT OFF, HURRIES
UP THE STAIRS AS THE OTHER
CLASSES BEGIN TO COME DOWN)   DISSOLVE

(FOURTH GRADE CLASSROOM)   FADE IN TO MRS.

    MRS. COLLINS: COLLINS' CLASS-

(OPENS "DAILY LESSON PLAN   ROOM. XCU OF

BOOK," PICKS UP PEN, WRITES)   "DAILY LESSON

SOUND: TWO TINY RINGS OF BELL   PLAN BOOK." HOLD

    MRS. COLLINS: TO GET COLLINS'

(LOOKS UP, AROUND, THEN BACK   HANDS OPENING IT,

DOWN AND BECOMES ENGROSSED   PICKING UP PEN

IN HER WORK)   AND BEGINNING TO

(A HUGE WHITE SCRIM IS NOW   WRITE

SLOWLY DROPPING TO SHUT OFF   CUT TO GET LS OF

THE SEATS FROM THE TEACHER'S   ROOM.

DESK. THE SCRIM IS A REAL   GET COLLINS AT

ONE, BUT AT A CRANK IN THE   DESK, WRITING

BACK OF THE ROOM NETSIL, THE
CARTOON CHARACTER IS CRANK-
ING THE CRANK--LARGE FOR
HIM--AND SLOWLY LOWERING
THE SCRIM. AS THE SCRIM
REACHES THE FLOOR, WE SEE
THE HUGE SHADOW OF NETSIL
ON THE SCRIM, STANDING ON
TOP OF ONE OF THE CENTER
DESKS, ONE HAND ON HIP, THE
OTHER OUTSTRETCHED, HOLDING
THE TUNING FORK)

    NETSIL:

(KICKS A BOOK TO THE FLOOR)

    MRS. COLLINS: CUT TO CU

(LOOKS UP SLOWLY, THEN   COLLINS

STIFLES A SCREAM)

    NETSIL:

That's all right, Mrs. Collins,   CUT TO COLLINS

Wishes are for teachers and chil-   AND NETSIL, PAN

dren I always say.   COLLINS TO DOOR

    MRS. COLLINS:

(RISES SLOWLY AND MOVES,
TERRIFIED, SLOWLY TOWARDS

THE DOOR) What do . . . you
mean . . . who are you?
    NETSIL:
Your wish . . . now don't tell me
you've forgotten. Really, you
must listen to yourself more carefully!
    MRS. COLLINS:
(EDGING CLOSER TO THE DOOR
WHICH IS NOW VERY NEAR) My
wish . . . to . . . restore the
gift of listening? (REACHES OUT
TO DOORKNOB)
    NETSIL:
Ah ha! So you do remember.
(SHARPLY) Don't!

    MRS. COLLINS: CUT TO XCU
(WITHDRAWS HER HAND FROM   COLLINS' HAND
THE DOORKNOB, BUT, WITH
HAND BEHIND HER EDGES SO
THAT HER BODY HIDES THE AC-
TION OF HER HAND)
    NETSIL:
(PLEADINGLY) Don't go. I'll   CUT TO COLLINS
leave if you truly don't want me.   AND NETSIL
But it's my duty to warn you, that
once you refuse to allow a wish to
come true . . . ka-plooey.
    MRS. COLLINS:
Ka-plooey?
    NETSIL:
Just that! Ka-plooey. No more
wishes granted. It's written down.
It's the law.
    MRS. COLLINS:
I . . . I've never heard of such a
law.
    NETSIL:
Of course you haven't. Just how
many wishes have you been granted?
    MRS. COLLINS: CUT TO XCU
(BEHIND HER BACK HER HAND   COLLINS' HAND
TIGHTENS AROUND THE KNOB
AND BEGINS TO TURN IT SLOW-
LY) Well, none, I guess.
    NETSIL:
That's exactly correct. None.   CUT TO COLLINS

And how many times have you
wished?
MRS. COLLINS:
Why . . . the same amount.
None. Oh, I used to wish a lot
when I was a child. You know,
money, clothes, a movie career
. . . the foolish things children
wish for.
NETSIL:
And . . . this wish for your
fourth graders. That was a child-
ish, foolish wish, also?
MRS. COLLINS:
Oh no! (PAUSE) I . . . I must
be losing my mind! I've been
working too hard. There's no one
here but . . .
NETSIL:
You (LIFTING UP THE SCRIM
AND CRAWLING UNDER, THEN
HOPPING UP ON EDGE OF PAPER
BASKET) and I. I'm Netsil, Mrs.
Collins.
MRS. COLLINS:
(OPENS DOOR A CRACK) I'm
leaving.
NETSIL:
Your wish! Don't you want your
wish?
MRS. COLLINS:
(PAUSES, CLOSES DOOR BUT
HOLDS ON TO KNOB) Yes . . .
no . . . yes, oh, this is too fan-
tastic.
NETSIL:
You're afraid! Certainly you're
not frightened of me?
MRS. COLLINS:
No, of course not. It's my eyes,
my imagination playing tricks on
me . . . That's what's so frighten-
ing . . . anything that can't be ex-
plained . . .
NETSIL:
Can you explain learning? What is
learning, Mrs. Collins? (PAUSE)

Oh, you can't . . . but you engage
in it everyday.   You aren't fright-
ened of it.   Then why . . .
    MRS. COLLINS:
I . . . I am frightened of it, really.
If only we knew more about learn-
ing, we . . . we could be so much
more effective as teachers.
    NETSIL:
What do you know about teaching?
    MRS. COLLINS:
You . . . You're impossible.
    NETSIL:
Are you still frightened?
    MRS. COLLINS:
(OPENS DOOR A CRACK)
    NETSIL:
I see you are.   Very well.   I'll
tell you how to get rid of me if I
. . . become dangerous.   (GOES
TO DESK, GETS SMALL PUSH
BELL FROM THE TOP.   OFFERS
IT TO MRS. COLLINS)   Here.
    MRS. COLLINS:
(TAKES IT WITH FREE HAND) My
bell . . . what . . .
    NETSIL:
Try it.   One ding and I'm gone.
Two dings and I come back.
(PAUSE)   Go ahead.   But . . . af-
ter this trial, you get only one
more ding and one more ding-ding.
    MRS. COLLINS:
I . . . I've just explained.   I'm
not afraid of you.   Why, you're so
small . . .
    NETSIL:
But I have very big ideas.
    MRS. COLLINS:
(PRESSES BELL: "DING") (THE
ROOM IS AS IT NORMALLY IS: NO
SCRIM, NO NETSIL)
    MRS. COLLINS:
(WALKS BACK OVER TO HER
DESK, REPLACES BELL . . .
LOOKS AROUND HER ANXIOUSLY
. . . UNDER THE DESK, IN THE

PAPER BASKET)
    MISS BIRCH: CUT TO DOOR
(APPEARS AT DOOR OPENS IT
SWIFTLY) Will you close the
front door, Wilma, when you leave?
Be sure it's locked.
    MRS. COLLINS: CUT TO COLLINS
(STARTLED) Oh! Oh, Miss   AND BIRCH
Birch, you startled me. Yes . . .
yes, of course. I'll be working
for a while yet.
    MISS BIRCH:
What have you lost?
    MRS. COLLINS:
Lost? Oh nothing. I mean, my
pen. I loaned it to one of the
. . .
    MISS BIRCH:
(NOT SUSPECTING) I've got to
hurry. Supposed to be at a meet-
ing fifteen minutes ago. All work
and no play . . . . (SIGHS, SMILES,
CLOSES THE DOOR AFTER HER)
    MRS. COLLINS: CUT TO MRS.
(STANDS FROZEN MOMENTARILY.   COLLINS
GOES TO DOOR . . . LOOKS OUT
. . . GOES BACK TO DESK.
SITS, LOOKS AT BELL. SIGHS.
DECIDES TO RING BELL, BUT
STOPS. GOES BACK TO HER
PLAN BOOK. OBVIOUSLY SHE
CAN'T DO ANY MORE. CLOSES
IT, SELECTS SOME BOOKS. OPENS
CLOSET, TAKES OUT COAT, HAT,
SCARF, PURSE. PLACES COAT
ACROSS CHAIR, PURSE ON DESK,
SEES BELL AS SHE PUTS SCARF
AROUND NECK. DECIDES TO
RING BELL. PLACES COAT AND
HAT BACK IN CLOSET. COMES
QUICKLY TO THE DESK AND WITH-
OUT HESITATION PRESSES BELL:
"DING-DING." IMMEDIATELY THE
ROOM IS SEEN AS BEFORE WITH
SCRIM DIVIDING IT. COLLINS
REACHES FOR THE BELL AGAIN.)

NETSIL: CUT TO NETSIL
(SLIDING DOWN ROPE ON MAP
AND DROPPING INTO CHALK
TRAY) Ah! Ah!
    MRS. COLLINS: CUT TO NETSIL AND
(WITHDRAWS HER HAND)   COLLINS
    NETSIL:
My, my! You are the cautious
one, are you not?
    MRS. COLLINS:
I . . . I'm better now. It's just
. . . never mind. Get on with
what you're about to do.
    NETSIL:
That's the spirit. Now, come
with me.
    MRS. COLLINS:
I'm not moving from this chair,
and the bell. (CLUTCHES BELL
TO HER)
    NETSIL:
But you must. We're only going   PAN NETSIL TO
to the other side of the scrim.   SCRIM
(HOPS TO DESK TOP. GRABS
BELL, JUMPS AWAY WITH IT)
    MRS. COLLINS: CUT TO COLLINS
My bell. What a despicable, dis-   AND NETSIL
honorable . . .
    NETSIL:
Tsh. Tsh. Why Mrs. Collins!
Your bell is here . . . on Melvin's
desk. Come back and see. (HIS
SHADOW APPEARS BEHIND THE
SCRIM, WE SEE HIM PLACE THE
BELL ON A DESK)
    MRS. COLLINS:
How do you expect me to trust you?
(RISES) Oh, very well. (WALKS
TO SCRIM. LIFTS IT UP. STOOPS
UNDER, WALKS TO DESK)
    NETSIL:
(PULLS BACK CHAIR FOR COLLINS
AS SHE SITS)
    MRS. COLLINS:
You do have very good manners.
But, why must I be here?

NETSIL:
I want you to see something. Look
at the screen.
    (SHADOW PLAY)   CUT TO SHADOW
COLLINS: (ENTERS THROUGH   PLAY
        DOOR, COMES AND SITS
        AT HER DESK, LOOKS
        UP AND ADDRESSES
        CLASS:)
        Now I want you to listen
        very carefully.
        Let's be quiet boys and
        girls.
        We're much too noisy.
        You really should pay
        better attention.
        You're not first graders
        anymore.
        You ought to be able to
        listen more politely to
        what's being said.
    MRS. COLLINS: CUT TO COLLINS
Why, that's me . . . how . . .   AND NETSIL
    NETSIL:
Shhh. Listen!
    (SHADOW PLAY)   CUT TO SHADOW
COLLINS: (HAND RINGS BELL   PLAY
        VIOLENTLY ON DESK)
        Boys and Girls! Have you
        forgotten our quiet signal?
        It looks as though some of
        you have!
        Peter if you do any more
        whispering, I'm going to
        send you straight to Miss
        Birch.
        Pay attention now.
        Are you listening?
        Of course you didn't under-
        stand what Millie said; you
        weren't listening.
    MRS. COLLINS: CUT TO COLLINS
Why . . . why are you showing me   AND NETSIL
this? You make me feel like . . .
like old man Scrooge!
    NETSIL:
Only much worse. Think of all the

lives you're affecting . . . have affected!

MRS. COLLINS:
(RISES, POISED TO STRIKE BELL)
I don't have to listen to this.
(PAUSE) There's that word again.

NETSIL:
Yes. Now I need to give you a
short history lesson. (PUTS ON
ACADEMIC CAP AND GOWN,
POSES WITH TUNING FORK)

MRS. COLLINS:
But what has this to do with my
wish about listening? My minor in
college was history.

NETSIL:
Let's call this a refresher course!
Watch the screen, Mrs. Collins.

MRS. COLLINS:
(RELUCTANTLY DOES AS SHE IS   CUT TO SCREEN
TOLD)
(SHADOW PLAY)
(CAVE MAN WITH SPEAR LEAVES
CAVE, WALKS THROUGH FOREST
THICK WITH TREES . . . LISTEN-
ING TO SOUNDS)
SOUND: FOREST SOUNDS ACCEN-
TUATED (CAVE MAN WALKS
CAREFULLY, STEALTHILY, LIS-
TENING)

NETSIL: (VO)
This guy was probably a thousand
times better at listening than we
are! Why, his stomach depended
upon it.

(SHADOW PLAY)
(MAN SUCCESSFULLY SPEARS
PREY, MAKES SOUNDS OF GLEE.
PUTS ANIMAL OVER HIS SHOUL-
DER, HEADS FOR CAVE . . .
ANOTHER HUNTER IN DISTANCE
SEES A BEAST IN BRANCHES
ABOVE CAVE MAN, ABOUT TO
SPRING . . . LET'S OUT A YELL
OF WARNING . . .)

NETSIL:
And . . . their lives, too.

(SHADOW PLAY)
(CAVE MAN DODGES SPRING . . .
ANIMAL GOES OFF . . . THE
TWO MEN COME TOGETHER AND
COMMUNICATE CRUDELY WITH
SOUNDS AND PANTOMIME)   DISSOLVE
NETSIL: FADE IN TO COLLINS
It seems fair to assume, anyway,   AND NETSIL
that these people were far better
listeners than we are today.   But
then, when they developed their
grunting into a crude sort of language, communication became easier for them . . . and listening
skills began to decline.   My guess
is that the more highly man developed his speech, the more listening-
lazy he became . . . or, to be a
bit more fair, since man probably
did not conscientiously choose to be
listening-lazy, let us say that man
became more careless in his listening.
        MRS. COLLINS:
What proof have you?
        NETSIL:
Proof? Proof? Now you do sound
like a teacher.   Very well, since
you are, I'll do my best . . .
(HOPS BEHIND SCRIM, HIS SHADOW   PAN NETSIL BEHIND
IS LIFE-SIZED NOW) Dr. Ralph   SCRIM.   HOLD ON
Nichols of the University of   SCRIM
Minnesota says he believes that
his guess is conservative when he
states that almost all of us listen
at precisely 25% level of efficiency
when we listen to a ten-minute
talk.   And the longer the talk . . .
(HE SHADOWS TWO LARGE BARS
ON THE SCRIM, DIVIDES BOTH
INTO HALVES, AND REMOVES
THREE QUARTERS.   THE RE-
MAINING QUARTER HE DIVIDES
AND REDIVIDES, UNTIL THERE
IS NOTHING) . . . practically
nothing! See? (PAUSE) Look.
This circle is a classroom full of

students . . . a whole lecture hall full of students (SHADOWS A LARGE CIRCLE ON SCRIM) in several universities who have done research on inefficient listening . . . Now this (PLACES A SHADOW OF A RECTANGLE ON THE SCRIM) rectangle represents a set of questions on the ten-minute lecture I'm about to give. (HIS SHADOW IS CAST BETWEEN THE TWO OBJECTS AND HE PANTOMINES A LECTURE FOR A FEW MOMENTS) Now, I give the students the questions to answer. (THE RECTANGLE IS PLACED OVER THE CIRCLE, THEN WITHDRAWN) When I collect the papers and correct them . . . what do I find? (REMOVES HALF OF RECTANGLE) Only about half are answered correctly! After two months? (DIVIDES THE HALF IN TWO AND REMOVES A PART) . . . about 25% correct! More proof? Well, Dr. Paul T. Rankin in his doctoral work at the University of Michigan in 1926, found adults in different occupations spending 70% of their waking hours in verbal communication! 9% of the verbal communication was in writing (PRODUCES A BAR GRAPH, SHADOWED ON SCRIM). 16% in reading, 30% in talking, and 45% in listening. More proof?

CUT TO MRS. COLLINS WHO IS WATCHING INTRIGUED
CUT TO SCRIM

MRS. COLLINS: (VO)
No . . . wait . . .

NETSIL:
(BEGINS WITH HIS LARGE SHADOW ON SCRIM, GRADUALLY BECOMES SMALLER AS HE APPROACHES THE SCRIM. SUDDENLY HE APPEARS "NON-SHADOW" ON THE OPPOSITE SIDE OF THE SCRIM) Yes?

PAN NETSIL TO COLLINS

MRS. COLLINS:
Your statistics are very interesting

and, no doubt, accurate and very
reliable.   But, I fail to see the connection . . . my classroom of
fourth graders here at Elm Hill
. . .

NETSIL:
But you asked me for proof.   And
dear me, I had hoped that you would
listen efficiently, these are not my
statistics . . . I thought I communicated that point clearly enough!

MRS. COLLINS:
You surely must realize Mr. . . .
a, Mr. . . .

NETSIL:
Netsil.   Just . . . Netsil.

MRS. COLLINS:
Certainly you must realize that,
with me, you have a beginner!
(SHE LOOKS UP AT HIS DISAP-
POINTED LOOK AND SMILES)
Would you care to ask me any ques-
tions?   You mentioned, I believe,
Dr. Nichols of Minnesota, Dr.
Rankin of Detroit and . . .

NETSIL:
(SMILING)   Wonderful . . . simply
wonderful!   And to think I was
about to press the bell . . . ding!

MRS. COLLINS:
(GRABS THE BELL)   Oh no!   Not
so easy.   You brought this on yourself . . . even though it was my
wish!   Tell me, do you have to
answer all wishes?

NETSIL:
Oh dear, dear, dear me no!   It's
impossible.   Why, in my special
category alone . . .

MRS. COLLINS:
Listening?

NETSIL:
Yes, listening.   Why the listening
wishes alone are fantastically high!
"I wish I could listen to what he's
saying" tops the list . . . it's unbelievable, the wishes here!   And

then, there's the "I wish I could
hear's" and the "Oh, I wish you
would listen's" and "I'd give anything if you could hear's . . ."
        MRS. COLLINS:
How do you ever decide?
        NETSIL:
My, my, my, my, my. I
couldn't. I don't. The Absorption
Machine does all of that. Absorbs
and then issues me my assignment
in a matter of split seconds.
        MRS. COLLINS:
But . . . how does it . . .
        NETSIL:
The most sincere, the neediest, the
wish that will cause the most good
to the greatest numbers . . . that
sort of thing. I'm supposed to work
only twelve hours . . . but I'm always on emergency call.
        MRS. COLLINS:
This sounds terribly . . . terribly
        NETSIL:
Human?
        MRS. COLLINS:
Well, yes . . . life-like, realistic,
if you will. This machine age, it's
the way of modern society, really.
(PAUSE) And yet, it's all fantasy
. . . A dream, while awake . . .
I am awake am I not?
        NETSIL:
(ANGRILY) Stop! Stop! Stop! Stop!
Stop! We will conclude immediately
if you insist upon referring to me
as a figment of your imagination!
        MRS. COLLINS:
(UNBELIEVING, BUT RESIGNED)
Very well. I apologize.
        NETSIL:
That's better, now shall we get on
. . . I would like some free time
to myself before another call comes
in . . .
        MRS. COLLINS:
What do you do in your free time?

NETSIL:
I listen, of course! Really, Mrs.
Collins if you're going to continue
to . . .
MRS. COLLINS:
Mr. Netsil . . .
NETSIL:
Just Netsil . . . Netsil.
MRS. COLLINS:
Netsil, a moment ago, when you
were telling about the wishes which
the . . . the Absorption Machine
handles, you kept mentioning listening and hearing. Are they inter-
changeable? Synonymous?
NETSIL:
A good point. A very good question! You can't really ask good
questions, you know, unless you
have listened very, very critically!
Now . . . hark! For some time
now you have been hearing that
noise from outside this room . . .
in the room next to ours, in the
hallway. You have heard it, but
you have not listened to it . . .
until now!
MRS. COLLINS:
(SITS UP PETRIFIED) The janitor!
The janitor! He mustn't find us.
He'll see . . . He can see us, can
he not?
NETSIL:
(UNCONCERNED) Of course he
can! You see, listening is different
. . . listening is thoughtful hearing!
MRS. COLLINS:
(RISES, POISED TO STRIKE THE   PAN COLLINS TO
BELL) He'll be in any moment   HER DESK
(HURRIES AROUND THE OTHER
SIDE OF THE SCRIM AND STANDS
BY HER DESK READY TO STRIKE
THE BELL) Can't you do some-
thing? Please Netsil, please fix it
so I can have another ding and ding-
ding!

NETSIL:
(WHO HAS FOLLOWED HER AND   CUT TO NETSIL
IS NOW RECLINING IN THE PAPER
BASKET, LEGS BENT OVER THE
EDGE) Nope . . . a wish is a
wish!
    MRS. COLLINS:
But . . . you're being grossly un-   CUT TO COLLINS
fair . . . think of the good . . .   AND NETSIL
how much you'll help these children
. . . the other children who will
come to me, their teacher . . .
    NETSIL:
Come now, you're being sentimental
and selfish, Mrs. Collins. Think of
all the other listening wishes that
are waiting. Besides, it's out of
my hands . . . That next ding will
put me back on call with the A. M.
    MRS. COLLINS:
A. M.?
    NETSIL:
Absorption Machine. (DUCKS DOWN
IN PAPER BASKET AS DOORKNOB
TURNS)   CUT TO XCU OF
                                         DOORKNOB AS IT
                                         SLOWLY TURNS
                                         FADE OUT
                                         END OF ACT ONE

                                         ACT TWO

(MOMENTS LATER)
    ERIC TILBY: FADE IN ON XCU
(OPENS DOOR, PUSHES PAPER   DOORKNOB TURNING
HAMPER INSIDE) Oh, 'xcuse me   CUT TO MS TILBY
M'ss Collins, Ma'm. I didn't
realize anyone were still here.
    MRS. COLLINS:
I . . . I had to work late this   CUT TO TIGHT SHOT
evening.   TILBY AND COLLINS
    TILBY:
(SURVEYS ROOM) Tha's all right,
I won't bother to sweep none . . .
I'll jist git the waste basket (PICKS
IT UP SWIFTLY AND DUMPS IT
UPSIDE DOWN IN HIS HAMPER)

MRS. COLLINS:
No! . . . Well, I do have some
more work . . .

NETSIL:
(WHISPERS FROM DESK DRAWER)
It's O. K., I made it.

MRS. COLLINS:
(PUSHES DESK DRAWER SHUT AS
ERIC TILBY TURNS AROUND) I'm
. . .

TILBY:
Oh, you don't have to tell me. I
can see you're rehearsin' a play. I
always tell my wife that you has
the best plays as anybody in the
school . . .

MRS. COLLINS:
(GAINING HER COMPOSURE) Thank
you, Mr. Tilby.

TILBY:
'Course, really M's Collins, you
hadn't oughta do nothing like this.

MRS. COLLINS:
(FRIGHTENED) Like . . . like
what?

TILBY:
(TEASES HER) It's really against
the law, ma'm, but I ain't gonna
report you . . .

MRS. COLLINS:
I . . . I'm sorry. I guess I
wasn't thinking . . . (NOT UNDER-
STANDING)

TILBY:
Climbing up to high places like them,
hanging that there curtain up . . .
s'posin' you was to fall? Now all
you have to do is call me, M'ss
Collins, and I'll do up the job in no
time at all. Now you call ol' Eric
next time. Don't want you a hurtin'
you'self none. (SMILES, PUSHES
HAMPER BACK OUT THE DOOR)
G'night M'am. Show must go on.

MRS. COLLINS: DOLLY UP TO CU
I'll call you Eric . . . thank you.   COLLINS
Good night. (COLLAPSES IN CHAIR)

SOUND: KNOCKING FROM INSIDE
DESK
    MRS. COLLINS:
The show must go on. (SIGHS,
HEARS KNOCKING, OPENS
DRAWER) Oh, I'm sorry . . .
Netsil.
    NETSIL:
(HOPS OUT ONTO DESK) Congrat-
ulations. You handled that very
well.
    MRS. COLLINS:
I . . . I feel as if I were doing
something bad . . . like a crimi-
nal!
    NETSIL:
You were!
    MRS. COLLINS:
What?
    NETSIL:
We were just discussing how ter-
ribly poor you listen!
    MRS. COLLINS:
I'm afraid I . . .
    NETSIL:
Lesson Number One: You heard
Mr. Tilby's voice talking, but you
only listened to . . .
    MRS. COLLINS:
I listened to everything he said.
    NETSIL:
Do you remember the sentence he
used which contained the word
"ain't?"
    MRS. COLLINS:
Eric's never been beyond second
grade, Netsil. He uses ain't and
he said "places like them" and
"hadn't oughta do nothing . . ."
    NETSIL:
But, the sentence with ain't. What
did he say?
    MRS. COLLINS:
I . . . I know Mr. Tilby hasn't had
much education, but when every anyone uses that word . . .

NETSIL:
You stop listening! Same as when
people use words like "communist"
or "unions" or "Pope" or . . .
loaded words, Mrs. Collins. Listening stops! Just the same as,
"Boys and girls, if you don't pay
attention to reading, some of you
will have to stay after school tonight."
Or . . . "Now, let's pay close attention to this chapter . . . we'll
have a test on it tomorrow!" See?
Lesson Number One!

MRS. COLLINS:
Netsil, you're really being unkind.
You've singled out two examples
only. Since you seem to know how
I teach, certainly you must be aware
of all that I've been doing to develop
better listeners!

NETSIL:
I agree with you . . . I do know
what purposes. But, I disagree
with your point that you're developing better listeners. Today for
example . . . you used words or
actions, like the two samples I just
cited, 23 times . . . 23 times you
cut off listening . . . today! So
far this week, 77 . . . last month,
641 . . .

MRS. COLLINS:
If you're going to spend the rest of
your time telling me what a bad
teacher I am, well . . .

NETSIL:
Quite the contrary . . . the A. M.
wouldn't have sent me to a bad
teacher! Come now . . . let's
look at your class . . . look at the
screen . . .   DISSOLVE AND FADE
                                          IN ON SCRIM
MRS. COLLINS:
(LOOKS)
    (SHADOW PLAY)   HOLD EACH SCENE
(RECORD PLAYER WITH A SMALL   BRIEFLY, THEN
  GROUP OF STUDENTS STANDING   DISSOLVE INTO
  AROUND, LISTENING)   NEXT

(STUDENTS READING A STORY TO
  THE GROUP)
(A READING GROUP . . . WHERE
  CHILD HAS TO BE SHOWN PLACE)
(TAPE RECORDER . . . UNUSED)
SOUND: BRING UP STREET NOISES.
GRADUALLY FADE OUT
(CLOSING OF WINDOWS BECAUSE
  OF STREET NOISE)
COLLINS: (VO) Listen for your
          places . . . (CLASS AT-
          TEMPTS TO SING A ROUND)
COLLINS: (PRONOUNCING SPELL-
          ING WORDS VERY DISTINCT-
          LY) watch, thought, through
COLLINS: (GIVING HOMEWORK
          ASSIGNMENT) Now, I've
          explained this twice before.
          Please listen! Your home-
          work for tomorrow will be
          . . .

BETTY ANN: Be quiet Melvin, I   CUT TO TIGHT SHOT
          can't hear the assignment   BETTY ANN AND
          . . .   MELVIN

MELVIN: Oh . . . if it's important,
          she'll say it again   FADE OUT
NETSIL: FADE IN TO NETSIL
There . . . that pretty well sums   AND COLLINS
it up doesn't it?
MRS. COLLINS:
Melvin's the worst discipline prob-
lem I've got.
NETSIL:
But the brightest?
MRS. COLLINS:
Yes. (PAUSE) Sums up what,
Netsil?
NETSIL:
Your direct attempts at teaching
listening.
MRS. COLLINS:
Yes . . . yes I suppose it does.
It's . . . it's inadequate, isn't it?
NETSIL:
Let's say that it's ineffective . . .
the ratio between the amount of
thought and the time given to it to

the results obtained.   Ineffective.
   MRS. COLLINS:
Netsil, just how can you teach listening?   What can be done?
   NETSIL:
Done? Before anything can be done,
we've got to know why people don't
listen and attack on that level!   Eh,
excuse me. (GOES BEHIND THE   PAN NETSIL BEHIND
SCRIM. HIS SHADOW IS NEARLY   SCRIM.
LIFE-SIZED NOW) Now . . . here   HOLD ON SCRIM
I am and there you are!   I have
something in this box . . . the box
is my brain (SHADOWS A BOX ON
THE SCRIM) . . . which I want to
communicate to you.   That some-
thing inside the box is the message.
So I take it out . . . (OPENS LID
OF BOX) Here's the message
(SHADOWS THE FIGURES OF FOUR
MEN ONTO THE SCRIM, SIDE BY
SIDE) Now, I have a decision to
make.   How shall I send the mes-
sage? With my voice? Written
symbols? Pictures? Sounds?
(PAUSE) I choose to do it with
pictures . . . therefore, my mes-
sage needs to . . . (LIGHTS GO
OUT)
   MRS. COLLINS: CUT TO COLLINS
What happened?
   NETSIL: (VO)
(LIGHTS COME ON) Interference.
You didn't get the message.   Or if
the message is interrupted like
this, (LIGHTS FLICKER ON AND
OFF)   CUT TO SCRIM
   MRS. COLLINS:
It's hard to . . .
   NETSIL:
Yes, exactly, it's hard to get.
Every time you tell your students
that you're going to test them on
some particular subject, some of
them are affected . . . much the
same way as you were by the lights
just then.   But . . . the message

continues regardless of the inter-
ference. And you receive it. Your
brain decodes it, and you get the
message . . . a message, anyway.
It may or may not be accurate in
terms of the sender's intention.
(THE FOUR MEN NOW HAVE A
"PLUS" SIGN BETWEEN THE
FIRST AND SECOND AND AN
"EQUALS" SIGN BETWEEN THE
SECOND AND THIRD)
    MRS. COLLINS: (VO)
One plus one equals two . . .
    NETSIL:
One of the simplest of all messages.
But if I had spoken . . . if I had
said those five words, say in
Turkish . . . or, even in English,
while the record player was turned
up high . . . (COMES OUT FROM   PAN NETSIL TO
BEHIND SCRIM)   COLLINS
    MRS. COLLINS:
I wouldn't have understood . . .
    NETSIL:
You might have received something
. . . certainly you would have
heard something . . . but, it's
almost certain you would not have
received my message accurately no
matter how thoughtful your listening!
It would have been either terribly
distorted by the noise or else lost
completely.
    MRS. COLLINS:
But in the classroom, with my students, well . . . that's why I like
to insist on as much silence as I
can so that my . . . my . . .
    NETSIL:
Messages?
    MRS. COLLINS:
Yes, so that my messages won't be
lost.
    NETSIL:
But it's the way you demand the
silence, the way you insist upon
listening. That kind of silence is

often noise, itself! Flickering
lights . . . blackout . . . your
message is lost.

MRS. COLLINS:
Certainly not to all . . .

NETSIL:
Right! Fortunately people still
have the right to choose that to
which they want to listen, though
we do not always get to choose
what we want to hear. Lesson
Number Two: The family in the
pew in front of you at church last
Sunday . . . the baby crying, the
three year old was about to tear
a page out of the hymnal, the
mother and father were discussing
the problem of going home or one
of them leaving with the crying baby.
You heard the minister and the whispering and the crying . . . had you
been trained in listening, you might
have shut out the family in the pew
in front of you, considered it
"noise," and listened to the minister's words. But, instead, you
followed the discussion until the
family left. You got only a portion
of the minister's message. Lesson
Two: Distraction is one of the
greatest causes of ineffective listening.

MRS. COLLINS:
But Netsil, now you're agreeing with
me! Oh, I'm all mixed up. First
you criticize me for keeping disturbances to a minimum and . . .
then you say that distractions are
the greatest . . .

NETSIL:
No! No! No! No! You weren't
helping children become better listeners by trying to keep disturbances
out of your classroom. You were
doing something which man cannot
do . . . you were trying to shut
out noise!

CHURCH SEQUENCE
SHADOW PLAYED
WITH NETSIL'S
VOICE OVER

MRS. COLLINS:
I suppose IQ has something to do
with it . . .
NETSIL:
Not as much as everyone would like
to claim. Standardized tests have
been given and the results reveal a
slight connection, but the relation-
ship between the two, listening and
intelligence, is so low that we have
classified it as a false assumption.
However, that brings me to Lesson
Three, Four and Five: (WAVES
HIS TUNING FORK AS A WAND)
Your class, Mrs. Collins. (SHAD-
OW PLAY BEGINS) You want to
launch into your unit on Indians
. . . so, you decide to talk about
Indians with the class with the pur-
pose of . . .
MRS. COLLINS:
Of finding some aspect of the sub-
ject which will interest all, or
most of them.
NETSIL:
But why Indians?
MRS. COLLINS:
History . . . social studies, of
course.
NETSIL:
Precisely. Now . . . look at the
screen, do you remember this?
(SHADOW PLAY)
COLLINS: Who has ever seen an
        Indian? A real live one?
NETSIL: (VO)
Good question. Now watch.
(SHADOW PLAY)
(HANDS WAVE FRANTICALLY.
SOME CALL OUT, "I HAVE
. . . ME TOO, THE CARNIVAL
. . . A PARADE")
COLLINS: Now wait a moment!
    We can't hear anything if
        we all talk at once. Susan?
SUSAN: Do you mean the Indians
        like out West or from

India?
(ALL HANDS STOP WAVING EX-
CEPT MELVIN'S WHO STILL
WAVES FRANTICALLY)
COLLINS: Melvin . . .
MELVIN: Well, when we went to
       our summer vacation, out
       through Texas and Colorado
       and Arizona . . . well, we
       saw lots of Indians on their
       reservations . . . I brought
       back a whole lot of souvenirs
       if you want me to bring them
       . . .
COLLINS: Melvin, I'm afraid you
       weren't listening very care-
       fully.   We were trying to get
       the answer to a different
       . . .

NETSIL: CUT TO NETSIL
Lesson Three: The listener was
overstimulated about the topic.   He
missed what followed.   But watch
what happens now, after you get
back on the track . . .
       (SHADOW PLAY)   CUT TO SCRIM
MELVIN: (SITS WATCHING GROUP
       AND TEACHER VERY IN-
       TENTLY, CHIN CUPPED IN
       HIS HAND)
NETSIL: (VO)
Think Melvin is listening now?
(PAUSE)   Note!   He's faking . . .
listen to what he's thinking . . .
MELVIN: (VO) Darn ol' Mrs.
       Collins, anyway.   I thought
       she said Indians . . . well
       I'll fix her . . . I won't
       bring any of my stuff for
       the Indian unit . . . the
       heck with Indians anyway
       . . . why don't we talk
       about inventors . . . yes
       . . . now that'd be a good
       unit . . . really exciting
       . . . we could make inven-
       tions and . . .

NETSIL: CUT TO NETSIL AND
Lesson Four: Faking attention.   COLLINS
You even told him how well he had
listened as he left for home that
afternoon.   But let's go back to
Melvin when he was talking about
American Indians . . . That's Les-
son Number Five.
      (SHADOW PLAY)   CUT TO SCRIM
BETTY LOU: The big fat bully, he
      doesn't even know what we're
      talking about.
SARA: He always gets the best
      grades and he doesn't even
      take any books home or do
      homework or even comb his
      hair.   He's always dirty.   I
      just hate Melvin Brent.
      NETSIL: CUT TO NETSIL AND
Lesson Five: Criticizing the speak-   COLLINS
er.   Even if Melvin had been talk-
ing about India, he wouldn't have
had very much of a listening audience anyway.   And, Melvin led us
into Lesson Six while he was talking about inventions . . . he called
the subject of the discussion dull
. . . he suggested it, rather, by
his enthusiasm about inventors.
Many poor listeners will call a subject dull and use that as an excuse
not to listen.   (HOPS AROUND IN   PAN NETSIL BEHIND
BACK OF THE SCRIM) Others try   SCRIM, HOLD FOR
to listen only for facts and miss the   SHADOW
whole idea of what's being said.   In
college, you used to try to outline
all the lectures . . . but what you
didn't know is that there were not
many of those lectures which were
outlined by the speaker in the first
place.   A summary would have been
better.   Lesson Seven and Eight!
Lesson Nine?   Take you and Melvin.
You probably speak around 100 to
125 words a minute.   Melvin can
probably listen to, or rather, think
about 300 to 400 words a minute

. . . Melvin has ample time to go
off on tangents and still get what
you have to say!

MRS. COLLINS: CUT TO COLLINS
(LOOKING A T SCRIM WHICH NOW
HAS HER CLASS SHADOWED ON IT)
What's happening now?

NETSIL:
A trip into the future.

MRS. COLLINS:
You're really making me out a
Scrooge, aren't you?

NETSIL:
Both have happy endings . . . Look!

MRS. COLLINS:
(SMILES, WATCHES)
(SHADOW PLAY)   CUT TO SCRIM
(CLASS SITTING VERY STILL . . .
A LONG PAUSE)

MRS. COLLINS: CUT TO COLLINS
But what are they doing . . . they   AND NETSIL
look frozen . . .

NETSIL:
The window's open. So is the door
. . . they're listening.

MRS. COLLINS:
But to what . . .

NETSIL:
They're recording every sound they
hear . . . then they're going to
concentrate on one . . . if they can.   CUT TO SCRIM
(SHADOW PLAY)
(MELVIN IS TELLING AN INVEN-   DOLLY IN ON "ROL-
TION STORY ON THE "ROLLER   LER FRAME"
FRAME")   DOLLY BACK TO

MRS. COLLINS: (VO)   GET CLASS WATCH-
A story?   ING

NETSIL: (VO)
Could be. No, Melvin's giving a
report on the steamboat . . .
(SHADOW PLAY)
(CLASS SITTING STILL AGAIN.
THREE PEOPLE ARE MAKING
DIFFERENT SOUNDS)

MRS. COLLINS: CUT TO COLLINS
They're still again . . . except for   AND NETSIL
Janet, Mike, and Carl.

NETSIL:
Those three are making different
sounds . . . the rest are trying to
separate them . . .
    MRS. COLLINS:
I'm doing this? Teaching this, this
. . .
    NETSIL:
You are.
    (SHADOW PLAY)   CUT TO SCRIM
SOUND: DIFFERENT SOUNDS COM-   XCU TAPE RECORD-
ING THROUGH . . . SIMULTA-   ER
NEOUSLY
    MRS. COLLINS: (VO)
I've recorded those sounds?
    NETSIL: (VO)
You have. It's a pantomime game
in sound you're playing with them.
There's a story behind one of the
sounds. They're to try to select it.
Try. Listen . . .
SOUND: THE "TAPED SOUNDS"
BROUGHT UP, THEN HOLD UNDER
CONVERSATION
    MRS. COLLINS: CUT TO COLLINS
(PAUSE) The water . . . someone   AND NETSIL
swimming?
    NETSIL:
Nope! You recorded that by splash-
ing your hands in the wash basin.
    MRS. COLLINS:
The music . . . a song?
    NETSIL:
Nope! Only parts of three different
songs . . .
    MRS. COLLINS:
A chicken . . . some voices saying
5 to 2 . . . sounds like a ball
score . . . a dog barking . . .
    NETSIL:
The chicken has just laid an egg,
and . . . But they have different
ideas. Watch.   DISSOLVE AND FADE
    (SHADOW PLAY)   INTO SHADOW PLAY
CARL: All good Americans like   ON SCRIM
       Yummy Cheese. Betty
       doesn't like cheese. Betty

       isn't a good American.

KAREN: I have one: Mrs. Collins
       doesn't like gum chewing.
       We had a gum-chewing con-
       test at Girl Scouts last night.
       Mrs. Collins doesn't like
       Girl Scouts.

    MRS. COLLINS: (VO)
Sounds like commercials. Pretty
bad logic, however.

    NETSIL: (VO)
Chase calls it guilt by association.
A pretty good lesson in discrimina-
tive listening.

    (SHADOW PLAY)

SARA: You said that dogs were
       mean animals. Do you mean
       Mr. Pritchard's dog that has
       to be tied up all the time?

WAYNE: Or my dog that you play
       with every day?

BETTY LOU: My dog is only mean
       when someone teases it . . .

    NETSIL: CUT TO COLLINS
Listening is part of speaking, too.   AND NETSIL
You're having them search for a
referent . . .

    MRS. COLLINS:
Stuart Chase again?

    NETSIL:
Stuart Chase. Becoming sensitive
to value judgments! You're doing
fine, Mrs. Collins.

    MRS. COLLINS:
Am I reading a story now?

    NETSIL: CUT TO SCRIM
Yes. But look carefully . . .
would you say that all are listening
to you?

    MRS. COLLINS: (VO)
Yes, all but those three.

    (SHADOW PLAY)   PAN CLASSROOM

COLLINS: (VO) (READS A STORY)   SCENE ON SCRIM TO

PETER: (COLORING A PICTURE)   GET PETER, BETTY

BETTY LOU: (WRITING A STORY)   LOU, AND MELVIN

MELVIN: (STARING OUT THE
       WINDOW)

NETSIL: (VO)
Who, would you say, isn't listening,
Mrs. Collins?
    MRS. COLLINS: (VO)
None of them . . . well, Peter and
Betty Lou?
    NETSIL: (VO)
Nope! Melvin and Betty Lou.
    (SHADOW PLAY)
BETTY LOU: (PASSES NOTE TO
        PERSON NEXT TO HER)
MELVIN: (VO) (THINKS OUT
        LOUD) Wonder who'll win
        the game tonight. Sure
        hope Mike can play. Mom
        said I could sleep over at
        Mike's tonight.
PETER: (VO) (LOOKS UP FROM
        COLORING PICTURE) If I
        would have written that story,
        I would have made it
        spookier . . .

NETSIL: Remember Lesson Four: Faking?	CUT TO NETSIL AND COLLINS

    MRS. COLLINS:
Netsil, there's so much . . .
    NETSIL:
You've been working on this one for
a long time . . . it's still a game,
but it'll pay off!

(SHADOW PLAY)	CUT TO SCRIM

STUART: I think it's O.K., but
        some sports are too rough
        for girls . . . (PAUSE)
        Janet?
JANET: You said that you think it's
        all right for girls to play in
        sports but some of them are
        too rough for girls. Right?
STUART: Right.
JANET: Well, some sports are too
        rough for some boys, too.
        (PAUSE) Carl?

MRS. COLLINS: What are they doing, Netsil?	CUT TO NETSIL AND COLLINS AT DESK

    NETSIL:
You've given them a topic . . .

"Girls Shouldn't Be Athletes."
They're discussing it.

  MRS. COLLINS:
But, isn't it a bit odd . . . the way
that they're going about it?

  NETSIL:
Odd . . . yes and difficult. But it
makes for better listeners . . .
and better contributors! Before
anyone can put in his ideas, he has
to repeat what the person before him
has said and . . . get his O.K. on
it. You'll use it more with them
later on, but it'll be more than a
game . . .

  (SHADOW PLAY)   CUT TO SCRIM

MELVIN: Girls aren't built right.
        They'd look funny in a foot-
        ball uniform . . . (PAUSE)
        Betty Lou?

BETTY LOU: You said that girls
        would look funny in football
        uniforms. What's that got
        to do with it? I think some
        boys look funny in tennis
        shorts!

MELVIN: Hey, Betty Lou . . . I
        said something else, too and
        you didn't get my O.K. to go
        on with your ideas.

BETTY LOU: Well, I've said it now.

MELVIN: Mrs. Collins . . . we
        can't go on . . .

  NETSIL: CUT TO NETSIL AND
Well, that finishes up my job . . .   COLLINS
I'll be going now . . .

  MRS. COLLINS:
But wait! You can't . . . I haven't
pushed the bell. My bell! Where
is it? I must have left it behind
. . . Netsil . . . (SEARCHES
AROUND DESK FOR IT . . . WHEN
SHE LOOKS BACK UP, NETSIL AND
SCRIM ARE GONE; HER ACTUAL
CLASS IS SITTING BEFORE HER,
THE BELL IS ON HER DESK AND
SHE IS RINGING IT NERVOUSLY)

MELVIN:
Mrs. Collins . . . we can't go on
. . . Mrs. Collins? Mrs. Collins,
you said you didn't need to ring the
bell for us to be quiet anymore.
      MRS. COLLINS:
(LOOKS UP FOR SCRIM . . . NO
TRACE. SEES CRANK IN BACK
OF ROOM, MOVES TOWARD IT)
Yes . . . Yes Melvin . . . so I
did, I'm sorry, I guess I stopped
. . . (WHEN SHE GETS TO PLACE
WHERE SHE SAW CRANK, SHE
FINDS IT GONE, TOO. BUT FOUR
HOLES, WHERE THE SCREWS
WERE, REMAIN) listening for a mo-
ment. Well . . . let's pick it up
with your comment, Melvin . . .
Does anyone remember what Melvin
said? (PAUSE) All right Ann . . .
(LOOKS OUT ON PLAYGROUND   XCU COLLINS
. . . NETSIL IS SCURRYING
AWAY VIA THE VARIOUS EQUIP-   CUT TO NETSIL ON
MENT ON THE PLAYGROUND. HE   PLAYGROUND
WAVES . . . COLLINS WAVES
BACK) I get the message, Netsil
. . . I'm receiving your signal loud
and clear!

THE END

Chapter VIII

THE TEACHING OF LISTENING
VI. SLOW LEARNERS

It is unfortunate that so little has been written about
the importance of teaching listening to children who for a
multitude of diverse reasons have difficulty in learning at the
same pace set for normal children by the curriculum. There
is probably no other group in school that has as much to
gain from knowing how to listen well. As Dr. Thomas Wood
Smith pointed out in his 1956 U.S.C. thesis [entry 1107 in
Duker, Listening Bibliography, 2nd ed., 1968], such children
are often treated as if their sole difficulty in language arts
was in reading. Consequently it is too often taken for
granted that they can listen and that using aural instruction
will solve all their communication problems. Such an approach is fallacious as much more often than not these
children are suffering from a handicap in all communicative
language arts skills. The fact that they perhaps listen better than they read does not justify the conclusion that they
therefore listen well.

The four selections in this chapter are all taken from
curriculum bulletins. The first passage is from a publication of the Richfield, Minnesota school system. The discussion of speech, listening, reading, and spelling in this passage emphasizes the need of establishing an atmosphere in a
summer session class for slow learners that does not arouse
fear or anxiety but builds confidence and assurance in a relaxed atmosphere.

The next three selections are taken from curriculum
bulletins prepared by the Division of Instructional Planning
and Services of the Los Angeles, California city schools. A
most useful suggested plan for appropriate sequencing of listening skills that may be used in teaching slow learners is
given in the first of these excerpts.

The third article in this chapter is a list of aims in

the teaching of listening to slow learners with suggested
teacher activities and materials that will aid in accomplish-
ing these aims.   The last excerpt is a useful summary of
the ways of teaching listening to low-index youngsters together with special emphasis on the teaching of attentive listening for particular purposes such as listening to directions.

PERSPECTIVES ON LISTENING

Carol Lohse and Mary Marquardt

From a Curriculum Bulletin of the
Richfield, Minnesota Public Schools

The objectives, materials, methods and activities of
a summer school language arts class must be directed
toward giving each student some measure of success.   This
includes success in social relationships as well as success
in the classwork.   Many of these students lack confidence in
both areas.   For these reasons, the first objective of a
summer school language arts teacher should be to create a
relaxed classroom atmosphere that allows students to feel
free to speak without fear of rejection.   As stated in the
Language Arts Curriculum Guide for the Richfield Public
Schools, "Perspectives on Speaking and Listening,"

> We must create and maintain an atmosphere of
> emotional acceptance.   Each student must feel that
> he is accepted as a human being.   At no time
> should a teacher's reaction to a student's oral pre-
> sentation threaten that student's feeling of self-
> worth.   Whatever intellectual judgments we must
> make must be preceded by emotional acceptance.
> Without this psychological assurance, a student
> cannot be free to develop meaningful skills and
> understandings.

Remedial language arts students should be given daily
experience in oral communication.   However, these students
are painfully aware of their own inadequacies.   Their
greatest fears are that they may be called upon to present
a speech or an oral book report.   If the student is to gain
self-confidence and realize some success in oral communica-

tion, he should not be placed in a spotlight which glaringly illuminates his inadequacies and increases his feelings of inferiority. Practice in speaking in an informal atmosphere with students who share his inadequacies will be more profitable and meaningful.

Skill in effective classroom discussion should be emphasized in attacking the basic language arts skills. Students should never be made to feel that the purposes of discussion are being presented to them as a "unit"; they should be made aware of classroom discussion as a skill that can be improved only through daily practice. Students should be helped to realize that effective discussion has order and direction; it is not indiscriminate chatter. Each student should be encouraged to offer his relevant ideas. Students appreciate a planned, orderly discussion in which more is accomplished and less "goofing around" occurs.

In addition to participating in total-class discussions, a student may gain self-confidence through an informal "buzz group." It is important, however, that the teacher realize that such discussions require direction. Students should not be organized into discussion groups without some questions which will provide purpose, direction and order for their exchange of ideas. Through buzz groups, students are allowed to freely communicate their ideas to a small number of their peers from the safety of their own desks. Because group discussions are valuable in developing their oral communication skills, the teacher should plan for such activities as often as the nature of the class, time and the relevancy of such an experience permit. The two-hour period of the summer school class provides time each day for preliminary class discussion, short buzz sessions, and regrouping for an exchange of ideas; immediate application of a skill insures better retention. Students who think slowly and who need practice in expressing their ideas orally may demand extra patience and consideration from the teacher and their classmates.

The development of several language skills is aided through speaking experiences. Oral communication furnishes opportunity for practice in usage; reading skills can be improved through oral reading; vocabulary and spelling assignments are made meaningful when the words are pronounced frequently by all students.

Drama is a form of literature which these students

enjoy and which can provide an effective means of improving
their oral communication skills.

Every teacher has experienced the frustration of presenting material which his students have not heard because
they "tuned out" the teacher in order to travel to lands of
worry or fantasy. It has resulted from his confrontation
with uninteresting material, or goals and assignments which
were meaningless to him.

Just as speaking skills can augment other areas of
communication, listening can also be valuable. Listening to
new vocabulary words used in context furthers understanding
of the word; always hearing correct usage encourages development of proper habits. In teaching speaking skills, the
instructor should point out that often words such as government, were, where, weather, whether are misspelled because they are either mispronounced or not heard accurately.
Brief exercises in both speaking and listening should be an
important part of spelling and vocabulary assignments.

The teacher must recognize his responsibility in teaching listening skills. He must take particular care to speak
distinctly in a pleasant, interesting voice which reflects his
enthusiasm for the subject. When giving directions, clarity,
conciseness and the patience to repeat are of vital importance.

Listening may be used effectively as an incentive to
read. If the student is eventually to want to practice his
reading skills, he must first find that he can enjoy and be
interested in information found in printed material. As suggested for younger, more reluctant readers, the teacher can
furnish this stimulus by reading aloud to the students. Brief
discussions can follow the reading, but the emphasis should
be placed on enjoyment and appreciation.

The value of listening in everyday relationships with
others should be pointed out to these students. As has been
stated before, these students want to get along with others
and "do the right thing." They don't want to be ignored;
they should appreciate similar desires held by all individuals.
Learning to listen as others speak and to react appropriately
is requisite to their desired social success.

TEACHING LOW INDEX CHILDREN TO LISTEN

Division of Instructional Services
Los Angeles City Schools

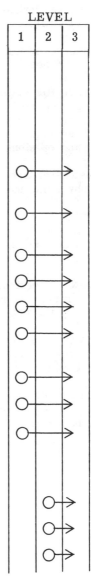

The difficulty level at which the teacher begins his instruction should be determined by diagnosis of pupils' needs and proficiencies. However, items listed in Level 1 should be maintained and reinforced when the pupil is learning Level 2 and Level 3 material; and Level 2 items should be maintained and reinforced when the pupil is learning Level 3 material.

	LEVEL	
1	2	3

Listen accurately to distinguish sounds of words.

Listen for cues to meanings of unknown words.

Visualize words, things, events spoken about.

Listen attentively to a speaker.

Listen for main ideas.

Listen to and execute directions.

Infer the meaning of words through context clues.

Listen to and appreciate rhythmic sounds.

Listen with courtesy.

Recall and recount important ideas listened to in reports, announcements, radio and television programs, motion pictures, and teachers' statements.

Take dictation by listening accurately.

Ask pertinent questions about a report or a film.

	LEVEL		
	1	2	3
Complete rhymes or jingles heard in class.		O→	
Observe the format of television and radio programs.		O→	
Observe influence of television on tastes and attitudes.		O→	
Listen for main and subordinate ideas heard in reports.			O
Listen critically to distinguish between facts and opinions.			O
Listen for and understand the role played by emotional or connotative words.			O
Listen to the voice of the reader in order to secure important clues as to the atmosphere, setting, and action of a story.			O
Listen attentively to the teacher or to the speaker on radio and television programs for correct speech patterns.			O
Listen to a skillful and fluent speaker in order to appreciate the beauty of spoken English.			O
Detect different forms of propaganda in television commercials and in newspaper advertisements.			O

SPEAKING AND LISTENING

From a Curriculum Bulletin of
the Los Angeles City Schools

General Suggestions for Teaching and Listening

Give low-index students plenty of oral instruction and drill in
language usage.

Give them many opportunities to participate in oral activities.
Discussion periods should be short but frequent.

If students speak a non-standard dialect, do not attempt to
have them cease using the dialect.   Instead, try to persuade
them to learn standard English as an alternate dialect to be
used in appropriate situations.

Every lesson is a lesson in listening.   Low-index students
particularly need help in knowing how to listen and what to
listen for.   Listening skills can be developed simultaneously
with other activities.   However, listening skills cannot be
developed incidentally.   Careful listening is a skill to be
developed, and the importance of this skill must be constantly emphasized.

Attentive Listening; Standards of Courtesy in Listening

Develop concurrently the standards of attentive listening,
standards of class discussion, and the standards of courtesy
in speaking.

To give students practice in attentive listening, dictate an
interesting paragraph to the class.   Write the key words in
the paragraph on the chalkboard.   As you dictate, point to
each key word as you say it, and have students write the
paragraph.   In dictation, say each sentence once at a natural pace; then, repeat it slowly as the students write it.
After students have completed the paragraph, write each
sentence on the chalkboard, pointing out correct punctuation.
Students should make necessary corrections in their work.
This activity builds listening skills, spelling skills, and
punctuation skills.   Recordings also can be used to develop
attentive listening.

Listening to Understand the Main Idea

Read an interesting article, anecdote, story, or news article
to students. Have them listen to recall details from the
story. After they have listened to the reading, have them
answer questions which ask who, what, when, why, or how.

Give the students a short oral quiz on the content of the
daily bulletin after it has been read.

Have the students describe a familiar personality or place.
Other class members listen and attempt to guess the subject
of the description. This activity gives students practice in
listening for details as well as practice in speaking.

List on the chalkboard words which help the listener follow
a speaker's ideas, words like first, next, then, secondly,
finally, at last, and also. Point out that these words function in the same way for reading materials. Tell the students that these words usually signal a new or additional
idea. Read a selection and have students point out these
words and the ideas which follow them.

List on the chalkboard words which help the listener detect
transition to a new idea or to a contrast of ideas. For example, words like furthermore, however, although, and on
the other hand, are signal words.

Listening for a Specific Purpose; Varying Approach to
Listening Depending on Purpose

Low-index students must be taught that listening to directions,
information, or explanations is not the same as listening to
ordinary conversation. Review the standards of listening.
Next, point out situations in which attentive listening is important. Tell them to listen for cue words which speakers
use when something important is about to be stated. Also,
tell them to watch the speaker's gestures and facial expressions for indications of important statements.

Listening Carefully to Directions and Following Those
Directions

Teach the students the following steps in listening to directions:

    1.   Listen attentively to the speaker.

2. Determine each step in the directions, and try to relate each step to preceding one.
3. Form a mental "picture" of each step and its place in the sequence of directions.
4. Ask the speaker to repeat the directions, if they are not understood.
5. If directions are not clear, ask questions.

It is likely that low-index students will not be able to recall all these steps; however, if they can remember one or two of the steps, their understanding of directions should improve. Some low-index students should select one of the first three steps, and concentrate on it.

Dictate the directions for drawing a simple pattern on a piece of paper. The students can compare their patterns with the original to determine how well they have followed the directions.

DISADVANTAGED CHILDREN'S NEEDS RELATED TO LISTENING

From a Curriculum Bulletin of
the Los Angeles City Schools

PURPOSES	TEACHER ACTIVITIES [and Materials]
To learn to listen	Listens to the children. Motivates them to listen through many approaches, including use of listening games, literature, and music. [Alexander, Cecil. All Things Bright and Beautiful. New York: Scribner, 1962.]
To learn to listen to and follow directions.	Sets listening goals with the children. Conducts instruction only after getting children's attention. Keeps directions simple; presents one at a time. Looks directly at the group and waits until talking has ceased before proceeding with directions. [Bonsall, Crosby. Listen, Listen! New York: Harper, 1961.]

PURPOSES	TEACHER ACTIVITIES [and Materials]
	Uses the tape recorder to give directions for small group lessons in the study center. [Tape recorder, records.]
To be introduced to literature. To learn to enjoy the beauty of language.	Uses poetry from time to time throughout the day. Encourages children to participate. Reads poetry to children. Permits them to express what they like about a poem and why, but does not require elaborate analysis or follow-up after each experience. [Armour, Richard. Animals on the Ceiling. New York: McGraw, 1966.]
To develop imagery. To learn new vocabulary.	Motivates the children to find, read, and share poems which they like. [Cole Williams. What's Good for a Six-Year-Old? New York: Holt, 1965.]
	Provides opportunities for choric and individual recitation of selected poems which the children especially like and wish to share. [Field, Rachel. Poems. New York: Macmillan, 1957.]
To develop familiarity with the sounds and patterns of standard English.	Tells stories and reads stories. [McEwen, Catherine. Away We Go! New York: Crowell, 1956.]
	Selects recorded stories for use with books in study center. Plays albums of stories. Listens to children retell stories. Builds standards for children in listening to each other. [Mother Goose. Brian Wildsmith's Mother Goose. New York: Watts, 1964.]
To hear different dialects.	Provides opportunities to listen to and compare dialects heard on radio or television programs. [Untermeyer, Louis. (Ed.) Golden Treasury of Poetry. New York: Golden Press, 1959.]

PURPOSES	TEACHER ACTIVITIES [and Materials]
To develop discrimination between sounds.	Uses games, music, sounds in the environment to develop aural discrimination:

high- low   fast- slow
loud- soft   same- different
[Song bells, Rhythm instruments, Record player, Records.]

Chapter IX

THE TEACHING OF LISTENING
VII. TEXTBOOKS AND MATERIALS

The first passage in this chapter is excerpted from
Dr. Kenneth L. Brown's doctoral thesis. This thesis was a
content analysis study of language arts textbooks for the
third through the sixth grades in the elementary school.
Some concept of the magnitude of the task undertaken by
Brown may be grasped by the fact that 15 series of language
arts textbooks for these four grades were examined, classified, analyzed, and reported on. The total number of pages
was a breathtaking 15,285 in 41 books which contained plans
for 7744 specific lessons.

The material presented in this excerpt which deals
with a portion of Brown's findings concerning the area of
listening establishes, I think, that not only was the quantita-
tive task an enormous one but that the qualitative task was
equally impressive. The patience, the painstaking care and
effort that went into this task result in a mass of useful
information concerning various ways of teaching a variety of
aspects of the listening process, alone or in combination
with other language arts skills.

Those readers who may wish to read further about
the content of these textbooks either about listening or about
any of the other language arts skills will find the thesis in
unabridged form a veritable treasure house of information
useful from the standpoint of both researcher and teacher.
No one could justifiably plan to write textbooks in the language arts without first giving careful consideration to this
material. A microfilm copy of the entire thesis may be
obtained at a modest cost from University Microfilms of
Ann Arbor, Michigan who will also furnish a photocopy, but
at a substantially greater cost.

The selection here from Dr. Brown's work begins
with a quotation from Helen K. Mackintosh (ed.), Children

and Oral Language, a joint statement of the Association for Childhood Education International, Association for Supervision and Curriculum Development, International Reading Association, National Council of Teachers of English. Washington, D.C., ACEI, ASCD, IRA, NCTE, 1964, p. 1-2.

The second and final selection in this chapter is by Professor Paul M. Hollingsworth of the University of Nevada who has done research in and has written extensively about listening. This article is included here because it is concerned with the effectiveness of materials which are sold in the form of kits. This amounts to a pre-packaging and pre-planning of the method of instruction. Such materials have proven to be very popular. Anyone who visits many classrooms in various parts of the United States sees them frequently. Foremost producers of such kits are Science Research Associates of Chicago, now affiliated with International Business Machines, and the Educational Developmental Laboratories of Huntington, New York, now a division of McGraw-Hill. A considerable amount of research has been performed concerning the effectiveness from an educational standpoint of using this type of material. Dr. Hollingsworth's report is one example of this type of research.

LISTENING CONTENT OF CHILDREN'S TEXTBOOKS

Kenneth L. Brown

"Although individuals and groups have long shared concern about effective written communication, those responsible for this bulletin now voice the need for equal concern for the effectiveness with which people listen and speak. Of the four English language arts, listening and speaking are the most frequently used means of communication. ... Because the effect of oral communication is so crucial, there is need to make careful appraisal of current practices in teaching children to express their ideas orally with clarity, sensitivity, and conviction. ...

The total oral communication skills must
be taught well at all levels of instruction so
that pupils may develop increased proficiency
as a continuing process. ... Articulate communication is essential not only for adequate
participation in society but also for self-fulfill-
ment. A balanced program with clearly defined goals and explicitly stated means for
achieving these goals must be developed."

Statement of the Problem

Recognizing that there exists increased concern for
speech education in the elementary school, what specific provisions for speech and listening training are made within the
language arts framework in the elementary grades? This
study examines the kind and quantity of speech and listening
content in language arts textbooks for grades three through
six. The specific questions asked are:

(1) What philosophy, broad objectives, and criteria
guide the authors and publishers of the textbooks? How do
they define the language arts and their general objectives?
What are the most important reasons for teaching speech and
listening in the language arts? What influence do the following factors have: knowledge of child development, emphasis
and balance of instruction, teaching sequence, interrelationships among language skills, and correlation of language
arts with the entire curriculum: How are the textbooks organized? How are the problems of evaluation and individual
differences handled?

(2) How much is speech and listening content emphasized? To what degree is the speech and listening content
presented apart from content relating to reading and writing?
How does the emphasis upon speech and listening compare
with the emphasis upon reading, writing, and the body of
content common to all areas of language arts instruction such
as word usage, grammar, vocabulary, literature, and sentence study? What is the emphasis within speech and listening content?

(3) What is the specific nature of speech and listening content? What objectives, principles, skills, understandings, and assignments are emphasized? Is there discernible grade placement of skills? Is there continuity of
instruction from one grade to the next? Is there an increase
in complexity of standards, understandings, and skills taught

from grade to grade?

Category 2.   Listening [see Fig. 1]: This category includes:

A. Lessons designed to call attention to listening directly by presenting guides for listening and/or discussing how we hear and listen, and how we can listen better.

B. Lessons designed to motivate the child to listen to stories for any of the following purposes:
   1. For picture words.
   2. For sentence beginnings.
   3. For sequence of events.
   4. For clues to meaning.
   5. For remembering details.
   6. For separating fact from inference.
   7. For discovering the mood and style.
   8. For anticipating the outcome.
   9. For discovering the central idea and purpose.
   10. For various parts of the story--introduction, development, conclusion and/or pictured incidents, or missed sequences.
   11. For evaluating the story in terms of standards presented.
   12. For enjoyment.
   13. For showing courtesy.
   14. For relating what is heard to what is known and observed.

C. Lessons designed to motivate the child to listen to poetry for any of the following reasons:
   1. To discover the rhyme pattern and rhyme words.
   2. To discover the mood.
   3. To discover word pictures or imagery in general.
   4. To discover visual imagery.
   5. To discover picture words.
   6. To discover sound words.
   7. To discover rhythm.
   8. To discover the main idea and meaning.
   9. To discover clues to evaluate the poem.
   10. To discover an answer to a question.
   This code is assigned only when listening to poetry for one of the listed reasons is sufficiently emphasized.

Fig. 1.--Schematic representation of the organization
of categories used to code content in language arts pupil
textbooks.

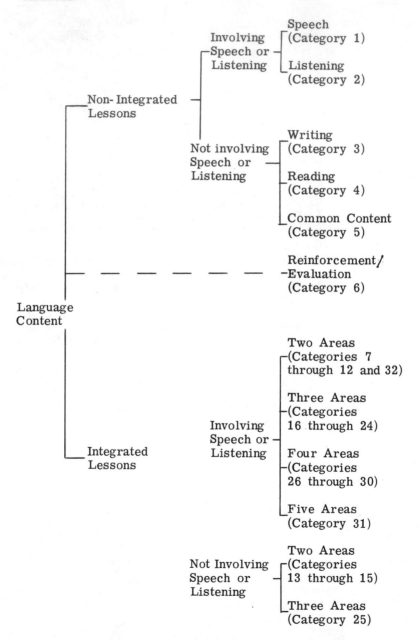

D. Lessons designed to encourage the child to listen
    for details, and for clues to <u>solve riddles</u>.

E. Lessons which encourage the child to listen in
    <u>conversation</u> and <u>discussion</u> courteously, to relate
    to others, and/or to summarize the main ideas.

F. Lessons which encourage the child to listen to
    <u>reports</u> and to <u>talks</u> to evaluate them in terms of
    <u>suggested standards</u>, to listen courteously, to
    listen for purposes of taking notes, for sequence
    of ideas, to evaluate general worthiness of con-
    tributions, and to follow directions.

G. Lessons which encourage the child to listen to
    <u>oral descriptions</u> for place relationships and/or
    <u>details</u>.

H. Lessons designed to encourage the child to listen
    to sentences and statements to <u>get meaning from
    the word order</u>, and/or to <u>answer questions</u>.

I. Lessons designed to help children to improve
    <u>auditory discrimination</u>, <u>auditory recognition</u> of
    initial and final sounds, recognition of vowel
    sounds, word endings, and recognition of sounds
    in spelling words, recognition of correct pronun-
    ciation, recognition of good voices and appropriate
    articulation.

J. Lessons designed to help children listen to a
    variety of materials for <u>specific kinds of words</u>
    such as synonyms, antonyms, picture words, and
    color words.

K. Lessons designed to help children listen to a
    variety of materials for details, for pertinent
    and/or accurate facts, to get information, to in-
    terpret meaning, and to choose the correct re-
    sponse, for cause-effect relationships, and/or
    time relationships, and to determine the reasons
    "why."

L. Lessons designed to help children to become
    more sensitive to sounds in the environment by
    listening for "sounds around us."

M. Lessons designed to develop interest and improve listening habits in relation to television, radio, and motion pictures, by presenting or suggesting the formulation of standards and criteria for the evaluation of such programs.

The categories which designate integrated lessons are defined by various combinations of the first five categories in Fig. 1. Each of these combinations is listed below.

1. SPEAKING AND LISTENING
2. SPEAKING AND WRITING
3. SPEAKING AND READING
4. SPEAKING AND COMMON CONTENT
5. LISTENING AND WRITING
6. LISTENING AND COMMON CONTENT
7. WRITING AND READING
8. WRITING AND COMMON CONTENT
9. READING AND COMMON CONTENT
10. SPEAKING, LISTENING, AND WRITING
11. SPEAKING, LISTENING, AND READING
12. SPEAKING, LISTENING, AND COMMON CONTENT
13. SPEAKING, WRITING, AND READING
14. SPEAKING, WRITING, AND COMMON CONTENT
15. SPEAKING, READING, AND COMMON CONTENT
16. LISTENING, WRITING, AND READING
17. LISTENING, WRITING, AND COMMON CONTENT
18. LISTENING, READING, AND COMMON CONTENT
19. WRITING, READING, AND COMMON CONTENT
20. SPEAKING, LISTENING, WRITING, AND READING
21. SPEAKING, LISTENING, WRITING, AND COMMON CONTENT
22. SPEAKING, LISTENING, READING, AND COMMON CONTENT
23. SPEAKING, WRITING, READING, AND COMMON CONTENT
24. LISTENING, READING, WRITING, AND COMMON CONTENT
25. SPEAKING, LISTENING, WRITING, READING, AND COMMON CONTENT
26. LISTENING AND READING

Category 2.   Listening Content
Listening content was emphasized in less than one per cent of the lessons and pages studied in all grades except the third where it was stressed in 1.16 per cent of the

lessons. Few lessons and pages were devoted to the various subdivisions of listening. Not any subdivision was emphasized in over eight lessons in any grade, nor were more than 13-3/8 pages devoted to a subdivision in any grade. Teaching listening directly receives the greatest amount of emphasis. The category ranked second varies according to the unit of measure. When content of lessons are compared, listening to stories for various purposes ranks second in frequency. When number of pages are compared, on the other hand, listening to television, radio, and movies ranked second. Listening to television, radio, and movies ranks third in lesson frequency. In page space, listening in conversation and discussion ranks third. Four subdivisions receive substantially more emphasis than the others: teaching listening directly, listening to stories, listening in conversation and discussion, and listening to radio, television, and movies. The remaining subdivisions seldom were emphasized in more than one or two lessons. Two subdivisions-- listening for specific kinds of words and listening to a variety of materials for specified purposes--were not found in any lesson in this category. Because of the nature of these activities, it is possible that they would be found more frequently in integrated content.

   Grade to grade trends. Few grade to grade trends can be noted on the basis of so few lessons. There is a decrease in emphasis on listening to stories from 36. 36% of the lessons and 35. 69% of the pages in third grade to 12. 50% of the lessons and 4% of the pages in fifth grade, and no emphasis in sixth grade. The only subdivision that is emphasized to some degree in each grade is listening to television, radio, and movies. Lessons that stress the teaching of listening directly do not even appear in the fourth grade. This subdivision ranks first in category two because it appears a total of fourteen times in grades three, five, and six.

   Agreement. There is little agreement among publishers and authors in emphasizing the various subdivisions. Only three books have two or more lessons in this category in grade three, four books in grade four, one book in grade five, and one book in grade six. The emphasis according to page space shows as little agreement. One book contains five pages or more on a subdivision in grade three, two books in grade four, and one book in grade six.

TABLE 1

NUMBER OF LESSONS AND PAGES IN EACH GRADE DEVOTED TO EACH SUBDIVISION
AND COMBINATIONS OF SUBDIVISIONS IN CATEGORY 2: LISTENING

Grade	3		4		5		6		Total	
Subdivision	L	P	L	P	L	P	L	P	L	P
A	5	13.3			2	1.5	7	13.6	14	28.4
B	8	12.0	3	3.1	1	.4			12	15.5
C	1	.5							1	.5
D			1	1.1					1	1.1
E					1	1.0			1	1.0
F	1	1.0			3	7.0	1	1.5	5	9.5
G	1	1.0							1	1.0
H	1	1.0							1	1.0
I	1	.5							1	.5
J										
K										
L	2	1.4			1	2.3	1	2.0	2	1.4
M	2	2.4	3	11.0					7	17.7
A-F			2	6.0					2	6.0

*All decimals are eighths of a page.

Category Seven: Speaking and Listening Content [see Fig. 1]
        The third category that emphasizes speaking and lis-
tening is category seven.   Lessons in this category differ
from those in categories one and two in that speaking and
listening are emphasized together.   The subdivisions are
combinations of those found in categories one and two:

   (1A & 2A)   Articulation and teaching listening directly
   (1A & 2I)   Articulation and auditory discrimination
   (1E & 2E)   Social amenities and listening in conver-
               sation/discussion
   (1F & 2B)   Conversation/discussion and listening to
               stories
   (1F & 2E)   Speaking and listening in conversation/
               discussion
   (1F & 2F)   Conversation/discussion and listening to
               talks
   (1F & 2M)   Conversation/discussion and listening to
               television
   (1G & 2B)   Telling and listening to stories
   (1G & 2F)   Telling and listening to reports
   (1H & 2B)   Giving talks and listening to stories
   (1H & 2F)   Giving and listening to talks
   (1H & 2M)   Giving talks and listening to television
   (1I & 2B)   Dramatizing and listening to stories
   (1I & 2F)   Dramatizing and listening to talks
   (1K & 2E)   Telephoning and listening in conversation
   (1M & 2M)   Listening to and participating in television
               and radio programs
   (1N & 2B)   Oral reading and listening to stories
   (1N & 2C)   Oral reading and listening to poetry
   (1N & 2G)   Oral reading and listening to oral descrip-
               tions
   (1R & 2H)   Asking questions and listening to answer
               questions
   (1F & 1K & 1P & 2E)   Conversation and discussion,
               telephoning, interviewing, and listening in
               conversation and discussion

        Giving and listening to talks (1H & 2F) is the sub-
division ranked first since 21.3% of the lessons in category
seven and 20.55% of the pages are devoted to this activity.
Second and third ranked are speaking and listening in conversation and discussion (1F & 2E), and telling and listening
to stories (1G & 2B).   Listening to radio, television, and
motion pictures, and giving oral reviews of them (1H & 2M)
is ranked fourth.   Fifth and sixth ranked are articulation

and auditory discrimination (1A & 2I), and listening to and
participating in television and radio programs (1M & 2M).
Other subdivisions were stressed in fewer than a total of
five lessons and ten pages.

As was the case with category two, few trends from
grade to grade can be noted because relatively few lessons
and pages are emphasized in category seven. Telling and
listening to stories (1G & 2B) decreases in emphasis from
23.33% of the lessons and 28.52% of the pages in third grade
to 5% of the lessons and 1.77% of the pages in sixth grade.
The activity of giving and listening to talks (1H & 2F) increases from 16.66% of the lessons and 10.51% of the pages
in third grade to 20% of the lessons and 21.33% of the pages
in sixth grade. Listening and speaking in conversation (1F
& 2E), an activity that ranked second or third depending
upon the unit of measure used, decreases in emphasis from
16.66% of the lessons and 24.02% of the pages in third grade
to no emphasis in sixth grade. Conversely, listening to
radio and television programs and giving oral reviews of
them (1H & 2M) increases from no stress in third grade to
emphasis in 45% of the lessons and 37.77% of the pages in
sixth grade. More subdivisions in category two receive
emphasis in third and fourth grades than in fifth and sixth
grades.

Little agreement exists among publishers on emphasis
on category seven. The most typical practice was for one
book to contain one lesson in each of the various subdivisions.
Exceptions to this are seven books which each contain one
lesson that emphasizes telling and listening to stories (1G &
2B) in grade three, and five books which contain one lesson
that emphasizes giving and listening to talks (1H & 2F).
Books that contain two or more lessons for any subdivision
are the exception more than the rule in all grades. A similar pattern exists for the page space unit of measure. When
each subdivision is emphasized, the most common practice
is for the books to contain from one to four pages; publishers seldom emphasize an activity in five or more pages in
any grade.

(1) Listening, an area which has been emphasized
more in recent years by speech teachers, is stressed even
though experts claim that it is the language art children use
most. Listening content is emphasized apart from other
areas of the language arts in .63% of the lessons and .57%
of the pages.

(2) When listening is stressed, it is related more often to speech content than presented alone; 1.26% of the lessons and 1.37% of the pages emphasize speaking and listening content together.

(3) The difference between emphasis on speaking and/ or listening content and emphasis on writing or common content is great; 31.21% of all the lessons and 27.27% of all the pages emphasize common content; 20.28% of the lessons and 18.8% of the pages emphasize writing.

Category 2: Listening Content: Teaching Listening Directly

Objectives. The most common type of lesson in category two is teaching listening directly. The goals of these lessons which appear in grades three, five, and six are: (1) to emphasize reasons for careful listening; (2) to be aware of the need to prepare minds as well as ears to listen; (3) to be a courteous listener; (4) to listen for facts and inferences to acquire understanding; (5) to listen to find answers to specific questions; (6) to listen to interpret idioms, labels, figures of speech, and colloquialisms; (7) to understand levels of abstractions; (9) to listen for picture words and sentences that begin in different ways; (10) to relate what is heard to personal experience; (11) to listen to follow directions; (12) to listen for sequence of ideas; (13) to take notes when listening.

Standards, skills, and understandings. Five general guidelines are stated frequently: (1) Look at the person who is speaking and show that you are interested in what he is saying. (2) Think about what the person is saying. (3) Be polite. (4) Sit quietly. (5) Clear the tops of your desks. (6) Avoid movements or noises that will interfere with the listening.

The following suggestions are made occasionally: (1) Sit in a comfortable position. (2) Think of your own experience to add to the story that is being read. (3) Ask questions if you do not understand what is said. (4) You must understand what you hear to be a good listener. (5) Always listen with a definite purpose--to get facts, to learn how to do something, to keep track of a conversation, and to be entertained. (6) The brain gives meaning and understanding to what you hear. (7) Listen for main ideas when you hear others talk. (8) Think of details as facts that make the main ideas clearer. One lesson attempted to teach how we hear.

Assignments. Two general types of assignments appear in this kind of lesson. One stimulates the child to participate in class discussion on such topics as why listening is important, what standards should be followed, and how to listen for different purposes. The second type of assignment places the child in a situation where he is encouraged to listen for specific purposes such as for facts and main ideas in a news report or sequence of events in a story.

Lessons that teach listening directly appear so infrequently that it is difficult to find continuity or a definite teaching sequence.

Listening to Radio, Television, and Movies

Objectives. Lessons in this group attempt to improve the child's listening habits by stimulating the formulation of standards for the evaluation of movies and radio and television programs. Objectives in this group of lessons are: (1) to help the child choose better programs; (2) to know that things that are looked at and listened to should be evaluated; (3) to know that television and radio programs may be worthwhile as entertainment or education; (4) to enrich experiences and listen for enjoyment.

Standards, skills, and understandings. The child is taught three basic understandings: (1) Many television and radio shows help you to learn about the world you live in. (2) When you decide whether or not a show is good, you are judging the show. (3) You are taking an opinion poll when you find out what many people think about something.

In addition, questions for judging a show are presented: (a) Did you learn anything new? (b) Was the program really funny? (c) Did the program hold your interest? (d) Did the characters talk and act like real people? (e) What did the program intend to do? (f) If a story was told, was it true? (g) Did you enjoy the program?

Assignments. Activities for the child to meet the objectives are: (1) Have a class discussion on favorite programs. (2) As a class, judge programs that are viewed. (3) Keep a list of mistakes in English that are heard on radio or television programs. (4) Write letters to a channel about programs you don't like. (5) Make a checklist for evaluating television programs. (6) Write a letter to a local radio or television station to find out whether the station

broadcasts educational programs, what they are, and when
they are broadcast.

Surveys show that the amount of time that children
watch television increases each year. A question that can
be raised is: Do the textbooks keep pace with this influential
listening activity?

Listening to Reports and Talks

Objectives. Listening to reports ranks third in emphasis. The objectives that are stressed in these lessons
are: (1) to visualize details and form mental relationships
accurately; (2) to listen to determine the reason why; (3) to
listen for sequence of ideas; (4) to show courtesy in listening;
and (5) to listen to follow directions.

Standards, skills, understandings, and assignments.
These recommendations are made to the child: (1) Clear the
tops of your desks. (2) Look at the speaker. (3) Think
about what the speaker is saying. (4) Listen to hear the
subject of the report. (5) Think of questions to ask when the
speaker is finished. (6) Don't make noises that will interfere with the listening of others. (7) Listen for the sequence
of ideas that are expressed. (8) Listen attentively to the examples the speaker gives.

The assignments structure a situation for the child to
listen and to evaluate the various kinds of talks and reports
given by classmates. A total of five lessons that emphasize
this kind of listening appear in grades three, five, and six.

Listening to Stories

Objectives. The purposes in having children listen to
stories are: (1) to be able to construct visual images while
listening; (2) to establish relationships between items mentioned; (3) to listen for color and sound words; (4) to realize that thinking and feeling are part of listening; (5) to listen for words that make the listener see, hear, and feel.

Standards, skills, and understandings. When judging
a story, these questions are posed: (1) Is it about something interesting? (2) Does it tell about one thing? (3) Does
it have a good beginning sentence? (4) Are the parts in right
order? (5) Do the sentences begin in different ways? (6)
Are all sentences joined by "and"?

In addition, these recommendations are stressed: (1) Look at the person who is telling the story. (2) Show that you are enjoying the story. (3) Clear your desks. (4) Sit quietly. (5) Listen for the names of the characters, the time and place of the story, interesting words that help to see pictures and to hear sounds, how each happening builds the story, and good conversation and humor.

Assignments. Listening to the teacher or a classmate read a story is the assignment that is stressed most. Generally, the purpose for listening is stated. Questions about the story are also listed for the child to discuss and answer. Re- organizing a story that is scrambled is a second type of assignment that is made.

Other Listening Lessons

The remaining subdivisions in category two appear infrequently so they are discussed together in this section. Listening in conversation and discussion is stressed in one lesson in grade five. The objective is to listen to ask questions. The child is advised: When you ask good questions, you show that you have listened carefully.

Listening to solve riddles appears in one lesson in grade four. No objective or standards are suggested. Instead, the lesson presents many different riddles for the child to attempt to answer.

Listening for sounds around us occurs in one lesson in grade three. Here the child is asked to listen for one minute and then to jot down all the sounds he heard.

One third grade lesson stresses listening to sentences for word order. The objectives are: (1) to listen for word order in sentences, and (2) to understand that the position of a word within a sentence determines its meaning. The concept that is stressed in this lesson is that sentences may have the same words but different meanings because words are located in different places.

Listening to oral descriptions is suggested once in third grade. The goals are: (1) to visualize details as we listen, and (2) to establish place relationships in our minds. The child is asked to make mental pictures as he listens to a story containing much description.

Finally, listening to discern qualities of good speaking voices appears in one third grade lesson. It is suggested that children listen for these kinds of voices: soft, sharp, cheerful, low, kind, rough, friendly, high, angry, pleasant, and loud.

To What Degree Is Speech and Listening Content Emphasized, and How Is It Emphasized?

1. If the number of lessons and page space are re-liable indicators of the emphasis upon a phase of the language arts in textbooks, writing, grammar, and review lessons are emphasized more than speech or listening. Only 10.16 per cent of the 7,744 lessons, and 10.62 per cent of the 15,285.5 pages studied emphasize speech content apart from other areas of the curriculum.

2. Listening content is emphasized apart from other areas of the language arts in .63 per cent of the total lessons, and .57 per cent of the total pages studied.

3. Listening and speaking are emphasized together, but apart from reading, writing, and common content, in 1.26 per cent of the total lessons and 1.37 per cent of the total pages studied.

4. The emphasis on writing and on common content is considerably greater than on speech or listening; 31.21 per cent of the total lessons and 27.26 per cent of the total pages emphasize common content--literature, research and study skills, observation, history of the language, vocabu-lary, word usage, grammar, and sentence study. Writing is emphasized in 20.28 per cent of the lessons and in 18.8 per cent of the pages.

5. The emphasis on speaking and writing decreases from the third through the sixth grade, but writing skills are always emphasized more than speaking.

6. The emphasis on common content and on review and test lessons increases from the third through the sixth grade.

7. Non-integrated content is emphasized more than is integrated content in all the grades; 63.85 per cent of the lessons stress non-integrated content; 16.01 per cent stress integrated content; and 20.13 per cent stress review and

evaluation.

8.   The amount of integrated content decreases from the third through the sixth grade, but non-integrated content remains the same.

9.   Integrated content that includes emphasis upon speaking and listening is stressed more than integrated content that does not.

10.   Categories that integrate two areas of the language arts are emphasized more than categories that integrate three and four areas.

11.   When speaking and listening are each integrated with other areas of the language arts, speaking is integrated more often than listening.

12.   Agreement among publishers on emphasis is highest for speaking and common content, and on common content alone.   Emphasis on speech and on writing varies greatly among the different books and grades.   Listening content is never emphasized in more than 5 per cent of the lessons and pages studied in any grade.

13.   The kinds of speech content that are emphasized most, in order of rank, are: giving talks, conversation and discussion, dramatization, storytelling, social amenities, articulation, enunciation, pronunciation, and telephoning.

14.   Speech content that is emphasized least includes: voice, bodily action, spontaneity, reading aloud, interviewing, and asking and answering questions.

15.   Choral speaking is emphasized in lessons that also stress literature appreciation.   In fact, choral speaking typically becomes the means of developing appreciation of poetry.

16.   Debating is not emphasized in any of the lessons studied.

17.   Materials on storytelling and on articulation, enunciation, and pronunciation decrease in emphasis from third through sixth grade.   Giving talks increases in emphasis.

18.   Speaking for specific purposes in various social
situations is emphasized more than tools or mechanics of
speaking.

19.   In the listening content, teaching listening directly is stressed most.   Listening to stories, to radio, television, and movies, and listening in conversation and discussion are also ranked high.

20.   In material that integrates skills in listening and
speaking, giving and listening to talks is ranked first. Speaking and listening in conversation and discussion, and telling
and listening to stories rank second and third respectively.

What Is the Specific Nature of the Speech and Listening Content?

21.   Eleven different kinds of talk are suggested:
(a) informal sharing of personal experiences; (b) show- and-
tell; (c) oral reports; (d) descriptions; (e) explanations; (f)
book reports and reviews; (g) announcements; (h) invitations;
(i) directions; (j) summaries; (k) sales talks.   It is apparent
that speaking to inform is more prevalent than speaking to
convince or to persuade.

22.   Conversation and discussion are closely related
in the books.   Nine kinds of lesson were found: (a) conversing to get acquainted; (b) conversing in a natural setting;
(c) conversing to initiate interest in a new unit of study;
(d) conversing to improve skills in conversation; (e) informal
class discussion; (f) discussing to share and pool information;
(g) discussing to make plans, hold conferences, conduct committee work, and to evaluate; (h) discussing to solve problems; (i) discussing in front of an audience.   Planning, evaluating, and committee work were emphasized most.

23.   Four kinds of dramatic activities were found. In
order of emphasis, they are: creative drama, formal drama,
puppetry, and pantomime.   Stories are used as the material
for dramatization in creative drama.

24.   Social amenities are emphasized in five different
kinds of lesson; (a) making introductions; (b) appropriate behavior in the library and on class trips; (c) greeting guests
and visitors; (d) acting as hosts and hostesses at a party;
(e) knowing when to use various polite phrases.   Introductions are stressed most.

25. Storytelling occurs in the following order: (a) telling original stories based upon a picture in the textbook; (b) retelling well known stories from textbook pictures; (c) telling special kinds of stories as folk tales or myths; (d) telling original imaginative tales; (e) telling stories in relay.

26. Lessons in articulation, enunciation, and pronunciation stress saying clearly the "ing" endings of words, the "wh" sound as in white, and the "ow," "t," and "d" endings of words. Many different words are listed for pronunciation drill.

27. Parliamentary procedure first appears in the form of conducting class meetings in fourth grade. The lessons stress: (a) qualifications, duties, and election of class officers; (b) order of business; (c) making a motion.

28. Lessons on telephoning emphasize courtesy, and making and receiving calls.

29. Volume, clarity, eye contact, posture, sequence, subject choice, and speaking in complete sentences are the standards that are stressed most in the speech content.

30. Lessons in listening stress these rules: (a) Look at the person who is speaking. (b) Be polite. (c) Sit quietly. (d) Clear the tops of your desks. (e) Think about what the person is saying.

SO THEY LISTENED: THE EFFECTS OF A
LISTENING PROGRAM

Paul M. Hollingsworth

In reviewing the literature, one finds many studies that indicate an interrelationship between listening and reading. There are also many studies that indicate that listening comprehension can be improved through instruction. This small study intends to provide further information about the effect a listening program has upon reading achievement, listening comprehension and study skills development.

The Problem
     The purpose of the current study was to compare the
effect the Educational Developmental Laboratories' Listen and
Read program has upon reading achievement, listening comprehension and study skills development with a control group
in which no formally planned program was given.

Procedures
     The pupils selected for the study were from the Payne
Training School, Arizona State University, Tempe, Arizona.
A table of random numbers was used to select 14 pupils for
the experimental group.   The remaining 14 pupils in the fifth
grade were the control group.

     Each fifth-grade pupil was given the Stanford Achieve-
ment Test, Intermediate Reading Test, Form K and the Otis
Quick-Scoring Mental Ability Test, Beta Test, Form EM.
The pupils' scores on these two tests were used to statistically equate the groups by an analysis of covariance.

     The listening exercises used in the current study were
commercially produced by Educational Developmental Laboratories.   The Listen and Read program has 30 tapes.   One
tape was given each Monday, Wednesday and Friday for a
period of ten weeks.   The tape and the workbook exercise
took approximately one hour each session.   The control
group continued with its normal school program.

     After the ten-week period had elapsed and the 30 lis-
tening lessons were given to the experimental group, both
groups were tested with the Stanford Achievement Test,
Intermediate Level Reading and Study Skills Sub-Tests, Form
J, and with the Sequential Tests of Educational Progress,
Listening Test, Form 4A.   The data obtained from the tests
were analyzed by using the analysis of covariance. The level
of confidence was set at the 5 per cent level.

Conclusions
     No significant differences were found beyond those ex-
pected by chance in reading achievement, listening comprehension or study skills development.   The null hypothesis
that no differences existed among members of the experimental group and the control group on the criteria could
not be rejected.   This study does not indicate that the
Educational Developmental Laboratories' Listen and Read
program did significantly affect reading achievement, listening comprehension or study skills development of these

fifth-grade pupils.

Recommendations
     A study done by Hollingsworth [entry 577 in Duker,
Listening Bibliography, 2nd ed., 1968] involving 535 eighth-
grade pupils in which he tested the effectiveness of the Educational Developmental Laboratories' Listen and Read program also showed no significant differences. In this study
ten of the 30 tapes were used and the Listen and Read program was modified to the extent that the reading part was
removed from the program.

     In view of the results of the current study, the study
cited above and the studies mentioned in the introduction, it
may be hypothesized that in order for improvement to take
place there must be more involvement by the teacher than
just merely turning on and off commercially taped programs.
For listening comprehension to be improved, reading achievement to be affected, and study skills developed, a planned
program in which the teacher reinforces and gives his pupils
many hours of practice in these skills may be necessary.

     So they listened--yes, but is this the complete task?
Could it be that skills necessary in listening must be strength-
ened throughout the school day by an alert teacher if the pupil is to benefit from listening programs?

Chapter X

TESTING LISTENING SKILLS

The teaching of listening has reached a substantially more advanced stage than has the evaluation of listening skills by means of tests.

The first test of listening skills was prepared by Donald D. Durrell and Helen B. Sullivan of Boston University in the middle 1930's. According to a letter from Professor Durrell to John C. Harvey which is included as an appendix to a master's thesis written by the recipient, publishers doubted that a test of listening would be marketable. Thus the test was renamed the Durrell-Sullivan Reading Capacity Test. Under that title the test has been widely used in the early grades of the elementary school from its publication in 1937 to the present. The philosophy underlying this test as well as the Durrell Listening-Reading Series of tests which will be discussed later on, is very clearly set forth in the first selection of this chapter by Dr. Durrell. It is quite unusual that one would be able to be so consistent in one's thinking during a period of over 30 years. It is a fact, however, that when Professor Durrell collaborated on the Durrell-Sullivan Reading Capacity Tests in the 1930's, his understanding of the interrelationship between reading and listening was qualitatively exactly the same as when the article included in this chapter was written three decades later.

All students of the listening process owe a great debt of gratitude to Dr. Durrell for his leadership in research activities in this field. I have often had occasion to deplore the fact that graduate work at both the master's and the doctoral levels is not coordinated in any way. This lack results in much useless repetition and, even worse, in a failure to explore logical next steps after the preliminary stages have been probed and reported on. Just as often as I have deplored this state of affairs, have I mentioned the fact that the investigations carried on at Boston University's School of Education under the aegis of Donald D. Durrell have been the exception to the rule.

The second section of this report consists of several sections excerpted from the thesis of Mary B. Brassard, Professor of Education at Tufts University. This thesis, sponsored by Dr. Durrell, is one that typifies the choice of a project that builds on what has gone before. The direct result of the investigation reported on in this thesis was the publication of the intermediate level tests in the Durrell Listening-Reading Series.

An excellent treatment of both the theory and the practical aspects of test construction is found in this thesis. The excerpts which Dr. Brassard generously allowed me to use, despite their length, should be useful to anyone seriously undertaking the construction of a test in any field. I consider this work a model of clarity, applied scholarliness, and thoroughness.

The first portion of the excerpts, "Present Tests of Listening Comprehension," is a thoughtful and informative appraisal of presently available listening tests: The Durrell-Sullivan, which I have already referred to; The Brown-Carlsen Listening Comprehension Test; and STEP: Listening.

This portion is followed by a succinct statement of the criteria for a test designed to reveal the relationship between listening comprehension and reading comprehension.

The third part of the excerpted material is an exposition concerning the way in which the vocabulary portion of a test such as the one prescribed in the previous section is designed. It would be difficult to overstate the amount of thorough and detailed work that was involved in carrying out the task outlined in this section.

The last part of Dr. Brassard's material is parallel to the part just described but is concerned with the development of measures of paragraph comprehension for the tests previously described.

The last section is taken from a Sacramento State College master's thesis by John C. Harvey. It is one example of the mass of research that has been done with the Durrell-Sullivan Reading Capacity Test as its basis.

LISTENING COMPREHENSION VERSUS
READING COMPREHENSION

Donald D. Durrell

Measures of pupil abilities in listening comprehension and reading comprehension offer useful information for educational planning. A high competence in each is essential for superior academic achievement; a weakness in either ability is detrimental to learning. A combination of results from listening and reading comprehension tests provides an estimate of the pupil's language learning potential. Since both abilities rest upon intellectual, sensory, and environmental factors, language learning potential may be improved through educational programs.

Useful comparisons between listening comprehension and reading comprehension may be made at different grade levels. In the early years of school, listening comprehension may be used as an index of pupils' growth in basic reading skills. Beginning reading is essentially a task of searching for speech patterns in print: letters and letter clusters are related to speech sounds; printed words and sentences are translated into speech. Competence in these abilities may be estimated by comparing reading comprehension with listening comprehension through a reading-listening ratio. If a pupil's reading skills are fully developed, he will have a reading-listening ratio of 100, indicating that his reading comprehension is equal to his listening comprehension. A nonreader has a reading-listening ratio of zero; various degrees of basic reading fluency are indicated by reading-listening ratios between zero and 100.

It is possible for reading comprehension to be superior to listening comprehension. In intermediate and upper grades many words come into reading vocabulary which might not be recognized in speech. A pupil may know the meanings of printed words such as oblique, temerity, acumen, incumbent, and echelon, but may not be sure of their pronunciation or may not recognize them in speech. A reading vocabulary higher than a listening vocabulary indicates a need for special instruction in speech and listening. When comparing reading and listening, the higher score in either indicates a potential for the other.

Dependable comparisons between listening and reading are possible only when the measures and conditions of testing are closely similar. Precisely equal tests must be used for both abilities; the format of the tests, the directions, the mode of response, and the time allotted to testing must be the same. Vocabulary selection must avoid words favorable to either: homonyms are more readily understood in print (flew-flue; stair-stare; pear-pair); homographs which depend upon accent (minute, record, address) favor listening. The form of response must not favor either reading or listening; pictures with simple labels, presented both in speech and print seem a fair solution to this problem. Obviously, reliabilities must be very high since the tests will be used for individual comparisons.

The desirability of comparable measures of reading and listening led the author and his associates to design such tests for grades one to eight. Three primary tests, standardized both for listening and for reading, cover grades one and two [3]. Intermediate forms are used for grades three to six; advanced forms are available for grades seven and eight [1, 2]. Primary forms include vocabulary and sentence tests; intermediate and advanced forms include vocabulary and paragraph tests. Single grade reliability coefficients for vocabulary tests are above .95, for paragraph tests above .90.

Listening-Reading Comparisons
When the same language comprehension tests are designed for use as listening tests and as reading tests and the several forms for each level are precisely equated, it is possible to make direct raw score comparisons between listening and reading. The following raw score means and reading-listening ratios are based on standardization populations of three to four thousand children at each grade level.

TABLE 1

Listening Versus Reading Vocabulary (Midyear scores)

	Listening	Reading	Reading/Listening Ratio
Primary Forms:			
Grade 1	75	37	49%
Grade 2	82	58	71%

	Listening	Reading	Reading/Listening Ratio
Intermediate Forms:			
Grade 3	46	35	76%
Grade 4	54	45	83%
Grade 5	61	55	90%
Grade 6	69	64	93%
Advanced Forms:			
Grade 7	130	122	94%
Grade 8	137	137	100%

In primary grades, listening vocabulary is much superior to reading vocabulary. Listening is a broader channel for acquiring information than is reading at this level, since reading skills are immature. At grade five, reading comprehension reaches ninety per cent of listening comprehension; the two abilities are equal in grade eight.

Mid-year raw scores and reading-listening ratios for longer units of language are shown in Table 2. In the primary forms, the tests are sentences; in intermediate and advanced forms, paragraphs are used.

TABLE 2

Listening Versus Reading Sentences and Paragraphs (Midyear scores)

	Listening	Reading	Reading/Listening Ratio
Primary Forms:			
Grade 1	31	15	48%
Grade 2	36	30	83%
Intermediate Forms:			
Grade 3	28	23	82%
Grade 4	33	30	83%
Grade 5	38	36	95%
Grade 6	41	42	102%

	Listening	Reading	Reading/Listening Ratio
Advanced Forms:			
Grade 7	31	34	110%
Grade 8	33	37	112%

In comprehension of longer units of language, primary and lower intermediate grades have listening comprehension superior to reading comprehension at about the same ratios as in vocabulary tests. From grade six on, the scores on reading paragraphs are higher than those in listening. Several factors may account for this superiority in reading to listening: silent reading speed at these levels is greater than the speed of speech, hence more time is available for "looking back" to check comprehension; many words are introduced in silent reading that may not yet be in listening vocabularies.

Normative Comparisons Between Listening and Reading
        Relationships between listening and reading are more meaningful when expressed in reading grade equivalents. This requires that both the listening comprehension raw scores and the reading raw scores use the same reading equivalent table. The resultant listening grade equivalents may be expressed as "Listening Equivalent to Reading Grade." Table 3 shows the results of changing the raw vocabulary scores of Table 1 into reading grade equivalents:

TABLE 3

Listening Equivalents to Reading Grade Versus
Reading Grade (Vocabulary)

	Listening		Reading		Listening
	Score	Equiv. to Reading Grade	Score	Grade	above Reading (yrs-mos)
Primary Forms:					
Grade 1	75	3.1	37	1.5	1.6
Grade 2	82	3.6	58	2.5	1.1

| | Listening | | Reading | | Listening |
	Score	Equiv. to Reading Grade	Score	Grade	above Reading (yrs-mos)
Intermediate Forms:					
Grade 3	46	4. 6	35	3. 5	1. 1
Grade 4	54	5. 4	45	4. 5	. 9
Grade 5	61	6. 2	55	5. 5	. 7
Grade 6	69	7. 1	64	6. 5	. 6
Advanced Forms:					
Grade 7	130	7. 9	122	7. 5	. 4
Grade 8	137	8. 5	137	8. 5	. 0

Listening vocabulary is a year and a half above reading grade at midyear first grade. It is still a year above reading at midyear in grades two and three; the differences diminish until they become zero at eighth grade.

Listening Equivalent to Reading Grade is a new and necessary concept in normative comparisons of listening and reading. Its use maintains the true relationships between the two abilities shown by raw score comparisons and reading-listening ratios. It answers the questions, "What would this listening score be in terms of reading grade?" or "What level of reading could this pupil understand if it were presented orally?"

Listening equivalent to reading grade avoids erroneous comparisons between listening and reading which result from the use of separate norms for the two abilities. The use of listening ages, grades, percentiles, or stanines does not eliminate the error. Separate norms for listening and reading equate unequal amounts of language comprehension. For example, if listening grade norms were used for the listening raw scores in Table 3, all of the listening grades would be exactly equal to the reading grades, despite the obvious inequalities in the two abilities. Table 4 shows the results of using normative tables for reading and listening in a single case.

TABLE 4

Normative Comparisons of Listening and Reading

Case A. Primary Level				Reading/ Listening Ratio
Listening:		Reading:		
Vocabulary score	78	Vocabulary score	78	100 (Ture)
Equiv. to reading grade	3.2	Reading grade	3.2	100 (True)
Listening grade	2.0	Reading grade	3.2	160 (Untrue)
Listening percentile	50th	Reading percentile	94th	188 (Untrue)
Listening stanine	5th	Reading stanine	9th	180 (Untrue)

This child whose listening and reading vocabularies are equal would be found to be a marked "overachiever" in reading if separate grade norms, percentile, or stanines were used for the raw scores in listening. The use of the listening equivalent to reading grade maintains the true relationship.

Summary

By designing language comprehension tests which are the same for listening and for reading, and by providing precisely equated forms of the tests, it is possible to make direct raw score comparisons and to compute reading-listening ratio. Listening vocabulary is much larger than reading vocabulary at all lower grade levels; only at grade eight does reading vocabulary equal listening vocabulary. Listening comprehension of longer units of language is superior to reading comprehension until sixth grade, when reading becomes higher than listening. When normative comparisons are made between the two abilities, it is essential to translate raw scores from both measures into grade scores, percentiles, or stanines by using the same grade equivalent tables. This results in a listening equivalent to reading grade which is directly comparable to reading grade.

References

1.   Brassard, Mary B.   "Listening and Reading Comprehension in Intermediate Grades," Ed.D. thesis, Boston University, 1968.
2.   Durrell, Donald D., Mary T. Hayes, and Mary B. Brassard.   Listening-Reading Tests.   New York:

Harcourt, Brace and World, Inc., 1969.
    3. Hayes, Mary T. "Comparable Measures of
English Language Comprehension in Reading and Listening in
Primary Grades," Ed.D. thesis, Boston University, 1957.

PRESENT TESTS OF LISTENING COMPREHENSION

Mary Butler Brassard

    The Brown-Carlsen Listening Comprehension Test[1]
[notes at end of section] published in 1953, was the first
standardized test designed solely to measure listening capacity. It is published for use in grades 9 through 12 and is
often used as a diagnostic and comparison test at the college
level. There are two forms, Am and Bm. Each form contains 76 items distributed in the following way in five areas
defined by the authors as those skills which constitute listening comprehension:

Skill Area	No. of Items
1) Immediate recall	17
2) Following oral directions	20
3) Recognizing word meanings	10
4) Recognizing transitions	8
5) Lecture comprehension	21

    The stimulus material is read by the examiner to the
students, who mark their responses on a separate sheet.
Eight thousand students in 28 high schools in 16 states were
tested, and these results were used for standardization.

    At the high school level the correlations between the
Brown-Carlsen Test and standardized tests of mental ability
ranged from .67 to .78. At the college freshman level,
correlations from .22 to .55 were reported. The lowest of
these correlations was found with the Wechsler Performance
Test, suggesting that the relation between listening comprehension and verbal IQ tests is higher. Both tests involve
listening comprehension and interpretation of visual symbols.

    When the Brown-Carlsen and the Nelson-Denny Reading
Tests were administered to college freshmen, the correla-

tions ranged from .31 to .38.   This suggested that listening
comprehension may be more closely related to IQ than reading comprehension.   It also suggested that listening skills
and reading skills are not identical and that measures of both
may be valuable in diagnosing difficulties in either field.

The Brown-Carlsen Listening Test has been criticized
by Lindquist on the limited method of the oral mode of presentation.   Since the answers are on a printed answer sheet,
Lindquist found that the test is one of silent reading as well
as of listening comprehension and concluded that no experimental data have been presented to show that the test measures anything not measured by a silent reading test. [2]

Lorge also criticized the oral administration of the
test because emphasis, control, and rate may differ among
examiners and thus affect the norms. [3] To make full use of
the scores, he felt that the relation between the difference
between listening and reading comprehension and intellectual
level would be the most meaningful interpretation.   Also, the
difference between the scores for listening comprehension and
for reading comprehension should provide definite evidence of
underachievement in either of the two skills.   Since the
Brown-Carlsen Test provides scores for listening ability only,
this score must be compared to a score on a reading test
which is developed with completely different materials and
populations.   A direct comparison of the two abilities is,
then, not possible, as correlations differ between the Brown-
Carlsen and every other test administered for comparisons.

The STEP Listening Test, 1956, [4] was the first designed solely to measure listening capacity in the intermediate grades 4, 5, and 6.   The tests were planned to
measure a student's skill in understanding, interpreting, applying, and evaluating what he listens to.   The tests were
designed by a committee which specified further that each of
these major aspects of listening skill can be broken down
into sub-abilities as follows:

    1.   Plain sense comprehension
        a.   Identifying main ideas
        b.   Remembering significant details
        c.   Remembering simple sequence of ideas
        d.   Understanding denotative meanings

    2.   Interpretation
        a.   Understanding implications of ideas

       b.   Understanding implications of significant details
       c.   Understanding interrelationships
       d.   Understanding connotative meanings

3.   Evaluation and application
       a.   Judging validity and adequacy
       b.   Judging necessity for supportive details
       c.   Criticizing content organization
       d.   Judging effectiveness of mood
       e.   Recognizing implications of ideas

The content includes: 1. direction and simple explanation, 2. exposition, 3. narration, 4. argument and persuasion, and 5. aesthetic material. There are two forms of the test, A and B, each containing 80 items of the multiple-choice type and requiring 70 minutes to administer. The student chooses the best of four answers which are printed on an answer form and also read orally by the examiner. Results are reported in percentile rank which describes the relative standing of a student in respect to other students of that grade. Comparison may also be made between the student's percentile rank on the STEP Listening Test and STEP Tests in science, social studies, mathematics, and reading. However, in comparing listening comprehension and reading comprehension in the STEP tests, comparisons are made between tests that have different contents and norms for either ability but not for both, which would permit a direct comparison and interpretation of the material.

In Buros' Fifth Mental Measurements Yearbook, Lindquist[5] finds that no comparable scale of scores for any other ability is provided. Layton[6] stated that in scoring, unequal units of increase in converted scores from grade to grade illustrate the lack of longitudinal meaning of these derived scores. The norms are not based on the same school for the sequence of any test. He criticized the statement by the authors that a comparable continuous measurement of educational development is made possible by these tests. He found that the tests do not provide this.

Thus, at the present time, there are no tests available which provide raw scores for both reading and listening comprehension based on comparable contents with the same population. No direct comparison can be made between listening comprehension and reading comprehension.

The first group tests, standardized to measure reading capacity and reading achievement, were developed by Durrell-Sullivan. [7] The tests consisted of two parts, word meaning and paragraphs. Test booklets provided for answers in the form of pictures. For the capacity test, the examiner read the word, and the student selected and marked the picture which portrayed the meaning of the word. In the paragraph section the examiner read the story, then asked questions about it. Students selected the picture which answered the question. The reading achievement test is a silent reading-multiple choice answer test. The paragraphs were narrative, expository, and explanatory. Norms were provided in terms of grades 1 through 6 and of chronological age. The tests are described in Buros' Mental Measurements Yearbook[8] as group tests measuring the child's capacity to learn to read in terms of his ability to understand the spoken language. The achievement and capacity tests are organized in the same way and standardized on the same population. However, the content is different for each medium and standardized scores are provided for each ability, based on different content. Direct comparisons are not possible between capacity and achievement.

For grades 1, 2, and 3 Hayes[9] has constructed English language scales comprised of vocabulary and sentences. Each test form has been administered as a reading test and as a listening test to controlled comparable groups. Norms are established for the two abilities, using the same content and similar population. Thus, direct comparisons between listening comprehension and reading comprehension may be made in the primary grades. At the present time, no such series of tests are available for the intermediate grades. Comparisons of the abilities must still be made using completely different tests for each ability.

References (numbers refer to entries in Duker, Listening Bibliography, 2nd ed., Scarecrow, 1968)

    1.   James I. Brown and G. Robert Carlsen, 148.
    2.   E. F. Lindquist, 736.
    3.   Irving A. Lorge, 753.
    4.   Sequential Tests of Educational Progress, Listening, 1069.
    5.   Lindquist, loc. cit.
    6.   Wilbur L. Layton. Review of Sequential Tests of Educational Progress. In The Fifth Mental Measurements Yearbook. (Edited by Oscar K. Buros.) Highland Park,

N. J.:   The Gryphon Press, 1959, p. 67- 74.
    7.   Donald D. Durrell and Helen Blair Sullivan, 340.
    8.   Oscar K. Buros, (Ed.) The Fifth Mental Measure-
ments Yearbook. Highland Park, N. J.:   The Gryphon Press,
1959.
    9.   Mary T. Hayes, 541.

PLANNING TEST CONSTRUCTION

Mary Butler Brassard

    The purpose of this study was to discover the rela-
tionships between listening comprehension and reading comprehension of intermediate grade children.   Since there were
no measures which permitted direct comparisons of the two
abilities, it was necessary to build an instrument which
could be administered as a listening test and as a reading
test.   Since a single test could not be given as a reading
test and as a listening test to the same child, two forms
were needed for each test so that each test could be equated
for both listening comprehension and reading comprehension.
The raw scores then would provide the common basis for
discovering the relationships between listening and reading
comprehension.

Criteria
    Many factors were involved in the building of the
measures.   The content of the tests, the length of time involved for both students and teachers, the type of scoring,
the format, page size, number of pages, and directions were
important to the design of the measure.   In order to provide
the most information within a reasonable length of time, the
measures were built on the following criteria:

    1.   The test should be a group test which could be
administered by the classroom teacher and scored either by
hand or by machine.

    2.   A category technique of testing should be used.

    3.   The test should have two parts, one to measure
vocabulary, the other to measure paragraph comprehension.

4.   There should be two forms for each test, one to be administered as a reading comprehension test, the other to be identical in content but administered as a hearing comprehension measure.

5.   Both forms should be the same in length and as nearly identical in difficulty as possible.

6.   Time allowed should be the same for both listening and reading comprehension tests.

7.   There should be multiple choice answers.

8.   Pictures should be used to designate the choices for answers.

9.   The preliminary tests should contain many extra items to allow for discards.

10.   Items should be selected in a range of difficulty from below third through sixth-grade level.

11.   Items of varying difficulty should be distributed throughout the measures.

12.   Directions should be as brief and simple as possible.

13.   The test should be one which can be administered in either one or two sections or settings.

14.   The listening measure should be read to the students by the classroom teacher or test examiner.

DEVELOPING VOCABULARY MEASURES
FOR READING-LISTENING TESTS

Mary Butler Brassard

Sources for Items

The customary method of constructing vocabulary measures is one of random sampling. Words are selected at random from a dictionary or from graded word lists.

This technique presumes to provide words typical of all the words in the English language. If the samplings are short, there is a question of validity of the sampling. There is no assurance of a balanced representation of the language with this method and it does not permit a category approach to testing. Thus, to build a vocabulary test which would be representative of the entire vocabulary in the English language, it was necessary to select items from a source which provides this structure and balance.

Roget's Thesaurus places all of the words and phrases of the English language in classes of language experiences according to their significance and the ideas which they convey. There are six major classes which are subdivided into 24 minor classifications. Each of these is further subdivided into a total of 1, 000 categories. The Thesaurus thus provides the source for accurate representation of the language and makes possible a classification technique for testing vocabulary items. The Thesaurus does not provide grade levels for words; therefore it was necessary to make preliminary studies which would be helpful in selecting items appropriate for intermediate grade children. Table 1 illustrates the plan of classification of words.

Selection of Items
Preliminary Studies
A selection of words suitable for the range of abilities in grades 4, 5, and 6 was necessary to fit the grade levels of the measure. A preliminary survey was made to gain as broad a background as possible in interests, vocabularies, and experiences to which children in the intermediate grades are exposed.

Children's Interests
Television and the increased availability of children's books have made for far more interests for children as well as for greater variety. J. Harlan Shores and Herbert C. Rudman (What Children Are Interested In, Chicago: Spencer Press, 1954) analyzed the reading interests of more than 11, 000 children. Questionnaires were completed by the students and revealed that, in general, children in the same age group have similar reading interests whether they live in the suburbs, the country, or the city. Few sharp differences appeared in the reading interests of boys and girls. A knowledge of children's interests is useful, but their interests are too varied and broad to be the sole criterion for building a vocabulary measure.

TABLE 1

PLAN OF CLASSIFICATION--ROGET'S THESAURUS

Class	Section	Numbers
I. Abstract Relations	I. Existence	1- 8
	II. Relation	9- 24
	III. Quantity	25- 57
	IV. Order	53- 83
	V. Number	84- 105
	VI. Time	106- 139
	VII. Change	140- 152
	VIII. Causation	153- 179
II. Space	I. Generally	180- 191
	II. Dimensions	192- 239
	III. Form	240- 263
	IV. Motion	264- 315
III. Matter	I. Generally	316- 320
	II. Inorganic	321- 356
	III. Organic	357- 449

Division

IV. Intellect	I. Formation of Ideas	450- 515
	II. Communication of Ideas	516- 599
V. Volition	I. Individual	600- 736
	II. Intersocial	737- 819

Section

VI. Affections	I. Generally	820- 826
	II. Personal	827- 887
	III. Sympathetic	888- 921
	IV. Moral	922- 975
	V. Religious	976- 1000

Vocabulary Lists
The vocabulary lists which were studied for possible grade level assignments of items selected for the vocabulary measure are listed in Table 2.

TABLE 2

VOCABULARY LISTS

Author	Source
Rinsland	Writing Vocabulary
Thorndike & Lorge	Reading Vocabulary
Fitzgerald	Spelling Vocabulary
Ribero	Reading- - Textbooks
Green	Reading- - Textbooks
Dale- Eicholz	Reading

It was not possible to assign definite grade placement to vocabulary items from these lists. The lists were based on different vocabulary sources- - reading, writing, spelling, speaking, and listening. The same word was often found at different grade levels according to the source used for the items. However, the lists did provide a general guide to the kinds of vocabularies which are familiar to intermediate grade children through the various media.

Textbooks
A sampling of textbooks and reading series for grades 4, 5, and 6 was made for subjects and areas of information which might be common to most intermediate grade students and thus helpful in selecting vocabulary items and writing paragraphs for the measure.

The social studies books published by Ginn, Silver Burdett, and Rand McNally were inspected, and a common pattern of subject matter was found. Each of the three different publishers treated the discovery, settling, and growth of the United States in grades 4 and 5. In grade 6, all covered Europe, the Soviet Union, and Asia. While the presentation differed among the publishers, there were many more similarities than differences.

A similar examination was made of science books published by three different companies: Lippincott, Macmillan, and Scott, Foresman. The same general pattern of subject matter was also found here. The same subject was not always offered at the same grade level by the three publishers, but by the end of grade 6, most of the publishers had presented the same subjects.

The fourth-grade basal readers from four different publishers were examined for common themes which might be found among them. Lyons Carnahan, Harper & Row, Lippincott, and Scott, Foresman presented stories dealing with history, adventure, nature, and famous people. An inspection of the glossaries showed that there was a wide disparity among the words offered by the four publishers although the books were all written for the fourth grade. The type of story seemed to determine the words which were used. Lyons and Carnahan presented words such as "accordion," "bellows," "buoy," "chapparral" and "guitar." The Harper & Row glossary contained items such as "awl," "fabulous," "pumice," and "trill." While the same general types of stories were offered, the vocabularies differed considerably.

This preliminary survey showed that these eight publishers covered approximately the same general content areas in their texts for grades 4, 5, and 6, and that there was more agreement rather than less about the level at which the information was offered.

Selection of Categories
        The selection of the categories was governed by the following criteria:
        1.   Each category was one which could be represented by a picture.
        2.   Each category contained a cluster of seven or more words to allow for discards after the preliminary testing.
        3.   Each category contained words which ranged from easy to difficult.
        4.   The same numerical balance of the Thesaurus was kept intact as much as possible.

Selection of Item
        Each of the six word classes in Roget's Thesaurus contains a different number of items. This numerical balance served as a guide for the number of categories to be selected from each of the six word classes in the Thesaurus as indicated in Table 3.

TABLE 3

BALANCE OF ITEMS IN THESAURUS AND
PROPOSED VOCABULARY MEASURES

Thesaurus Word Class	No. of Categories	Proposed No. of Categories	Proposed No. of Items
I. Abstract Relations	179	17	105
II. Space	136	14	79
III. Matter	134	14	77
IV. Intellect	150	16	84
V. Volition	220	18	129
VI. Affections	181	17	106
Total	1,000	96	580

     Possible test items were then selected from the Thesaurus. Each category was examined and those which seemed most suitable and best fitted to the criteria were collected. Each entry was printed on an index card. The class, subclass, and number of the category were printed at the top of the card, and a cluster of words which ranged from easy to difficult was listed below the category as shown in Table 4. Five hundred eighty cards were developed in this manner, keeping to the balance in the Thesaurus. The vocabulary sections of the measures were then built, page by page.

Construction of the Vocabulary Measures
     The criteria required multiple choice answers for the tests. A two- or three- choice answer form was rejected as this could permit a correct response either by guessing or by chance. A four- choice answer eliminated these factors to a greater extent. At this point, it was necessary to set up certain guides to direct the selection of the four categories and the items for each page.

     1. Each category on a single page represented a different word class from the Thesaurus.
     2. Each category on a given page was different from the other three.
     3. Each vocabulary item was clearly different from the other items on the same page.
     4. No confusing multimeaning words appeared on a single page.
     5. No homonyms were selected.

TABLE 4

SAMPLES OF THE 580 CATEGORY CARDS

Word Collection

SPACE   II. SPACE
I. GENERAL
expanse
stretch
capacity
room
scope
range
infinity
ample
extensive
everywhere

DISCLOSE   IV. INTELLECT
I. COMMUNICATION
divulge
reveal
acknowledge
allow
concede
grant
admit
own
confess
avow
expose

RELATIONSHIP I. ABSTRACT
II. RELATION
kindred
parentage
lineage
kinsman
kin
uncle
aunt
niece
family
generation
fraternity
clan
tribe
matriarch
patriarch

WATER   III. MATTER
I. GENERAL
wet
moisten
dilute
dip
immerse
merge
plunge
souse
soak
drawn
sprinkle
macerate
lave
inundate
irrigate

A master list which would meet these criteria was built. Four different categories were selected for each page, and the balance among the categories in the Thesaurus was maintained as closely as possible. Ninety-six different categories were arranged to provide the 24 pages of vocabulary items.

Table 5 presents the master list of category placements. Each entry is followed by the number of the classification in Roget's Thesaurus from which it was drawn. The key indicates the category classification in Roget.

Each set of four categories was distributed on a single page which had been divided into four sections. A suggested sketch was made for each category, and a wide selection of vocabulary items was listed under each such heading. Table 6 shows the arrangement of the four categories on a single page.

Each page was examined for ambiguities, multimeaning words, homonyms, or any items which could cause confusion. On some pages two categories conflicted and it became necessary to exchange this category with one from another page to avoid confusing items. Table 7 shows some of the types of changes which were made on some of the master pages.

Each category on this page is taken from a different word class in the Thesaurus. However, Think and Plan conflict when choices must be made among the sub-items. The meanings of "reason" could lead to placement under either Plan or Think. The same is true of "study," "scheme," and other entries. Another category was selected to replace Plan on this page. Enough, also from Class V, Volition, presented no ambiguities with the three other categories on this page.

Other changes were made in the key words for some of the categories. Some of the items listed under the category heading were clearer and easier to illustrate than the Roget heading. In these cases, the item and category heading were interchanged. For example, Big was changed to Size. Similarity was replaced by Likeness, which is a more familiar word to children. Other changes were made for purposes of illustrating each category, such as See for Seeing and Pleasure for Happy. Table 8 is a preliminary master page which contained no ambiguities and met the criteria established for the measures. (Text cont., p. 275.)

TABLE 5

MASTER LIST OF CATEGORY PLACEMENTS

Page				
1	Hardness III	Choice V	Experiment IV	Pleasure VI
2	Dwelling II	World III	Measurement IV	Pain VI
3	Difference I	Receptacle II	Illustration IV	Persuade V
4	World III	Think IV	Enough V	Sad VI
5	Strength I	Space II	Plan V	Fear VI
6	Length II	Softness III	Writing IV	Sale V
7	Order I	Passage II	Relax V	Accuse VI
8	Fold II	Darkness III	Teach IV	Courtesy VI
9	Family I	Garment II	Cultivate III	Insufficient V
10	Group I	Uncertain IV	Waste V	Courageous VI

11	Imperfect I	Solve IV	Worship I	Dirt V
12	Similarity I	Burial III	Trap IV	Dislike VI
13	Equality I	Speed II	Cold III	Disease V
14	Big I	Inquire IV	Improve V	Punishment VI
15	Part I	Expands II	Animal III	Choice V
16	Violence I	Knowledge IV	Guide V	Reward VI
17	Time I	Seeing III	Work V	Church VI
18	Smallness I	Motion II	Knowledge IV	Music III
19	Increase I	View III	Construction II	Love VI
20	Decrease I	Conceal IV	Money V	Amusement VI
21	Morning I	Arrival II	Plant III	Thief V
22	Twist II	Sign IV	Worship I	Pleasure VI
23	Destroy I	Prairie III	Activity V	Pity VI
24	Separation II	Book IV	Opponent V	Pain VI

KEY: I. Abstract Relations. II. Space. III. Matter. IV. Intellect. V. Volition. VI. Affections

TABLE 6

ARRANGEMENT OF CATEGORIES

I	III
EQUAL	**COLD**
27	383

I EQUAL 27	III COLD 383
similar	inclement
symmetry	gelid
balance $2+2=4$	glacial
match	polar
homologous	bitter
co-ordination	hibernal
parity	bleak
identity	arctic
poise	frosty
evenness	keen
same	

II SPEED 274	V DISEASE 655
velocity	illness
acceleration	infirmity
celerity	contagion
expedition	complaint
canter	malady
haste	ailment
sprint	disorder
spurt	attack
scamper	invalidism
volt	infection
permicity	morbidity
hie	distemper

TABLE 7

SAMPLE OF CHANGES MADE ON MASTER PAGES

III

WORLD

318

universe
firmament
luminaries
galaxy
mundane
solar
creation
nature
globe
heavens
sun
planet
orbit
cosmic
satellite
equator
earth
sphere

V

PLAN

626

scheme
design
conspire
contrive
devise
project
organize
sketch
cast
arrange
plot
intrigue
invent

IV

THINK

451

reason
muse
study
cogitate
discuss
digest
contemplate
deliberate
speculate
ponder
consider
reflect

VI

SAD

837

dejected
melancholy
despondent
dismal
lugubrious
gloomy
mournful
pensive
sober
saturnine
disconsolate
solemn
rueful

TABLE 8

FORMAT FOR VOCABULARY AND CATEGORIES

I	V
LIST	WORSHIP
86	990

I		V
catalogue		aspire
inventory		revere
syllabus		pray
file		invoke
register		supplicate
enumeration		propitiate
manifest		praise
scroll		beseech
schedule		
tally		
register		
index		
score		
census		
docket		

IV	V
SOLVE	DIRT
480	653

IV		V
educe		soil
ravel	$2 + 3 = ?$	squalor
verify		smudge
elicit		grime
evolve		mire
disclose		decay
fathom		contamination
interpret		impurity
recognize		slag
identify		slough
trace		compost
		dregs
		putrefaction

Each page of the measure was built and examined in this manner. Many changes and substitutions, such as those already described, were made. Twenty-four pages with four categories on each page filled the requirement of 96 categories, holding to the balance in the <u>Thesaurus</u>.

Preliminary Testing
Individual Testing

Sample pages were constructed for preliminary testing. The four categories with their appropriate identifying illustrations were placed across the top of the page. A key indicated the category and picture which belonged together. Sample pages included 40 to 50 words to allow for a wide range of words for each category and to indicate the approximate number of words necessary for the cluster of items for each category.

Both the picture and identifying title were printed on the listening measure and on the reading measure. The vocabulary items were printed only on the reading measure. The vocabulary items were read by the examiner for the listening test.

Directions for the listening measure were: "Listen to each word I say and then fill in the answer space under the heading which best fits the word." Directions for the reading measure were as follows: "Look at each word and then fill in the answer space under the heading which best fits the word."

Sample pages were tried out with individual children. Two students of average ability from each of grades 4, 5, and 6 were selected by the classroom teachers. One student took the measure as a reading test, the other as a listening test. After the test was administered, each student reviewed the measure, item by item, with the examiner. The two fourth-grade students found the format required too much time for selecting answers. Each referred to the key and then to the numbered column to select the answer. The fifth- and sixth-grade students felt that the test would be simpler to follow if the word and identifying picture were placed together in a box at the head of each answer column. With this change made, the students found that the design of the measure and the directions were clear and easy to follow.

After more pilot tests with individual students, the entire test was screened by a group of reading specialists for items which might cause confusion. The format of the test was altered so that the category and its identifying picture appeared in the same box, still offering four choices. The revised vocabulary forms were then administered as group measures.

Group Testing

A fourth-, a fifth-, and a sixth- grade teacher in one school building selected ten students from each of their classrooms to take the preliminary group tests in listening and reading. The students were average or near average in ability. Five students from each classroom were placed in one group, which took the group measure as a listening test. The other 15 students were given the measure as a reading test. The tests were corrected and the scores recorded in number of correct responses. Table 9 presents these data.

TABLE 9

RESULTS OF PRELIMINARY GROUP TEST

Grade	Raw Scores	
	Listening	Reading
4	16	11
	18	13
	18	13
	20	17
	20	16
Subtotal	92	70
5	17	13
	20	14
	21	20
	26	21
	27	24
Subtotal	111	92
6	19	14
	21	18
	22	20
	29	28
	30	28
Subtotal	127	108
Total Scores	330	270

The results of the preliminary group testing showed that the measures given as a reading test to one group of intermediate grade children and as a listening test to a comparable group of children discriminated between listening comprehension and reading comprehension at each of the grade levels and between the grades.

One more change was made as a result of the group test. Children may choose the right answer by recognizing that the word has a noun, verb, or adjective ending, although they do not know the meaning of the word. For this reason, the final form included only two parts of speech--nouns and verbs.

Final Forms
Two forms of the vocabulary measure were necessary in order to provide raw scores for listening and for reading on the same measure. Thirty-two categories were selected for Form A and 32 for Form B as shown in Table 10. Four different categories were placed on each page, with five vocabulary items for each category. On some pages, this page balance could not be maintained, but it was possible in most instances. For the final forms, the Thorndike-Lorge word list served as the basis of arrangement. The clusters in each form were in order of average frequency according to Thorndike-Lorge, and the words within each cluster were put in order of frequency of usage as far as it was possible.

Two final forms--A and B--were constructed to measure listening comprehension and reading comprehension in the present study. Each form contained eight original selections to measure paragraph comprehension.

For the reading measures, the vocabulary section contained four categories with 20 items to classify on each page. Categories and items were printed on each page for a total of eight pages. The paragraph selections were also printed. Each page contained the paragraph and answer form.

As listening measures, the vocabulary design remained the same as that for the reading measure. However, the items to be classified did not appear in print. These were read by the examiner. Since the paragraphs also were read by the examiner, two answer forms were placed on each page of the booklet, making it possible to print the eight answer forms on four pages.

Each form was designed and published as a reading comprehension test and as a listening comprehension test.

TABLE 10

FINAL CATEGORIES FOR VOCABULARY COMPREHENSION

Form A

Strength	Place	Plan	Fear
World	Thought	Enough	Sad
Order	Passage	Rest	Accuse
Hardness	Give	Experiment	Pleasure
Difference	Container	Picture	Persuade
Fold	Dark	Teach	Polite
Home	Water	Measure	Pain
Length	Soften	Writing	Sell

Form B

Part	Expand	Animal	Choose
Equal	Speed	Hot	Sickness
Excite	Tell	Inhabitant	Reward
Family	Clothing	Country	Not Enough
Size	Question	Improve	Punishment
Likeness	Grow	Trap	Dislike
List	Solve	Worship	Dirt
Group	Uncertain	Wasteful	Courage

TABLE 11

FINAL FORMAT FOR VOCABULARY COMPREHENSION TESTS

(Reading) or (Listening)

		House	Cook	Move	Flower
1. bake 2. daisy 3. window 4. travel 5. tulip 6. push (etc.)	[items left blank for listening test]				

DEVELOPING MEASURES OF PARAGRAPH MEANING
FOR READING- LISTENING TESTS

Mary Butler Brassard

In reviewing the literature and tests of reading comprehension and listening comprehension of paragraphs, it became apparent that paragraphs which were already in print were usually employed to test listening comprehension. The Durrell-Sullivan Reading Capacity Test and the STEP Tests of Listening were the most frequently used published tests. Sometimes the Durrell-Sullivan Test was administered in its entirety; sometimes only selected paragraphs were given. However, both of these tests of paragraph comprehension provide different content for listening comprehension and for reading comprehension and are thus subject to the criticism of current tests set forth in the discussion of the need for equated measures.

Many of the results of other research studies were based on paragraphs which were selected from commercially prepared materials. The Gates Reading Skill Series, McCall-Crabb Series, and SRA Laboratories provided paragraphs which ranged from easy to difficult in content and measured a variety of comprehension skills. However, these materials are widely used for instructional purposes in the schools. They are subject to prior knowledge and study and can, therefore, be familiar to some students and so penalize those to whom they have not been exposed.

A third source of listening comprehension paragraphs was found in doctoral dissertations for which the authors had constructed their own tests. However, these were not available in published form, nor had they been administered as both reading comprehension and listening comprehension tests.

It was obvious, then, that original paragraphs which could be administered as both reading and listening measures, not subject to prior exposure and learning situations, were needed to provide comparable raw scores of reading comprehension and listening comprehension.

Criteria

The guidelines set for the general design of the measure required a group test which could be administered by the classroom teacher and scored either by hand or by

machine. In addition to the guides developed for the total
measure, the following criteria were established to obtain the
information necessary for making direct raw score comparisons between listening comprehension and reading comprehension of paragraphs:

    1.   Paragraphs were constructed around topics of
interest to intermediate grade children.
    2.   Paragraphs were constructed around topics which
require no previous knowledge.
    3.   Material which appeared in text and reading books
for this age group was avoided as much as possible.
    4.   Each paragraph was approximately 250 words in
length.
    5.   The content in each paragraph allowed at least
eight items for testing.
    6.   A comparison technique was used in building the
paragraphs and test items.
    7.   A four-place multiple-choice answer was provided
for each item.
    8.   There were no specific numbers or dates to re-
call.
    9.   There were at least eight paragraphs for each
form of the test.

Sources for Paragraphs

    The surveys of children's literature and textbooks
which had been carried out prior to the construction of the
vocabulary measures served as guides to areas which are of
interest to children at the intermediate grade level. Further
investigations of children's interests and background knowledge
were carried out among a sampling of the population to be
tested.

    A questionnaire was constructed to provide information
on the following three points:

    What do you like to do best after school?
    What kinds of books or stories do you like best?
    What kind of television programs do you like best?

    This survey questionnaire was administered to children
from grades 4, 5, and 6 who attended the Boston University
Reading Clinic. The same investigation was carried out in
a school which contained three classrooms for each of the
intermediate grades, arranged in heterogeneous grouping.
The responses to the three questions were collected and

placed in general categories. These were listed in rank order of choice, as shown in Table 1.

TABLE 1

TOPICS OF STATED INTERESTS OF
INTERMEDIATE GRADE CHILDREN

Activities Out-side of School	Favorite Book and Story Topics	Favorite Types of TV Programs
Sports	Animals	War
Baseball	Mystery	Mystery
Football	Sports	Westerns
Tag	Indians	Cartoons
Hide-n-Seek	Biographies	
Punch ball	Fairy Stories	
Published Games	Myths	
Bingo	Legends	
Concentration	Ghost Stories	
	Different People	
	Different Places	

Another group of sixth graders was asked to prepare a composition comparing any two people, places, or things of their choice. The following subjects were compared, as shown in Table 2.

TABLE 2

SUBJECTS COMPARED BY SIXTH GRADERS

Sports	Places
Skating-hockey	Jungle-city
Skin diving: now and	North-South
20 years ago	Town-city
Tennis-ping pong	
Skating-skiing	People
Softball-baseball	Indians of different tribes
	Ancient-modern
Animals	
Domestic-wild	

The information gained from these sources served as a general guide in selecting topics around which to build the paragraphs.

Preliminary Paragraphs
Format
An initial paragraph was written to fit the criteria and the stated interests of the intermediate grade children. There were four choices for each item in the vocabulary section of the measure and the same number of choices was kept for the paragraphs to eliminate guessing and random responses as much as possible. True-false and yes-no responses were not possible for this pattern; pictures were not practical. Printing the four choices with each question was suitable for the reading comprehension test but not for the listening comprehension measure. The student can review the possible choices after he has read them but not after he has heard them. Printing the possible responses on an answer form makes the measure one of reading ability as well as listening comprehension. The child who has reading difficulties does not have the opportunity to indicate a true level of listening comprehension unless he hears the questions and possible answer choices.

These difficulties were eliminated by developing an answer form which offered the following choices: (1) true of one; (2) true of the other; (3) true of both; (4) answer not given, or, true of neither. For the fourth response it was necessary to make a choice between "True of neither" and "Answer not given." "True of neither" was rejected because it could cause some confusion, especially if the student had additional or different information about the topics in the paragraph. "Answer not given" eliminated this complication and was chosen for the fourth option.

This answer form fitted the paragraph design of comparisons and contrasts. Instead of questions, statements were made based on the content of the selection. Each statement could be answered by one of the foregoing choices. The statements were printed on the reading form of the test page; they were read by the examiner for the listening measure.

Preliminary Testing
An initial paragraph was written to try out the comparison technique and the answer format. Table 3 portrays the initial format for the paragraph comprehension measures.

Two students of average ability were selected from each of grades 4, 5, and 6. One partner took the test as a reading measure, the other as a listening comprehension measure. The directions were: "Here are some stories

TABLE 3

TRIAL PARAGRAPH FOR INDIVIDUAL TESTING

Reading- Listening Test
Sample Format of Paragraph Testing

What is brought about by force may be removed by the same action. This can be seen in the rule of Mazentius. He governed the people without thinking about the needs or wishes of the people. The masses rose against him and drove him from the country. Latinus, who counted Saturn among his ancestors, displays another sort of kingship. He was just and gracious, always consulting with the senate to promote the common good.

Check the correct column:

A -- if the statement is true of Mazentius.
B -- if the statement is true of Latinus.
C -- if the statement is true of both.
D -- if the answer is not given.

	A	B	C	D
1. He was descended from Saturn				
2. He governed arbitrarily				
3. He was expelled				
4. He rebuilt the empire				
5. He came to the deserved end of all tyrants				
6. He was a ruler				
7. He displays the proper character of a king				
8. He was concerned for the welfare of his people				
9. He ruled for many years				

which tell about people, places, or things which are alike in
some ways but different in other ways. After each story
there are statements for you to classify. You do this by fill-
ing in the answer space under the right heading." The examiner and the student then reviewed the paragraph and answers.

The students found that it was easy to compare the
two people in the paragraph and then make choices about
each statement. The format worked well for both listening
and reading. However, they felt the answer block would be
clearer if the A, B, C, D choices were placed at the head
of the answer columns. It was time-consuming to consult a
key and then look back to response columns. The answer
form was changed to this format and more paragraphs were
written for a group trial.

Selection of Topics
Initial Paragraphs
Two, possibly three, forms of the measure were
to be built. A master list of possible topics was compiled
from the results of the questionnaire; comparison paragraphs,
which had been completed by the students, and preliminary
paragraphs were written around the following subjects, as
shown in Table 4.

TABLE 4

SUBJECT MATTER LIST OF PRELIMINARY PARAGRAPHS

Origins of alphabets	Mystery	School
History	Adventure	Construction
- Phoenician	Animals	Occupation
- business	Space	Other countries
Latin	Undersea exploration	Other customs
- printing	Colonial times	Forests
- tools	Transportation	- how people
Mythology	Morse code	live
- 3 original myths	Legends	- how vegeta-
Sports	- original	tion differs
- boxing	Ghost Stories	- differing
- tennis	- original	weathers
- skiing		
Food		
- of desert people		
- of jungle people		
Character		
- fiction		

TABLE 4 (cont'd.)

SUBJECT MATTER LIST OF PRELIMINARY PARAGRAPHS

    - sports figures
Success
    - fiction
    - famous men
Art
    - of Indians
    - Pueblos
    - Mound Builders
Fairy Stories
    - 3 original

      Initially, three paragraph selections were written about each specific subject. The purpose was to prepare three different forms of the measure which would be as similar as possible for difficulty and comparisons. The following pages illustrate the content and questions for three different selections about the Mound Builders. Each selection contains different information about the same subject and is followed by at least eight comprehension questions.

PARAGRAPHS FOR PRELIMINARY TESTING

Paragraph No. 14

      One by one many of the Indian tribes moved away from their homes. Some were driven away by enemy tribes. Others were killed by the white man. Some were wiped out by disease.

      For hundreds of years no one knew why the Pueblo Indians had left their homes. Their cities were built to last forever. They were good farmers. Their enemies could not reach them. The mystery was finally solved by a man who studied the rings of the trees where the Pueblos had lived. There was a terrible drought between 1277 and 1299. All of the crops died. The corn and beans on which the Pueblos relied for their food were gone. So the Pueblos had to leave their homes to find food. They never came back.

      The Mound Builders were another kind of Indian. They built fine hills and buildings of earth. They made beautiful

pottery, beads, and knives. They were also very good
farmers. Yet they too died out. The young men began to
hunt buffalo. They used this animal for food and clothing.
Soon all the men stopped farming and building their beautiful
mounds and beads. And so the Mound Men too left their
homes and never returned.

	True of Pueblos	True of Mound Builders	True of Both	Answer Not Given
1. They were beaten by other Indians.				
2. They were good farmers.				
3. They left to hunt buffalo.				
4. They moved to find food.				
5. They made beautiful jewelry.				
6. Their enemies were not men.				
7. They were killed by white men.				
8. Their homes burned down.				

Paragraph No. 15

Many of the American Indian tribes had fine workmen.
The Pueblo Indians in the southwest built apartment-like
houses in the cliffs. Some of the houses were really cities.
They had land for farming set out by the houses. Dams
were shored up to catch and hold rain water. Ditches were
dug to carry the water to the farms. The Pueblos were
fine farmers and builders. Many of their apartment houses
are still standing today.

The Mound Builders erected hills of many different
shapes in the eastern section of America. The mounds were
made of earth in many shapes. One mound is built along
the edge of a high cliff by the side of a river. It is in the
form of a serpent with an egg in its mouth. In the egg are
burnt stones. This means that this part of the mound was

used as an altar. Mounds were built for many different purposes. They still can be seen in some places although
people still cannot understand how the Indians were able to
construct such beautiful hills.

	True of Pueblos	True of Mound Builders	True of Both	Answer Not Given
1. They built only on lowlands.				
2. Sometimes their buildings were religious monuments.				
3. They were skilled builders.				
4. Some of their buildings are standing today.				
5. They traveled.				
6. They were farmers.				
7. They built mainly on cliffs.				
8. Many of their people lived together in one building.				

However, upon inspection of the writings, it seemed
likely that children could gain information about a specific
topic on one measure which would be helpful to them when
they were tested on another form of the listening or reading
comprehension test.

Revised Paragraphs
Four more paragraph selections were written about
different topics and were tried out on thirty students from
grades 4, 5, and 6. At each grade level the teacher was
asked to select five pairs of students who represented the
range in ability from low to very high. Each partner was
matched with another of the same ability. One set of partners took the measure as a listening test, the other partners
as a reading comprehension test.

Samples of the revised paragraphs and format may be seen on the following pages.

REVISED TRIAL PARAGRAPHS

Donald and Paul were friends. They had entered a travel contest and each of them had won a trip as a prize.

Donald had written about the life of a sea captain. His prize was a trip to Bermuda on an ocean liner. Now he could compare his story to real life. He was to be the cabin boy and run errands for the captain.

Paul had written about a pilot on an airplane. His prize was a trip to Bermuda, too, but he was going to fly down. He would leave two days later than Donald but both boys would arrive there on the same day. Then they would spend the week together, touring the island.

	True of Donald	True of Paul	True of Both	Answer Not Given
1. He won a contest.				
2. He left for Bermuda first.				
3. He would work on the trip.				
4. He wrote about the pilot on an airplane.				
5. He wrote about some form of travel.				
6. He was going by train.				
7. It will take him longer to reach Bermuda.				
8. He will be a cabin boy.				

Many people have interesting stories to explain how the writing of their country began.   In China they tell how a wise man invented their alphabet.   He saw the patterns of the stars in the sky, the marks on the back of the turtle, and the footprints of the birds in the garden.   From these shapes he drew the characters which the Chinese use in writing.   In India a Hindu god made his own letters so that he could write down his teachings.   He drew his patterns from the lines in the human skull.   It is said that he traced the first letters of the Hindu alphabet with his fingers on leaves of gold.

	True of Chinese	True of Hindu	True of Both	Answer Not Given
1. Each country appoints a group of wise men to make an alphabet.				
2. Shapes from the stars may be found in this alphabet.				
3. This alphabet has many straight lines.				
4. This man wanted to write down his own lessons.				
5. These letters are like shapes we see in nature.				
6. This country has a legend to explain its alphabet.				
7. Some of these letters are like the lines in the head.				
8. The shapes of some of these letters can be seen in animals.				
9. This alphabet is more scientific.				

After the group testing, the measures were scored by adding the total number of correct responses.   Table 5 re-

ports the scores for listening comprehension and reading
comprehension for each of the paragraphs administered at
each grade level.   Table 6 compares the total raw scores
for listening and for reading.

TABLE 5

RAW SCORES FOR LISTENING AND READING
COMPREHENSION OF PARAGRAPHS

Paragraph	Grade	N	Listening	Reading
A	4	10	23	15
	5	10	26	24
	6	10	33	30
B	4	10	22	14
	5	10	17	12
	6	10	30	25
C	4	10	12	8
	5	10	19	12
	6	10	20	16
D	4	10	21	15
	5	10	24	17
	6	10	29	24

TABLE 6

TOTAL RAW SCORES FOR FOUR PARAGRAPHS

Grade	N	Listening	Reading
4	10	78	52
5	10	86	65
6	10	112	95
Total		276	212

An analysis of the raw scores showed that there were
276 correct responses for the measure given as a listening
test and 212 correct responses when the measure was administered as a reading test.   The measures did discrimi-

nate between listening ability and reading ability. Examination of the raw scores for each ability at each grade level also showed that the measures discriminated between grade levels as well. Grade 4 students had 78 correct responses for listening; grade 5 students, 86; and grade 6 students had 112 correct replies. The same general discrimination appeared in the reading scores.

Paragraph Revisions

The group testing had demonstrated that the technique and format of the paragraph comprehension tests were successful. The original list of topics was revised, and while three paragraph selections of the same general nature were still retained for placement, one in each of the proposed forms, the treatment of the topics was changed. Each topic now served as a broad rather than a specific area of interest, and related to the curriculum for intermediate grades.

Forty-two paragraphs were written to meet the criteria which had been set for them. Each selection compared two people, places, things, or situations. Each selection provided enough information to allow at least eight items for testing comprehension. The paragraphs were written to cover a range of difficulty on both content and questions from below third grade to above sixth grade level.

The paragraphs were then examined by a group of reading specialists, and appropriate changes were made where content or questions were not clear.

Table 7 presents the final organization of topics for the paragraph comprehension tests.

TABLE 7

TOPICS AROUND WHICH PARAGRAPHS WERE BUILT

No. of Paragraphs	Topic	Curriculum Area
3	Alphabets/Word Origins	Social Studies
3	Mythology	Literature
3	Fairy Tales	Literature
3	Animal Stories	Lit., Sci., & Soc. Stud.
3	Ghost Stories	Literature
6	Sports	Literature
3	Legends	Literature
3	Adventure	Literature & Soc. Stud.

TABLE 7 (cont'd.)

TOPICS AROUND WHICH PARAGRAPHS WERE BUILT

No. of Paragraphs	Topic	Curriculum Area
3	Space Stories	Science
6	Different Peoples	Social Studies
6	Different Places	Social Studies

Twenty-four paragraphs were selected from the total number--eight for Form A, eight for Form B, and eight for Form C. All paragraphs were matched for subject matter and curriculum balance when distributed among the three forms. Difficulty ranged from very simple to difficult. No two selections of the 24 contained information which would be helpful in answering another paragraph selection.

Table 8 shows the final subject matter chosen for the paragraph comprehension tests.

TABLE 8

FINAL SUBJECT MATTER FOR PARAGRAPH COMPREHENSION TESTS

Curriculum Area	Subject	Number of Selections		
		Form A	Form B	Form C
Language	Juvenile Story	1	1	1
	Fiction	1	1	1
	Mythology	1	1	1
Social Studies	History	2	2	2
	Geography	1	1	1
Science	Science	1	1	1
	Animals	1	1	1

THE DURRELL-SULLIVAN READING CAPACITY TEST
AS A MEASURE OF INTELLIGENCE

John C. Harvey

Satisfactory academic achievement is becoming more difficult with the great demands being made by the various pressure groups for literate people in occupations which did not exist a generation ago. If those who have the responsibility of the education program are to fulfill technological demands, it is of paramount importance that early and continual identification of pupils take place.

Individual evaluation for the purpose of obtaining intelligence ratings for all pupils is not feasible. Trained psychometrists are scarce; the time involved and funds necessary to conduct an individualized testing program are not realistic when viewed in terms of the numbers of students involved.

Group intelligence tests which can be administered, corrected, and interpreted by teaching personnel seem to be the only suitable solution at the present time. Even this type of testing program has its limitations as all group intelligence tests rely heavily upon the testee's ability to comprehend the printed word. Reading achievement has not, in a system of compulsory education, kept pace with the intellectual ability of each child. Donald Durrell states:

> It follows that the group intelligence test involving a great number of reading items should not be used as a basis for intellectual accomplishments quotients. It [the intelligence test] appears to be a reading test incorrectly labeled. ["The Influence of Reading Ability on Intelligence Measures," J. of Educ. Psych., 24:412-16, 1933, p. 416.]

In this study an attempt was made to show that the Durrell-Sullivan Reading Capacity Test, a non-reading test, will give a realistic and quick appraisal of an individual's intellectual capabilities, independent of reading achievement.

Procedures
In order to collect the data necessary to find a possible answer to the problem of this thesis, the following steps were used:

1. All teachers involved in the testing portion of the prob-
    lem were orientated to the testing instruments and the
    importance of giving them in accordance with the direc-
    tions contained in the test manuals.

2. The California Test of Mental Maturity, Intermediate
    Level, was given to all third- and fifth-grade pupils
    during October, 1957.

3. During the same month of 1958, this test was given to
    all fifth-grade pupils who had been fourth graders the
    previous year, and all fourth- and sixth-grade pupils
    new to the school.

4. All testing was done in the pupils' own classroom and
    by the teacher who adhered to the test manuals supplied
    with the test.

5. Third-grade pupils indicated their choice of answers by
    marking directly in the test booklets. Teachers con-
    verted the raw scores into intelligence quotients.

6. Fifth-grade pupils used the IBM answer sheet; these
    were electronically scored in the office of the Solano
    County Superintendent; raw scores were converted into
    intelligence quotients.

7. Of the 314 pupils who received the California Test of
    Mental Maturity, 237 pupils were given the Durrell-
    Sullivan Reading Capacity Test, Form A, Intermediate
    Level.

8. Like the maturity test, the capacity test was given by
    the teacher in the classroom. The teacher computed
    an assumed intelligence quotient from the mental age
    equivalent norms furnished in the manual.

9. The Wechsler Intelligence Scale for Children was ad-
    ministered by a certificated school psychologist to 27
    pupils who had been administered both maturity and
    capacity tests.

10. Correlations were secured by using the Pearson-Product
    Moment formula. The three sub-test intelligence quo-
    tients (obtained by dividing an equivalent mental age by
    the chronological age) of the Durrell Capacity Test were
    compared with the three intelligence quotients of the

California Mental Maturity Test and the three intelligence
quotients of the Wechsler Intelligence Scale for Children.

Procedures

Immediately prior to any testing program, it is the policy
of the district that all teachers involved review the directions
for administering and correcting tests.   In this study all
teachers concerned were informed of this writer's intentions
of utilizing the results; they were reminded of the importance
of adhering to printed directions.

The California Short Form Test of Mental Maturity,
1957 Revision, Intermediate Level, was given to all third-
and fifth-grade pupils during October of 1957.   Because third-
grade pupils tend to have difficulty in transferring answers
from the test booklet to a machine-scored answer page, they
were directed to indicate answers directly in their test booklets.   Due to their previous testing experience utilizing
machine scoring procedures, all fifth graders were instructed
to mark their answers on the IBM answer sheet.

Third-grade teachers, using the scoring key and
manual, carefully. scored each test booklet, obtained mental
ages for each sub-test and computed mathematically the intelligence quotient by dividing the obtained mental age by the
pupil's chronological age.

Fifth-grade answer sheets were sent to the office of
the Solano County Superintendent.   That office scored each
answer sheet electronically and computed intelligence quotients; thus, the fifth-grade teachers had no further responsibility for the testing program after they had administered the
tests to the pupils.

One year later, during October of 1958, all fifth-
grade pupils who had been fourth graders and all fourth- and
sixth-grade pupils new to the school received the same test
by the method described previously for the fifth-grade testing
program.

Mental Maturity Tests were administered in the classroom by the pupils' own teacher, except for new fourth and
sixth graders who were assigned to one of the fifth-grade
teachers for the testing period.   Outside distractions were
held to a minimum during testing, no interference was permitted from outside, and the physical environment of the
room was adequate.   Each teacher followed the manual of

directions during the test administration.

Because it would have been impractical to check each test booklet, answer sheet, mental age, and intelligence quotient for errors, a random sampling was made by this writer and all samples were found to be correct.

Test booklets and machine-scored answer sheets which gave evidence of misunderstanding of the proper procedures or a lack of ability by the pupil to follow directions were not considered valid and consequently were withdrawn from this study.

During the same month, October, 1958, two hundred thirty-seven white fourth-, fifth-, and sixth-grade pupils who received the maturity test, were given the Durrell-Sullivan Reading Capacity Test, Form A, of the Intermediate Level. All tests were administered in the classroom by the teacher who had been briefed on the test, its purpose and possible future as an indicator of intelligence. The manual of directions for administering and scoring the test, which accompanied the test booklets, was used and followed within the limits prescribed. All outside distractions were held to a minimum and interruptions were not permitted from the outside while testing was in progress. Teachers corrected each test booklet by using the answer key which accompanies the manual, and obtained equivalent mental ages from the raw scores for the Word Meaning sub-test, Paragraph Meaning sub-test and total test results. Test booklets which indicated failure by the pupil to follow directions were not considered in this study. This writer made a random sampling of the test booklets, raw scores, and equivalent mental age scores for the purpose of detecting errors which might affect the correlations.

An assumed intelligence quotient was obtained by the following formula:

$$\text{Assumed Intelligence Quotient (AIQ)} = \frac{\text{Mental Age Equivalent (MAE)}}{\text{Chronological Age (CA)}} \times 100$$

A school psychologist administered the Wechsler Intelligence Scale for Children to twenty-seven white pupils who had received both the Durrell-Sullivan Reading Capacity Test and the Short Form of the California Test of Mental Maturity. Each of the twenty-seven had been referred by the classroom teacher for various reasons such as possible mental retardation, high academic potential, difficulties with reading, or general lack of interest in all learning situations. All testing took place in a room where there were no interruptions or outside influences which would have affected the final results. After each test was scored, verbal, performance, and full-scale intelligence quotients were obtained.

Correlations Obtained Between The Durrell-Sullivan Reading
Capacity Test and Two Intelligence Tests: The California
Short-Form Test of Mental Maturity and the
Wechsler Intelligence Scale for Children

In order to obtain correlations between the Durrell-Sullivan Test and the two intelligence tests, the Pearson Product-Moment formula was selected. This formula was chosen because a ratio or correlation between two variables was to be determined; one variable was an assumed intelligence quotient of the Durrell-Sullivan Test and the other was a sub-test intelligence quotient of either of the two intelligence tests. The variables of the Durrell-Sullivan Test were divided into two categories, sex and grade level, and correlated with similar categories of the California Mental Maturity Test. In addition, both sexes and combined-grade level correlations were obtained. (See Table 1.) This procedure was used in finding the correlations existing between each sub-test and the total scores of the Durrell Word Meaning, Paragraph Meaning, and Total and the three parts of the California Maturity Test: Language, Non-language, and Total. In all, there were 90 correlations involving 237 white pupils.

Test results from a total of 27 pupils were involved in correlations between each score of the Durrell-Sullivan Reading Capacity Test (Word Meaning, Paragraph Meaning, and Total) with each of the three intelligence quotients of the Wechsler Intelligence Scale for Children (Verbal, Performance, and Full Scale). No attempt was made to make distinctions on the basis of grade levels or sex as was done with the California Mental Maturity Test. Tables 2, 3, and 4 show the ninety correlations obtained.

Ninety correlations were obtained between the California Short-Form Test of Mental Maturity, Intermediate Level of the 1957 Revision, and the Durrell-Sullivan Reading Capacity Test, Intermediate Level (Form A). These correlations ranged from .29 for the word test of the Durrell-

TABLE 1

Comparison of Grade Level and Combined Grade Level
Correlations Between the Durrell-Sullivan Reading Capacity
Test and the California Short-Form Test of Mental Maturity
Involving 237 Fourth-, Fifth-, and Sixth-Grade Pupils

| | | California Test of Mental Maturity | | |
	Durrell-Sullivan	Language	Non-language	Total
Total	Word Meaning	.558	.372	.521
Fourth	Paragraph Meaning	.594	.465	.597
Grade	Total	.605	.451	.597
Total	Word Meaning	.639	.325	.553
Fifth	Paragraph Meaning	.593	.284	.483
Grade	Total	.683	.384	.589
Total	Word Meaning	.588	.470	.626
Sixth	Paragraph Meaning	.657	.456	.641
Grade	Total	.688	.497	.667
Combined	Word Meaning	.537	.374	.524
Grade	Paragraph Meaning	.577	.419	.561
Totals	Total	.594	.432	.578

TABLE 2

Comparison of the Intelligence Quotient Ranking of the 27
Fourth-, Fifth-, and Sixth-Grade Boys and Girls on the Word
Meaning Test of the Durrell-Sullivan Reading Capacity Test and
the Sub-Tests of the Wechsler Intelligence Scale for Children

Case No.	Durrell-Sullivan: Word Meaning	Wechsler Intelligence Scale for Children		
		Verbal	Performance	Total
1	99	77	104	89
2	62	91	86	88
3	110	84	100	91
4	115	109	128	120
5	68	57	65	57
6	80	69	71	67
7	62	63	67	62
8	104	80	87	82
9	112	109	104	107
10	109	92	97	94
11	144	131	110	123
12	135	125	121	125
13	117	82	90	85
14	92	97	85	91
15	133	124	108	118
16	81	81	62	70
17	99	90	101	95
18	144	128	107	120
19	96	71	111	96
20	104	81	94	86
21	96	71	111	96
22	106	95	96	95
23	100	85	78	80
24	81	81	99	88
25	131	108	106	107
26	102	115	121	120
27	99	90	72	80
Rank Correlation with Wechsler Intelligence Scale for Children		.80	.66	.88
		.36	.57	.21
		.60	.76	.48

TABLE 3

Comparison of the Intelligence Quotient Ranking of the 27
Fourth-, Fifth-, and Sixth-Grade Boys and Girls on the
Paragraph Meaning Test of the Durrell-Sullivan Reading
Capacity Test and the Sub-tests of the Wechsler Intelligence
Scale for Children

Case No.	Durrell-Sullivan: Paragraph Meaning	Wechsler Intelligence Scale for Children		
		Verbal	Performance	Total
1	99	77	104	89
2	76	91	86	88
3	104	84	100	91
4	133	109	128	120
5	85	57	65	57
6	80	69	71	67
7	71	63	67	62
8	85	80	87	82
9	121	109	104	107
10	99	92	97	94
11	130	131	110	123
12	161	125	121	125
13	98	82	90	85
14	88	97	85	91
15	133	124	108	118
16	88	81	62	70
17	95	90	101	95
18	144	128	107	120
19	112	71	111	96
20	106	81	94	86
21	112	71	111	96
22	120	95	96	95
23	106	85	78	80
24	89	81	99	88
25	118	108	106	107
26	108	115	121	120
27	118	90	72	80
Rank Correlation with Wechsler Intelligence Scale for Children		.77	.69	.82
		.40	.48	.32
		.64	.69	.57

TABLE 4

Comparison of the Intelligence Quotient Ranking of the 27
Fourth-, Fifth-, and Sixth- Grade Boys and Girls on the Total
Test Scores of the Durrell- Sullivan Reading Capacity Test and
the Sub- Tests of the Wechsler Intelligence Scale for Children

Case No.	Durrell-Sullivan: Total	Wechsler Intelligence Scale for Children		
		Verbal	Performance	Total
1	100	77	104	89
2	70	91	86	88
3	107	84	100	91
4	124	109	128	120
5	76	57	65	57
6	82	69	71	67
7	68	63	67	62
8	96	80	87	82
9	118	109	104	107
10	109	92	97	94
11	130	131	110	123
12	145	125	121	125
13	100	82	90	85
14	91	97	85	91
15	131	124	108	118
16	87	81	62	70
17	99	90	101	95
18	144	128	107	120
19	105	71	111	96
20	106	81	94	86
21	105	71	111	96
22	114	95	96	95
23	103	85	78	80
24	78	81	99	88
25	128	108	106	107
26	105	115	121	120
27	105	90	72	80
Rank Correlation with Wechsler Intelligence Scale for Children		.81	.70	.84
		.34	.51	.29
		.59	.71	.54

Sullivan Test correlated with the non-language of the California test for the fourth-grade boys to a high of .70 obtained when the total assumed equivalent intelligence quotient of the Durrell-Sullivan test was correlated for the boys of the sixth grade.

A survey of correlations indicates that, in general, high correlations are obtained not from the non-language test of the California Test, but the language test which involves the testee in a reading experience which he may be unable to perform.

No differences can be shown on the basis of sex or grade level, which would indicate that neither test would be more reliable for one group than for another.

All correlations obtained, even the r of .29, are significant at both the five per cent and one per cent levels of confidence.

Significant at the five per cent and one per cent levels of confidence were nine correlations obtained between the Durrell-Sullivan Reading Capacity Test, Intermediate Level, Form A, and the Wechsler Intelligence Scale for Children.

Only one correlation, the Word Meaning Test of the Durrell-Sullivan Test versus the Performance scale of the Wechsler Intelligence Scale for Children, denoted a moderate relationship with an r of .65. All other correlations ranging from .69 to .88 indicated high to very high relationships. The correlation of .88 was obtained between the Word Meaning Test of the Durrell-Sullivan and the Total Score of the Wechsler Intelligence Scale for Children. These results are considered conditional and not absolute indices of relationship.

Summary, Conclusions, and Recommendations for the Use of
the Durrell-Sullivan Reading Capacity Test

I. SUMMARY

Two sets of correlations were obtained in this study. One set involves 237 white fourth-, fifth-, and sixth-grade pupils who were given two standardized tests. The Durrell-Sullivan Reading Capacity Test and the California Short-Form Test of Mental Maturity. The second set of correlations was obtained by comparing the test results of twenty-seven pupils who were given the Durrell-Sullivan Reading Capacity Test and the Wechsler Intelligence Scale for Children.

All correlations were obtained by using intelligence quotient scores and the Pearson Product-Moment formula. Equivalent mental ages obtained from the raw scores of the Durrell-Sullivan Reading Capacity Test were converted to equivalent intelligence quotients.

II.   CONCLUSIONS

On the basis of the investigations made and reported in this study, the following conclusions can be drawn:

1.   There appears to be a significant relationship between the non-reading Durrell-Sullivan Reading Capacity Test, a group test, and the individually administered Wechsler Intelligence Scale for Children.

2.   It is apparent that a group intelligence test requiring reading penalizes those who do not have the reading skills necessary to read and comprehend a group intelligence test.

3.   The Durrell-Sullivan Reading Capacity Test may be considered an indicator of a person's intellectual capacity to learn to read printed symbols. Therefore, this test may be utilized, along with careful observations, to predict a child's capacity for learning to read.

Chapter XI

RELATIONSHIPS BETWEEN LISTENING
AND OTHER PSYCHOMETRIC FACTORS

Whether factors are related to each other in one way or another is always a matter of interest. Sometimes such a relationship sheds light on more effective ways of teaching or testing skills. Often it is possible to use the psychological principle of transfer of training in teaching a skill when these relationships have been discovered, analyzed and understood.

In this chapter excerpts from only a few studies concerned with this intriguing aspect of listening are presented.

The first excerpt is from a doctoral dissertation by Richard S. Hampleman. This excerpt does not describe in any degree of detail the procedures used in this study of the relationship between reading and listening. Instead only the findings of the research are presented along with Dr. Hampleman's recommendations for further research.

The second excerpt is also brief but certainly not because Dr. Evertt's study is not a very interesting one. The one page excerpt from her doctoral study gives only the results obtained but the methods used in reaching these was carefully planned and carried out in a conscientious and scientific manner. Accordingly it is a well-justified conclusion that the findings reported here deserve a high degree of credence.

Dr. Maurice S. Lewis, who is a Professor of Education at Arizona State University, has long had an unusual interest in the area of listening and has made substantial contributions to knowledge about this area. In 1954 he wrote a doctoral study at Colorado State College of Education entitled, The Construction of a Diagnostic Test of Listening Comprehension for Grades 4, 5, and 6. The test constructed as part of this study, while it has never been published, has

been used by a number of graduate students in their works
on listening and is deservedly one of the better known and
highly regarded unpublished tests of listening skills.   The
excerpt used in this chapter is taken from Dr. Lewis' second
doctoral study in which he explored the effect on certain
reading skills of the teaching of these same skills in the
area of listening.   This has become an even more important
contribution than that made by his first study for there are
many children who resist reading instruction because of the
failure they associate with their previous experiences with
such instruction.   If it were possible to approach such boys
and girls with listening instruction there might well be hope
for reading improvement in some hard-core cases.   The excerpt gives a clear picture of Lewis' experiment and its outcome.

        The fourth excerpt is taken from a doctoral study
written at Arizona State University under the sponsorship of
Dr. Lewis.   Here Dr. Ann E. Jackson investigates a multi-
plicity of relationships with listening ability.   The data re-
sulting from her carefully performed research are presented
in a number of informative tables which are included in the
excerpt reproduced here.

        The study by Dr. Graham from which the last excerpt
is taken is a carefully planned and well executed study.   It
investigates the effect on the growth in listening skills relating to verbal communication of lessons in listening to music.
Pupils at the elementary school level were used as subjects.
The findings suggest that there may be yet another avenue by
which the reluctant reader may be approached.

COMPARING LISTENING AND READING COMPREHENSION

Richard S. Hampleman

        The purpose of this investigation was to compare lis-
tening comprehension ability with reading comprehension ability of fourth- and sixth-grade children as this relationship
was affected by differences in mental age, chronological age,
grade level, difficulty of material, length of passage, and
sex.   There were 490 pupils in grades four and six of the
eight schools selected.

Findings

1. The reliabilities of the tests used were sufficiently high to serve as fairly precise group measuring instruments. The average of four reliability coefficients for the 50-item Power of Comprehension Test was .85. The average of four reliability coefficients for the 25-item Length of Passage Test was .82.

2. Tests of homogeneity of variance have shown that the eight sub-classes of subjects used in the study were not significantly different from one another so as to represent different populations. Since this tests one of the basic assumptions under which this study was made, conclusions dependent upon such an assumption can be validly drawn.

3. Analyses of variance indicated that there were no significant differences between the listening and reading groups in chronological age and mental age. This result gave two pieces of evidence that the randomization process used in the study was effective.

4. Grade level had a significant effect upon the score made by pupils on the Power of Comprehension and Length of Passage tests.

5. There were no significant differences between the scores made by boys and girls on Power of Comprehension and Length of Passage tests.

6. A significant interaction was observed between the classifications of type of presentation and difficulty of material for the Power of Comprehension Test. This may be explained by the fact that the difference between the two levels of difficulty is greater when presented as a listening test than when presented as a reading test. Another way to explain this same finding is that the superiority of listening over reading is mainly observed on the easy part of the test.

7. The classification of difficulty of material is independent of grade level but not of sex. Difficulty of material is observed to be interacting with sex. The explanation of this interaction is that the superiority of easy over hard material is greater for girls than for boys. Girls make much lower scores than boys on the hard material.

8. Controlling mental and chronological ages of pupils increases the superiority of the scores made by sixth graders

as compared with those of fourth graders on the Power of Comprehension Test. Such control also increased the differences between listening and reading. Controlling these two variables likewise results in boys becoming superior to girls on the total test. The difference is accounted for chiefly because of differences on the hard material.

9. On the Length of Passage Test controlling mental age increases the superiority of listening over reading. It also causes fourth graders to surpass sixth graders on the total test. This may be explained by the fact that, with mental age controlled and chronological age still operative, the effect of having relatively brighter pupils in fourth grade is achieved. The most important factor to bear in mind with this finding is that listening maintains its superiority over reading with mental age controlled.

For the population tested in this study, the following conclusions may be safely drawn from the findings:

1. Sixth grade pupils are significantly superior to fourth grade pupils in both listening and reading comprehension.

2. Listening comprehension is significantly superior to reading comprehension for fourth and sixth grade pupils of both sexes.

3. For fourth and sixth grade pupils, listening comprehension shows a greater superiority over reading comprehension with easy material than with hard material.

4. Boys are superior to girls in comprehending the hard material in this study. However, although this result may reflect a true difference between boys and girls on hard material, it may indicate only that the hard material contained more information of interest to boys.

5. Varying the length of passages of story-type material produces no apparent differences in the ability to comprehend such passages.

6. The relationship between listening and reading comprehension does not appear to be altered by length of passage.

Recommendations
1. More attention should be given to oral presentation of subject-matter materials with elementary school children.

2. Further research is needed to discover whether boys actually surpass girls in the comprehension of difficult material, or whether the boys' superiority in this study may

have been caused, instead, by the fact that the difficult material was better suited to the interests of boys.

3. The factor of interest in materials should be the object of future research. Several studies, including this one, have implied that interest may be a more important factor in comprehension than the variables studied.

LANGUAGE STRUCTURE AND LISTENING

Eldonna L. Evertts

The oral reading of the pupils was evaluated by the investigator and rated as excellent, good, average, fair, and poor. These ratings were given a numerical ranking from 1 to 5 and were recorded. A listening test developed by Milton E. Marten [entry 801 in Duker, Listening Bibliography, 2nd ed., 1968] was used to determine the level of listening comprehension. The number of questions answered correctly constituted the score. The range of correct answers was from 2 to 16, with a median of 10. The number of questions answered correctly in the Listening Test constituted the pupil's raw score. These scores were transferred to an arbitrary five-point rating scale, and the ratings were recorded.

There was a relationship between listening comprehension and the structure of children's oral language. The structure of children's oral language as measured by the frequency of use of the 26 common structural patterns was more closely related to listening comprehension than any other variable. Pupils who were rated excellent in listening comprehension used the 26 common structural patterns more frequently than pupils who were rated poor. Fewer short utterances were used by those who ranked high in listening comprehension. These same pupils had a greater average use of movables and subordinate elements and a longer mean sentence length than pupils in the low group. There was no significant difference according to the chi square test of significance in the use of movables or elements of subordination and listening comprehension.

THE EFFECT OF TRAINING IN LISTENING FOR CERTAIN PURPOSES UPON READING FOR THOSE SAME PURPOSES

Maurice S. Lewis

The teacher of reading in the elementary school must concern himself with what to teach, when to teach it, and how to teach it. This is true in the case of teaching children to read for certain purposes. Almost all authorities in the field of reading agree that children should learn to read for different purposes. Most authorities stress the importance of such training in the intermediate grades.

We have two modes of presentation which may be used. In one, the material may be presented orally, that is, read to the pupils by the teacher, while the pupil listens for one or another purpose. In the other, the material may be presented in printed form, and pupils read for a particular purpose.

It is the aim of this study to determine the effect of training in listening for certain purposes upon reading for those same purposes. It is the writer's hypothesis that children can be taught to read effectively for certain purposes by providing a definite program in listening for those purposes.

Purpose

The purpose of this investigation is to determine the effect of training in listening (1) to get the general significance of a passage, (2) to note the details presented on a given topic by a passage, and (3) to predict the outcome of a passage upon the ability of intermediate grade pupils to read for those same purposes.

Method

The data for this investigation were obtained from a control group type of experiment during a period of eleven weeks. The first week was devoted to testing for the purpose of matching the groups. The following six weeks were used for the experiment itself. A final test was given in the seventh week, and a delayed recall test was given in the eleventh week. The steps taken were as follows:

The 357 pupils used in the experiment represented the total enrollment in twelve intermediate grade classes of two schools. They were chosen because they were under the supervision of the investigator and close contact could be maintained with teachers and pupils during the course of the experiment.

In each of the two schools a fourth-, a fifth-, and a sixth-grade, fused-program teacher is responsible for the reading, language, social studies, science, spelling and writing instruction of the upper unit pupils. Each teacher meets two groups daily, one in the forenoon and one in the afternoon. This departmentalized type of organization made it possible for each teacher to teach one experimental and one control group, thus minimizing the effect of teacher differences upon the experiment.

The 357 pupils in the two schools were given a mental ability test, and a reading test which tested the ability to read for the three purposes listed. From the scores made on these two tests one group was designated experimental and one control for each teacher. No attempt was made to match groups exactly at the beginning of the experiment, because it was contemplated that many would have to be eliminated for reasons such as moving and absence.

The Instructional Program
        Both the experimental and the control groups received their regular instruction in reading. In addition the experimental groups received the scheduled training in listening. This training was not given to the control groups. Neither received training in reading for the three purposes.

The program of training in listening included a series of 30 lessons, each approximately fifteen minutes in length. These lessons were given one each day for a period of six weeks. They were read orally by the regular teacher of reading, but not during the time regularly allotted to the teaching of reading. Each lesson included: (1) one selection in which the pupils were asked to listen to get the main idea in the selection; (2) one selection in which the pupils were asked to listen to note the details, and (3) one selection in which the pupils were asked to listen to see if they could predict the outcome of the story. After each selection was read the pupils were asked to answer the questions pertaining to the selection on a check sheet provided. The check sheets were corrected by the pupils and the results recorded

on an individual progress chart.   Check sheets were re-
checked later by the teachers to make sure that they were
accurately scored.

The listening exercises for the 30 lessons were taken
from Gates- Peardon, Practice Exercises in Reading.   The
first 30 exercises for each grade were used.

1. Reading to Get the General Significance

Significant gains were shown by the fifth- grade, sixth-
grade, and total experimental groups between the pretest and
final test.   In the control group significant gains were made
by the fourth grade and the total group.

A comparison of the experimental and control group
shows:

    a.   There is no significant difference between any of
the comparable groups on the pretest.

    b.   The fifth- grade, sixth- grade and total experimen-
tal groups are superior to the comparable control
groups on the final test.

    c.   There is no significant difference between the
comparable experimental and control groups on
the delayed recall test.

2. Reading to Note Details

The fifth- grade and total experimental groups made
significant gains between the pretest and the final test.   Of
the control groups a gain is shown only by the total group.

A comparison of the experimental and control groups
shows:

    a.   There is no significant difference between any of
the groups on the pretest.

    b.   The fifth- grade experimental group is superior
to the fifth- grade control group on the final test.

    c.   The total experimental group is significantly
superior to the control group on the final test.

    d.   There is no significant difference between the
groups on the delayed recall test.

3. Reading to Predict Outcomes

Generally better gains were made in this type of reading by experimental groups than by control groups, between
the pretest and the final test.   Control groups did somewhat

better than experimental groups on the delayed recall test.

A comparison of experimental and control groups
shows:

a. There is no significant difference between the
    groups on the pretest.
b. The fifth-grade experimental group is superior to
    the fifth-grade control group on the final test.
c. The total experimental group is superior to the
    total control group on the final test.
d. There is no significant difference between any of
    the comparable groups on the delayed recall test.

4. Total Paragraph Reading
    The experimental groups made somewhat better gains
between the pretest and the final test than the control group.
The control group did better on the delayed recall test than
the experimental group.

A comparison of the experimental and control groups
shows:

a. There is no significant difference between any of
    the comparable groups on the pretest.
b. There is no significant difference between the
    fourth- and sixth-grade groups on the final test.
c. The fifth-grade experimental group is superior to
    the fifth-grade control group on the final test.
d. The total experimental group is superior to the
    total control group on the final test.
e. There is no significant difference between com-
    parable experimental and control groups on the
    delayed recall test.

AN INVESTIGATION OF THE RELATIONSHIP BETWEEN
LISTENING AND SELECTED VARIABLES

Ann Elizabeth Jackson

The art of listening well is a requisite in modern society. Technological changes which have taken place in the
past two decades have called forth a whole new need in the

use of this receptive language art. As with any learning, a basic background of knowledge and skill is required to practice the art with any degree of success. Teachers must be as fully informed as possible about the effect of variables on listening.

THE PROBLEM

Statement of the Problem
The major aspects of the problem of this study were: (1) to determine the relationship between two independent tests of listening comprehension; (2) to determine the relationship between each of the tests of listening comprehension and reading, intelligence, personality adjustment, teacher assigned marks of scholastic achievement and teacher assigned marks of adjustment in school; (3) to determine if a difference exists in the listening comprehension of boys and girls, between children from families of varying sizes, and between first or only children and children who have a different serial placement in a family, and; (4) to determine if a significant improvement takes place in ability to comprehend through listening during a school year in classrooms in which there is no planned listening instruction.

Hypotheses Tested
The following null hypotheses were tested:

1. There is no significant relationship between two independent tests of listening comprehension.

2. There is no significant relationship between listening comprehension, as measured by two independent tests of listening comprehension, and reading to appreciate general significance, reading to understand precise directions, reading vocabulary, level of comprehension, and reading to note details, as measured by tests of reading; to social adjustment, personal adjustment, and total personality adjustment, as measured by a test of personality; to non-language intelligence, language intelligence, and total intelligence, as measured by a test of intelligence; to scholastic achievement, as determined by a grade-point average of marks in reading, arithmetic, spelling, language, writing, social studies, health, and science assigned by a classroom teacher; and to adjustment in school, as determined by a grade-point average of marks in conduct and attitude assigned by a classroom teacher.

3.   There is no significant difference in listening comprehension, as measured by two independent tests of listening comprehension between boys and girls; between children who are only children or first children in a family and children who hold some other serial placement in a family; and between children from small, medium, or large- size families.

4.   There is no significant improvement in the listening comprehension of children, as measured by two independent tests of listening comprehension, during the school year when no planned instructional program in listening was prescribed.

STUDIES USING MEASURES OF LISTENING

Studies Using Measures of Listening Developed as Independent Projects

Researchers using STEP: Listening have also used a variety of other measures to determine relationships between variables.   At the elementary level the results have not been consistent, perhaps because of the variety of measures and the variety of population, or because no major study has attempted to determine relationship as a primary purpose.

Lewis developed two forms of a listening test for intermediate grades.   The tests administered to 200 fourth, fifth, and sixth graders had correlations of . 68 for form A and . 76 for form B with the Nelson- Denny Reading Test [1see end of section].

Baldauf and Anderson reported on a 1961 study made with 420 fifth graders to determine the relationship between listening comprehension and school achievement.   A coefficient of correlation of . 57 was determined between listening comprehension, measured by STEP: Listening, and word meaning and paragraph meaning of the Stanford Achievement Test.   Correlations between the listening measure and total achievement was . 82.   It was concluded that verbal comprehension appeared to be the largest factor contributing to the inter- correlations between the achievement variables.   The correlation between the mental ability test and listening test was . 52. [2]

Toussaint investigated inter- correlations among reading, listening, arithmetic computation and intelligence in a 1961 study. [3]   The measures of listening were STEP and the Durrell- Sullivan Reading Capacity Test which had a correla-

tion of .70 for the 172 students in the intermediate grades.
The measures of intelligence were a group test and an individual measure. The correlations between each of these and
listening ranged from .24 to .63 with higher relationships between the STEP: Listening and the individual measure of intelligence.

Investigators using the STEP: Listening measure test
have reported various correlations. Toussaint's study was
extremely interesting because both the highest and lowest
correlations of the studies reviewed in this research were
from the Toussaint study. STEP: Listening and SRA Primary
Mental Abilities yielded a correlation of .40, between STEP:
Listening and Stanford-Binet the correlation was .63.

The Durrell-Sullivan Reading Capacity Test yielded
correlations of .24 with SRA Primary Mental Abilities and
.46 with Stanford-Binet.

The highest relationship in the study was between the
two listening tests with a correlation of .70.

The relationship between reading and each of the listening tests was .67 and .58 with the higher relationship
again with STEP: Listening.

The study showed that arithmetic computation alone
offered little predictive value for reading but should be considered in combination with listening and intelligence when
estimates of reading potential are to be made.

In 1964 Ross[4] reported attempting to identify factors
that contribute to listening ability by using STEP: Listening
and a variety of other measures. He identified 43 poor listeners and 47 good listeners in the fifth, sixth, and seventh
grades through the use of the listening test.

Ross selected variables of personality, mental maturity, reading test and mathematics test scores, sociometric
measures, socioeconomic status and assessment of behaviour
by present teachers. The relationship between listening ability and verbal intelligence, .76, was stronger than between
listening and non-verbal intelligence, .28. Correlation with
total intelligence was .51.

Later in the report Ross made an interesting statement:

We commonly assume that the direction of
relationship is from intelligence to listening. How
bright the child is determined by how well he listens. It is interesting to conjecture whether the
opposite might not be true. The child who, for
one reason or another, never learns to listen lives
in a self-made cell isolated from the world about
him. As surely as if he lived in a hidden moun-
tain village or in a hut in the desert, he is cut off
from the stimulating influences that contribute to
optimum development of his intellect.

Coefficients of correlation between listening and adjustment were: total adjustment .42, personal adjustment
.34 and social adjustment .44. The good listeners were
chosen more frequently as work and play partners and teachers ratings indicated the teachers' awareness of these relationships. A relationship of .74 was determined between
listening and reading. Ross does not give separate correlation figures for the high and low listeners although he does
say that there was a difference in each factor in favor of the
high listener.

Studies Using Measures of Listening Developed as Part of a Study

One of the earliest studies at the elementary level
was conducted by Rankin in 1926.[5] He developed a series
of tests of listening and a test of reading comprehension
which had a correlation of .48. The materials were administered to 113 fifth graders and 143 seventh graders.

The general conclusion indicated here is that
reading and listening abilities are quite closely associated, but that their correspondence is far from
perfect. That is, the abilities are sufficiently independent, on account of differences either in nature or nurture, so that individuals may stand high
in one ability and not in another.

The test of intelligence which Rankin administered to
the group yielded a correlation coefficient of .56 with the
test of listening.

Hollow reported a study in 1955[6] which was designed
to determine the value of instruction in listening for intermediate grade children. Parallel forms of a listening test
were constructed by the investigator as was the instructional

program in listening. A listening pretest had correlations of
.55 with a test of reading comprehension, .47 with reading
vocabulary, and .36 with total language. The listening test
was designed to measure the listeners' ability to summarize,
to draw inferences, to recall facts, and to remember ideas
in sequence. Hollow reported a coefficient of correlation of
.42 between listening and intelligence.

There was no significant difference between the means
of the scores of boys and girls on the listening tests. Size
of family made no significant difference. Best performers
on the first listening test had an average of 2.72 brothers
and sisters while poorest listeners had an average of 3.16
siblings, but the difference was not statistically significant.

Pratt's study in 1956[7] was an attempt to test and
teach listening. The experiment involved 40 classrooms
chosen at random from a variety of school systems. Intelligence tests, reading achievement tests, and a specially
constructed listening test were administered.

Pratt, using his own listening test and the Pintner
General Abilities Test as a mental test, found a correlation
of .66 between the measures. Pratt said, "Intelligence
seems to play about the same role in listening that it does
in reading, arithmetic, social studies and science." The
measure of reading was the Iowa Silent Comprehension Reading Tests; he reported a correlation of .64 between listening
and reading.

Lundsteen reported a research study[8] in 1963 concerned with ways to teach and measure critical listening of
263 fifth and sixth graders. The instructional program and
the test were both constructed for the study by the researcher. Correlation between the Stanford Achievement Test of
Reading and the Critical Listening Test was .47. Critical
listening is "a highly conscious process involving analysis, a
questioning attitude and keeping a standard in mind while
judging."

The Lundsteen study reports correlations between the
California Test of Mental Maturity and the Lundsteen Test of
Critical Listening to be: verbal .43; non-verbal .26; total
.39. Using the same population Lundsteen reports a correlation of .64 between her listening test and the Pratt test of
general listening.

COMPARISON OF LISTENING AND SELECTED VARIABLES

Measures of listening and studies using measures of listening have been limited at the elementary level. Only one standardized test is available by name although at least one other test has been used as a standardized measure. Most of the tests used to measure listening have been a part of the study which included some other areas of investigation, usually the efficacy of a program of listening instruction.

Correlations between variables have been determined only as a part of a study with some other purpose or in a study in which only a few relationships were to be investigated. Reading has received the most attention from investigators in determining relationships. Intelligence has been reported with some frequency as a variable with a relationship to listening; however, this has usually been because the investigation used the scores of the tests for other purposes in the studies.

Reported correlational studies which have been frequently quoted are at all levels and are not suited for comparison because of the differences in the age levels of the populations.

Listening and Reading

Listening and reading are both receptive areas of the language arts and as such share comprehension, evaluation, and interpretation. Reading can be done at the individual's own rate of speed and rereading can take place at any time to clear up misunderstanding or to fix in mind a desired point. The listener is at the mercy of the speaker who is in control of rate, amount of emphasis, and interaction. For the listener there is only one opportunity to obtain the message and establish pertinent information.

The National Education Association study, Deciding What to Teach, [9] includes a section about reading in which the comment is made: "Reading skills are part of a large complex of communication skills. They are closely related to the skills required for effective listening and for oral and written expression."

Listening and Personality

Individual differences can never be overlooked when one works successfully with human beings.

Beery has a rather lengthy discussion about the inter-relationships between listening and the other language arts area, and mentions their relationship to personal development.

> The interrelationships among the language arts point to the need for a s chool program that teaches them in harmony with each other and with the larg-er purposes which language serves in the develop-ment of the individual and his relationship with others. [10]

A study which has used a personality test at the ele-mentary level was done by Ross[11] with good and poor listen-ers. He found correlations between STEP: Listening and the California Test of Personality, as follows: total adjustment .42; personal adjustment .34; social adjustment .44.

Listening and Intelligence

Investigators have been concerned with the relationship between listening and intelligence.   The very manner of ad-ministration of both kinds of tests has made comparison ob-vious.

The studies which have been reviewed in this chapter have generally included a correlation between listening and intelligence.   Correlations between listening and reading seem to be somewhat closer than correlations between listening and intelligence.

Listening and Scholastic Achievement

Nichols[11] reported a low correlation between teacher-assigned marks and listening.   Canfield[12] reported a coeffi-cient of correlation of .74 at the elementary level.   Ross[13] used academic marks as a factor but does not report a co-efficient of correlation.   He says, "Academically good listen-ers surpassed poor listeners.   Good listeners' school marks in reading and arithmetic were significantly higher than those of poor listeners."

Listening Differences Between Boys and Girls

In the primary grades the ability to read is generally different between boys and girls with the latter having an ad-vantage.   Studies in listening have shown no distinct advan-tage to either sex at any grade level.

The technical report of STEP: Listening indicates that on listening tests boys and girls performed similarly throughout the range of grades for which they have information.

Scores in Hollow's[14] study of fifth graders showed the mean or the boys' initial listening score to be 33.17, the mean of the girls' scores 32.71. The difference of the means was not significant.

Caffrey[15] found mean scores of all listening tests to be higher for boys at the secondary level. Hampleman[16] found boys' listening ability superior to girls in materials he called "hard." He surmises that the difference may have been due to a greater interest in the materials by the boys. Nichols[17] reported this kind of finding also, although he suggested his difference might be due to greater motivation by males.

King[18] investigated differences in ability of the sexes in listening and reading comprehension in the primary school of England. He reported that girls did not react more to either method of presentation but that boys returned significantly higher scores (.01 level) on materials presented orally.

Lundsteen[19] reported that girls appeared to be better critical listeners than boys. The difference was significant.

Listening and Serial Placement in a Family

Research about the listening ability of first or only children has been negligible. The most reliable information in this area comes from the speech development studies which indicate more mature language patterns for only children.

Listening and Size of Family

Bean[20] investigated the psychology of language and reports that

> If it is true that children improve faster in language through their association with children, as is supposed, then through contact only with adults, one of its causes is the necessity for more adequate expression of their thoughts that are intended to be understood by children.

He continues by saying that the fastest growth would be with both children and adults because adults would present new words and idioms while children would have conversation about topics of interest to them.

Hollow[21] and Nichols[22] reported no significant differences in listening ability because of family size.

Improvement in Listening Ability

The studies which report change in listening ability have been concerned with an instructional program in listening. Taylor[23] infers that listening ability does not improve in the later intermediate grades and junior high school as much as reading.

> Below the sixth or seventh grade, individual students will tend to prefer reading as soon as their reading proficiency reaches or exceeds the level of their listening proficiency. If their reading development is slow, they will continue to rely most heavily on listening beyond the seventh grade.

The change in learning to listen will in itself depend on many variables. The assumption does appear to be reasonable that some change would take place as a normal life process.

SUMMARY

The literature on listening includes few studies at the elementary level which have investigated correlations of more than a few variables. The range of correlations has been nearly as wide as within the grade level limitations as it is when grade levels have been ignored.

The variables of reading and intelligence have received the greatest amount of attention from investigators. The availability of testing devices in those fields and the interest in reading in the school situation have probably prompted the more extensive investigation of those relationships.

Other variables seem to merit recognition only as they can supplement a study. There is very little specific information concerning the relationship of listening to the personal life of the individual.

The following instruments were used as measurement tools in this investigation: [see p. 326]

TABLE 1

COEFFICIENTS OF CORRELATION BETWEEN LISTENING
TESTS ADMINISTERED IN THE FALL AND IN THE SPRING
OF THE SAME SCHOOL YEAR

	Lewis	STEP	Comparative Data*
Fall mean	25.64	57.03	
Fall S.D.	6.330	11.491	
Fall S.E. of mean	.422	.767	
Coefficient of Correlation			.7525
Spring mean	28.04	61.56	
Spring S.D.	6.886	9.810	
Spring S.E. of mean	.460	.655	
Coefficient of Correlation			.7350

*Significant at the .01 level of confidence.

TABLE 2

COEFFICIENTS OF CORRELATION BETWEEN SCORES ON
TESTS READING ABILITY AND SCORES
ON TESTS OF LISTENING

Reading	Lewis*	STEP*
General Significance	.4985	.4418
Understanding Directions	.5549	.5754
Note Details	.5211	.4882
Vocabulary	.6625	.6637
Level of Comprehension	.7008	.6803

*All correlations were significant at the .01 level of confidence.

TABLE 3

COEFFICIENTS OF CORRELATION BETWEEN SCORES ON
TESTS OF SOCIAL, PERSONAL, AND TOTAL PERSONALITY
ADJUSTMENT, AND SCORES ON TESTS OF LISTENING

Adjustment	Lewis*	STEP*
Social	.4255	.4471
Personal	.4448	.4272
Total Personality	.4692	.4720

*Significant at the .01 level of confidence.

TABLE 4

COEFFICIENTS OF CORRELATION BETWEEN SCORES ON
LANGUAGE, NON-LANGUAGE, AND TOTAL INTELLIGENCE,
AND SCORES ON TESTS OF LISTENING

Intelligence	Lewis*	STEP*
Language	.7405	.7064
Non-Language	.6399	.6689
Total	.7470	.7470

*Significant at the .01 level of confidence.

TABLE 5

COMPARISON OF SCORES BETWEEN BOYS AND GIRLS ON
THE LEWIS LISTENING TEST AND THE STEP
LISTENING TEST

Test	Measure			t Score*
Lewis	Mean	25.6330	25.6522	
	S.D.	6.1236	6.5210	
				.0225
STEP	Mean	57.0261		
	S.D.	10.5868	12.2875	
				.0128

*Differences not significant at the .05 level of confidence.

TABLE 6

COMPARISON OF TEST SCORES OF LISTENING ABILITY
OF FIRST OR ONLY CHILDREN AND OTHER
CHILDREN IN A FAMILY

Test	Measure	Only child or first child	Children other than first or only	t Score*
Lewis	Mean	25. 9615	25. 5465	
	S. D.	5. 5503	6. 5453	
				. 4126
STEP	Mean	58. 1538	56. 6977	
	S. D.	9. 4856	12. 0117	
				. 7983

*Differences not significant at the . 05 level of confidence.

TABLE 7

COMPARISON OF TEST SCORES OF LISTENING ABILITY
OF CHILDREN FROM SMALL AND MEDIUM FAMILIES

Test	Measure	Small size families	Medium size families	t Score*
Lewis	Mean	27. 0169	25. 9278	
	S. D.	5. 1139	6. 5034	
				1. 0195
STEP	Mean	58. 9153	57. 9588	
	S. D.	8. 4739	10. 7050	
				. 5802

*Differences not significant at the . 05 level of confidence.

TABLE 8

COMPARISON OF TEST SCORES OF LISTENING ABILITY
OF CHILDREN FROM SMALL AND LARGE FAMILIES

Test	Measure	Small size families	Large size families	t Score*
Lewis	Mean	27.0169	24.0441	
	S.D.	5.1139	6.6850	
				2.7598
STEP	Mean	58.9153	54.0882	
	S.D.	8.4739	14.0092	
				2.2870

*Differences significant at the .05 level of confidence.

TABLE 9

COMPARISON OF TEST SCORES OF LISTENING ABILITY
OF CHILDREN FROM MEDIUM AND LARGE FAMILIES

Test	Measure	Medium size family	Large size family	t Score*
Lewis	Mean	25.9278	24.0441	
	S.D.	6.5034	6.6850	
				1.7994
STEP	Mean	57.9588	54.0882	
	S.D.	10.7050	14.0092	
				1.9977*

*Difference significant at the .05 level of confidence.

The Sequential Tests of Educational Progress, Listening, 4A.[24] This was one instrument used as a measure of
listening. Form 4A was used in the fall and spring. A
parallel form of the test was available but was not used.

Listening Comprehension Test, Grades Four, Five,
and Six Form A.[25] A diagnostic test of listening comprehension constructed by Lewis was the second measure of listening. Alternative forms of the test were available; however, the same form was used both fall and spring to be
consistent with the use of the other listening test.

A list of possible factors to be used in designing the
test was submitted to a panel of 21 authorities in the field
of language arts. On the basis of their recommendations
and the judgment of the investigator the test was designed to
measure five listening skills: (1) ability to get the main
idea from a selection; (2) ability to recall facts and details;
(3) ability to make inferences from the facts presented in a
selection; (4) ability to recognize word meanings from context; and (5) ability to follow directions.

Subjective validation of selections and related questions were carried out with a group of pupils from fourth-,
fifth-, and sixth-grade classes. The coefficient of reliability
computed by the alternate forms method was .78. Item
analysis was made to determine the internal consistency of
the test. The average item correlation was .24 for form A.

The Gates Basic Reading Tests[26] are made up of five
tests which measure: (1) Reading to Appreciate General
Significance; (2) Reading to Understand Precise Directions;
(3) Level of Comprehension; (4) Reading to Note Details; and
(5) Reading Vocabulary. These reading tests were selected
for the study because they consist of tests which are nearly
comparable in content to those of the two listening tests. Alternate forms are available, however, form 1 was used in
both fall and spring testing.

The 1953 revision of the California Test of Personality, Form AA,[27] is a group test which was used as the
measure of personality adjustment. Separate scores are
computed for personal adjustment and total test. The test
has been organized in terms of logical analysis of compo-
nents and the experience and judgment of those involved in
making the test.

Reliability coefficients were computed using the Kuder-Richardson formula. Coefficients of reliability for form AA are: personal adjustment .93; social adjustment .92; total adjustment .94.

In 1963 the short form of the California Test of Mental Maturity[28] was used to determine intelligence. The test has scores for language, non-language, and .95 for total.

References (numbers refer to entries in Duker, Listening Bibliography, 2nd ed., Scarecrow, 1968).

1. Maurice S. Lewis, 720.
2. Harold M. Anderson and Robert J. Baldauf, 51.
3. Donald L. Cleland and Isabella H. Toussaint, 1188.
4. Ramon Ross, 1021.
5. Paul T. Rankin, 983.
6. Sister Mary K. Hollow, 578.
7. Lloyd E. Pratt, 970.
8. Sara W. Lundsteen, 764.
9. National Education Association. Deciding What to Teach. Project on the Instructional Program of the Public Schools. Washington, D.C.: National Education Association, 1963, p. 123.
10. Althea Beery, 67.
11. Ralph G. Nichols, 873.
12. Robert G. Canfield, 172.
13. Ross, 1021.
14. Hollow, 578.
15. John Caffrey, 161.
16. Richard S. Hampleman, 510.
17. Nichols, 873.
18. W. H. King, 663.
19. Lundsteen, 764.
20. C. H. Bean. "An Unusual Opportunity to Investigate the Psychology of Language." Journal of Genetic Psychology 40: 181-201, 1932, p. 195.
21. Hollow, 578.
22. Nichols, 873.
23. Stanford E. Taylor, 1173.
24. Sequential Tests of Educat. Progress (STEP), 1069.
25. Lewis, 720.
26. Gates Basic Reading Tests. New York: Bureau of Publications Teachers College, Columbia University, 1958.
27. California Test of Personality, Form AA. Devised by Ernest W. Tiegs, Willis W. Clark, and Louis P.

Thorpe.   Monterey, California: California Test Bureau,
1953.
     28.   California Test of Mental Maturity, 1963 revision.
Devised by Elizabeth Sullivan, Willis W. Clark, and Ernest
W. Tiegs.   Monterey, California: California Test Bureau,
1963.

LISTENING AND SOCIAL VALUES

Jewell H. T. Hancock

     The problem of this study was to provide through the
instrumentality of critical listening and directed discussion
an answer to the question: To what extent can certain social
values be changed?

     The chief purposes of this study were:

     1.   To discover what social values are held by sixth-
grade children.

     2.   To select materials to be read to children to
help them to modify their thinking and behavior relative to
social values.

     3.   To gain better understanding of the three impor-
tant aspects of such values, namely: (1) where the values
come from; (2) what the values are doing for us; and (3) why
we hold on to them.

     4.   Through skillful leadership in listening and di-
rected discussion to enable children in the study to bring into the open their personal experiences as a basis for a discussion of their values.

     5.   To determine the extent to which the children
changed their social values after concentrated listening and
discussion.

     The population consisted of sixth-grade children en-
rolled in Negro schools in Tyler, Texas.   The study group
was composed of 82 boys and girls, grouped heterogeneously
in self-contained classrooms.

It has been suggested that the social studies teacher deals with the most complex of all phenomena-- man's behavior as a member of social groups-- and it is in this area that the greatest need for understanding, knowledge, wisdom and insight exists. It is particularly significant in times of crises that the fundamental assumptions on which we base behavior be as clear and precise as we can make them. The obligation for inculcating such social values as leadership and responsibility has come to rest more heavily on our schools and teachers.

The findings from recent investigations have revealed that many children do not know how to respond in socially accepted ways. Several of the studies were seeking to find out whether a child knew the right response to a situation and whether he would expect another child to act according to that knowledge. The fact that a child does not always know the correct response and does not always expect others to make what he thinks is the right response should be of serious concern to all those who work with children.

An attempt was made to utilize reading materials in which social values were evident and questions on textbook materials in such a way that the child would be able (1) to identify himself with the characters in the story and to recognize how the emotional experiences of the characters in the story provided an extension of his own experience; (2) to note the kinds of behavior that are practiced and rewarded; and (3) to identify and understand satisfactions that come as a result of different kinds of approval and disapproval of behavior.

The three-group method was used in this experiment. This is an extension of the two-group experimental method which permits one of the three groups to receive an intermediate or lesser form of the experimental factor. The three groups were designated as Experimental Group I, which was taught social values through listening to specific stories, directed discussion and questioning; Experimental Group II, which was taught social values as identified and pointed up in textbook materials; and Control Group, which received no specific instruction on social values.

In Experimental Group I the social values drawn from The Behavior Preference Record were pointed up, defined and discussed in the class. Problems checked on The SRA Junior Inventory provided a point of departure for exploring and assimilating the values of leadership and responsibility.

To provide for continuity of the children's learnings
and to structure the environment for listening and discussion
relative to the selected reading material, four units were
planned for Experimental Group I.

In accordance with the unit themes drawn from problem situations a series of lessons was planned for the reading material. Only materials were selected in which the
concepts of leadership or responsibility were implicit.

Once per week for 24 weeks a story or other imaginative reading material was read by the investigator to 28
sixth-grade children in a self-contained classroom. The discussion pattern followed a modified form of the following sequence:

1. Introduction of the story. A clarification of new
terms. Information about where the story can be located.
An approach which ties the story with the experience of the
particular group of children.

2. A reading of the story by the researcher.

3. A retelling of what occurred in the story to be
sure that each child understood.

4. A probing into what happened in feelings.

5. A stimulation of the children to identify similar
incidents from their experiences, and to bring in similar experiences from radio, television, travel, etc.

6. Provide opportunity (1) for the exploration of the
consequences of certain behavior and feelings; (2) for asses-
sing incentives of children and other groups; and (3) for
seeking new or broader meanings embodied in leadership
and responsibility such as unselfishness, self-reliance, approval of friends, and rewards.

7. Formulating conclusions and generalizations about
the consequences of certain behavior and feelings. Telling
what he liked best in the story and what he liked least.

This method or plan encouraged the children to think
about their beliefs in connection with a particular pattern of

behavior, allowed the acceptance of some values if the consequences seemed constructive, encouraged the questioning
and rejection of others where the consequences warranted.

A total of 28 lessons were planned, but only 24 were
used in the study. Many of the books which contained the
stories had to be secured from publishers and were not
available in the public school libraries. In such cases, the
books were left in the classroom for the children to explore.

Great effort was made to provide an environment
which would facilitate the learning of democratic values, for
it is in the propitious environment that children can build
feelings, ideas and behaviors which lead to a comfortable,
responsible and creative life.

FINDINGS

Leadership

1. Boys and girls subjected to the experimental variable of listening and discussion made greater gains in the
social value of leadership than the control group when comparisons were made among groups.

2. Boys and girls subjected to the experimental variable of textbook materials made greater gains in leadership
than the control group when comparisons were made among
groups.

3. When each experimental group of boys was compared separately with the control group the gain in leadership was not significant.

4. Girls taught through listening and discussion did
not make significant gains in leadership when compared with
the control group.

5. Girls subjected to the experimental variable of
textbook materials made significant gains in leadership when
compared with the control group.

Supporting evidence from the checklist of critical incidents concurred roughly with the above findings.

Responsibility

1. Boys and girls who received the experimental
variable of listening and discussion made significant gains in

responsibility over the control group when comparisons were made among groups.

2. Boys and girls who were subjected to the experimental variable of textbook material made greater gains in responsibility than the control group when comparisons were made among groups.

3. Boys taught through listening and discussion made significant gains in responsibility when compared with the control group.

4. Boys taught through the use of textbook materials did not make significant gains in responsibility when compared with the control group.

5. When each experimental group of girls was compared separately with the control group the gain in responsibility was statistically significant.

6. Girls in the experimental groups demonstrated more significant gains in the social value responsibility than did the boys.

Evidence from the checklist of critical incidents supported the above findings to a significant degree.

The boys showed more improvement in critical thinking than did the girls.

CONCLUSIONS

1. Children in the sixth grade have acquired certain social values which they will express in a permissive environment.

2. Desirable modifications of social values can be brought about through a listening and discussion approach and through textbook materials. This method should provide for the use of the self-perceived problems and social values of children as a point of departure. Further, the technique should provide for the internalizing of social values.

3. There was considerable evidence of desirable modification in social values among these sixth-grade children which could not be tabulated in exact figures. The children demonstrated an openmindedness and a questioning at-

titude toward various behavior patterns which had heretofore received little or no attention.

4. Some individuals involved in the study did not show growth in social values as measured by the test used and in the setting of this particular experiment. It was not expected that uniform results would be achieved even if there had been uniform treatment.

5. The instructional techniques which were used in this study are effective classroom procedures for modifying social values.

LISTENING TO MUSIC AND TO LANGUAGE

Justyn L. Graham

The problem of the study was to determine the extent to which listening could be improved in individual fourth- and fifth-grade pupils through the use of a series of lessons designed to teach identifiable listening skills in the area of music.

The study was delimited in the following ways: (1) the lessons in listening were constructed in the area of music; (2) the daily lessons were approximately ten minutes in length; (3) the instructional period encompassed five consecutive weeks of the school year; (4) the population of the study consisted of 318 pupils in grades four and five; (5) the regular classroom teachers administered the listening tests and presented the prepared lessons as directed in the manual; (6) the lessons were constructed around the four listening skills found to be mentioned with greatest frequency in the literature.

Pupils making up the population of the study were randomly assigned to an experimental group or a control group.

Preliminary meetings were held with the 13 participating teachers to orient them to the plan of the project. Materials which each teacher would use were distributed and assistance was given in helping the teachers to interpret the materials properly.

Alternate forms of the Hollow Test of Listening Comprehension were administered by the classroom teachers as
a pretest prior to the initiation of the instructional period
and as a post test at the close of the instructional period.
Although the alternate forms of the listening test were reported by the author of the test to be comparable instruments
for measuring listening (r = .88), a precaution was taken to
prevent any possible variability of the forms from affecting
the results of the experiment. One-half of the experimental
and of the control pupils were administered Form A initially
and the other half of the experimental and control pupils,
Form M. At the close of the experimental period, the procedure was reversed.

The study utilized a teacher replication technique of
instruction. This means that each teacher taught the listening lessons to the pupils in her classroom who were assigned
to the experimental group and also taught, for an equal
amount of time, a period of library reading to the pupils
who were assigned to the control group. A tape recorder
was utilized by the teacher during the instructional period
for the experimental group.

Because teachers, administrators, and supervisors
need valid information which will give them greater insight
into problems of teaching listening, the study answered the
following questions:

(1) Can listening be taught through the use of lessons
     in listening to music?
(2) To what extent can listening be improved in indi-
     vidual fourth- and fifth-grade pupils?

Findings
      The statistical technique analysis of covariance was
selected as the method of treatment to be applied to the raw
score data collected.

The F statistic of 90.0459 indicated a difference between the experimental and control groups which was significant at the .05 level.

The F statistic of 3.9838 was significant at the .05
level which suggests that Form M of the Hollow test was
more sensitive to measuring gains in listening than Form A.

Conclusions
        1.   The fact that pupils in the experimental group made significant gains through lessons in listening to music indicates that transfer took place and also raises interesting questions concerning transfer in other academic areas.

        2.   Psychological researchers are in the process of developing projective personality tests which utilize ambiguous sound stimuli as a method of personality assessment. It was suggested by the writer that some of the pupils may have used lessons in listening as a vehicle to meet psychological needs.

        3.   Ability to listen seems to be a trait which is unevenly distributed among elementary school pupils.   Research findings in this area have implications for every teacher who would like to nurture more effective listening habits in her pupils.

GENERAL INFORMATION SHEET

        The teaching of listening skills through the use of music in grades four and five is a cooperative learning project involving pupils, teachers, and administrators.

        Each teacher will work from the Manual of Directions accompanying Form A and Form M while administering the Listening Test and from the Teacher's Manual while teaching the lessons in listening to the pupils assigned to the experimental group.   It is important that the teacher be familiar with the material before it is presented to the pupils.   The test is administered orally throughout.   The sample exercises may be discussed in class.   All other work is to be done independently.   Each story and accompanying answers may be read only one time unless some outside disturbance makes it impossible for the teacher to be heard and understood. Pupils will use separate answer sheets to record their answers.   The answer sheets should be collected immediately following the completion of the test.

        Physical conditions in the room should be adjusted prior to the initiation of the test or lesson.   The seating should be arranged so as to enable pupils to work independently.   The DO NOT DISTURB sign (which has been provided for you) should be placed on the classroom door while the listening test or listening lesson is in progress.   Pupils should be allowed a "break" of five or ten minutes when the test is about half over.

The listening lessons are presented in four units; six lessons in each unit. Each lesson is presented in four parts: Objective, Preparatory period, Presentation period, and Post-listening period. The teacher will make the purpose of the lesson known to the pupils at the beginning of each lesson. The preparatory period will be a short interval of "instructional talk," aimed at "setting the scene" for the presentation period which follows. With the exception of two lessons, a tape recorder will be utilized by the classroom teacher during the presentation period of the lesson. The recorder should be placed where it can be seen by all the pupils in the classroom. During the post-listening period, the pupils will have an opportunity to discuss and react to the listening lesson which was played. The questions, appearing in the Teacher's Manual, should be used to lead and guide discussion of the lesson. The discussion should be conversational in nature, involving as many pupils as possible. Pupils may give answers which are basically the same, as those listed should be accepted as correct. Further questions and discussion on the part of the pupils should be encouraged.

Each teacher will work from the Teacher's Manual which has been prepared to supplement the lessons which are presented on magnetic tape. The information in the lesson plan appearing in small letters is instructional material for the teacher. The material written in capital letters is to be read to the pupils. The teacher will need to be familiar with the lessons before presenting them to the children. The lessons are approximately ten minutes each in length. The teacher will have a degree of control over the time element in the lessons.

The design of the project calls for the control group to receive daily instruction in library reading taught by the classroom teacher. This period should equal the time required to instruct the experimental group as described in the previous paragraphs. The two treatment groups will be instructed separately. Each pupil assigned to the control group must have a library book which he can read during this library reading period. The teacher may give assistance to the pupils as needed, helping with words, aiding in making a book report, and otherwise maintaining a desirable classroom situation. Here again, physical conditions of the room should be adjusted prior to the reading period and the DO NOT DISTURB sign placed on the door.

Please keep a careful record of attendance. No make-up or home assignments will be required. Pupils enrolling in your classroom during the project period may be random-ly assigned to one of the two treatment groups by flipping a coin; heads will put him in the experimental group, tails will place him in the control group.

The pupils should understand that:

1. This is a new learning experience which they will have fun doing. We hope it will enable them to become bet-ter listeners and better learners.

2. Listening requires effort on the part of the learn-er. It is not always easy to be a good listener; whereas, hearing is something which we do all the time while we are awake.

3. The scores they make on the listening tests and the work they do in the listening lessons and/or reading period will not appear on their grade cards.

4. A letter has been prepared for each pupil to take home and give to his parents. It will help mothers and fathers to have a better understanding of what we are doing.

MANUAL FOR TEACHING LISTENING LESSONS IN MUSIC

The following material is a manual for your use in teaching lessons in listening. The manual should be fol-lowed closely. Each of the lessons will require approximate-ly ten minutes to complete. In 23 of the lessons, a tape recorder will be utilized by the classroom teacher during the presentation period. Because of the nature of the mate-rial in one of the lessons (No. 1, Following Instructions), the teacher will present the lesson without using the tape recorder. The tape recorder should be placed where all of the pupils can see it as well as hear it.

Each lesson has its own directions. The teacher should study the material prior to the time for the listening lesson. Instructions and directions are to be given only one time. Information may be repeated if a class bell or other noise has made the teacher's words inaudible. In the les-sons which require the pupils to do some writing, paper will be furnished. It is to be distributed to the pupils prior to the beginning of the lesson.

Adjust the physical conditions of the room before the listening lesson begins. Interruptions during the lesson should be avoided.

Please make note of any event or occurrence which might have an influence on listening during the experimental period (the period during which the listening lessons or library reading is being taught).

LISTENING LESSONS--MUSIC

Unit I.   "Listening for Details" (Lesson No. 1)

Objective: To develop the ability to listen in order to detect likenesses and differences in rhythm patterns.

Preparatory period: WE ARE GOING TO HEAR SOME SHORT RHYTHM PATTERNS. IF THE PATTERNS ARE ALIKE, YOU WILL WRITE "YES" ON YOUR PAPER. IF THE PATTERNS ARE DIFFERENT, YOU WILL WRITE "NO." LISTEN FIRST TO THE EXAMPLE. Play the example. NOW WRITE YOUR NAME AT THE TOP OF YOUR PAPER.

Presentation period: Play the rhythm patterns as presented on the tape recording. Allow pupils five to ten seconds to write their answers (yes or no) to each rhythm pattern.

Post-listening period: Re-play the tape and check the answers. Each child should check his own paper. Collect the papers.

ANSWER KEY-
Unit I.   "Details" (Lesson 1)
1. Yes   4. No
2. No   5. No
3. No   6. Yes

Unit I.   "Listening for Details" (Lesson No. 2)

Objective: To develop the ability to listen in order to distinguish likenesses and differences in pitch.

Preparatory period: TODAY WE WILL LISTEN TO TWO NOTES. IF THE SECOND TONE IS THE SAME AS THE FIRST, YOU WILL WRITE "YES" ON

YOUR PAPER; IF IT IS DIFFERENT, YOU WILL
WRITE "NO." LISTEN FIRST TO THE EX-
AMPLE. Play the example. WRITE YOUR
NAME AT THE TOP OF YOUR PAPER.

Presentation period: Play the tone patterns as presented on
the tape recording. Allow pupils five to ten
seconds to write their answers (yes or no) to
each tone pattern.

Post-listening period: Re-play the tape and check the answers. Each child should check his own paper.
Collect the papers.

ANSWER KEY-
Unit I. "Details" (Lesson 2)

1.	Yes	4.	No
2.	No	5.	No
3.	Yes	6.	No

Unit I. "Listening for Details" (Lesson No. 3)

Objective: To develop the ability to listen so as to distinguish likenesses and differences in short melodies.

Preparatory period: IN OUR LISTENING PERIOD TODAY,
TWO SHORT MELODIES WILL BE PLAYED.
IF THE SECOND IS LIKE THE FIRST, AN-
SWER "YES" ON YOUR PAPER: IF IT IS DIF-
FERENT, ANSWER "NO." LISTEN FIRST TO
THE EXAMPLE. Play the example. WRITE
YOUR NAME AT THE TOP OF YOUR PAPER.

Presentation period: Play the melodies as presented on the
tape recording. Allow pupils five to ten seconds
to write their answers (yes or no) to each mel-
ody.

Post-listening period: Re-play the tape and check the answers. Each child should check his own paper.
Collect the papers.

ANSWER KEY-
Unit I. "Details" (Lesson 3)

1. Yes   4. Yes
2. No   5. Yes
3. Yes   6. No

Unit II.   "Identifying the Main Idea or Theme" (Lesson No. 1)

Objective: To develop the ability to listen for the main idea
                or theme (melody) in a selection of music.

Preparatory period: Arouse interest in today's exercise by
                placing the prepared illustrations of a tree on
                the chalk board or in a place where it can be
                seen by all members of the class.   BOYS AND
                GIRLS, YOU WILL NOTICE NOT ALL THE
                BRANCHES OF THE TREE ARE THE SAME
                SIZE.   SOME OF THE BRANCHES ARE MUCH
                LARGER AND VERY IMPORTANT FOR THE
                GROWTH OF THE TREE. SMALLER BRANCHES
                STEM FROM THESE LARGE ONES.   THEY
                ARE A PART OF THE TREE, TOO, BUT ARE
                NOT AS IMPORTANT TO THE WELL- BEING
                OF THE WHOLE TREE.   IN OUR LISTENING
                TODAY, WE WILL BE INTERESTED IN HEAR-
                ING THE MAIN PARTS OF TWO FAMILIAR
                SONGS.   YOU MAY THINK OF THEM IN THE
                SAME WAY AS THE MAIN PARTS OF A TREE.
                AS YOU LISTEN TO THESE TWO S ONGS, NO-
                TICE HOW THE FIRST MELODY, OR MAIN
                THEME, IS HEARD AGAIN.   SEE IF YOU CAN
                HEAR W HEN THE MAIN IDEA OR THEME IS
                REPEATED.

Presentation period: Play "Lullaby" by Brahms and "Dixie"
                by Emmett as presented on the tape recording.

Post- listening period: Discuss with the class the theme or
                main idea as illustrated by these two familiar
                melodies.   Direct the class to hum the theme
                to each of the melodies.   NOTICE THAT THE
                MAIN THEME IN EACH OF THESE SELEC-
                TIONS IS REPEATED A NUMBER OF TIMES.
                THIS IS HOW WE CAN TELL IT IS THE MAIN
                THEME OR THE SELECTION.   THE MUSIC IN
                EACH PIECE SEEMS TO BE BUILT AROUND
                THIS IMPORTANT LITTLE TUNE WHICH IS
                HEARD IN DIFFERENT WAYS THROUGHOUT

THE SELECTION.   Play the selections again.
Ask the pupils to raise their hands when they
hear the themes.   Ask the pupils if they can
think of other familiar songs which have main
themes.   Permit pupils to sing, whistle, or
hum tunes which readily show main ideas.   If
no one can think of a song, suggest "The Birth-
day Song" and "For He's a Jolly Good Fellow."
Perhaps a few children will volunteer to sing or
hum one or both of these songs which exemplify
the main idea.

Chapter XII

RESEARCH ON LISTENING

In this final chapter it is my purpose to present excerpts from three research studies that exemplify a variety of research approaches. Obviously there are many other kinds of research; these excerpts, at best, represent only a small sample but it is hoped that they will impress the reader with the flavor of genuine dedication to the discovery of facts by means of scientific research.

The first excerpt is taken from a study supported by the Office of Education. Here Dr. Stodola and his associates investigated the effect of different types of presentation of a listening test. The approach to and the results of this study will be of interest to anyone who may contemplate the administration of any test to a large population.

The second excerpt is from a study by Dr. Edwin Vineyard and Robert B. Bailey in which the interrelationships between listening, reading, intelligence, and scholastic achievement were investigated. The results were obtained by the use of first and second order partial correlations and are clearly and understandably presented in the excerpts reproduced in this chapter.

The last excerpt in this book is taken from a study by Professor Eleanor E. Maccoby of Stanford University and Karl W. Konrad. This research has as its basis the work of Dr. Donald E. Broadbent, the well-known English psychologist who has written widely on various aspects of communication, hearing, and listening. It was the purpose of this study to ascertain whether Broadbent's findings concerning selective listening were valid for young children as well as for adults. Some readers may find that this article requires more careful reading than they are accustomed to. All readers will be repaid for a careful study of this important article about research in the field of listening.

342

ADMINISTERING A LISTENING COMPREHENSION TEST THROUGH USE OF TEACHER-READERS, SOUND FILM, AND TAPE RECORDINGS

Quentin Stodola, Donald F. Schwartz, and Ralph H. Kolstoe

With the increased interest in improving listening habits, there is a need to be sure that scores on presently available listening tests are accurate indicators of pupil listening ability. Teachers want to train pupils how to listen effectively, but how can teachers plan lessons to improve listening if they are not able to measure present skill in listening with confidence? Furthermore, how can research workers measure comparative success of various ways of teaching listening if they are not able to trust test results?

In the listening tests presently available, the teacher reads selections aloud to the pupils and then asks questions on what has been read. .In this kind of test administration, what is the danger of excessive variation in presentation causing a variation in test scores quite apart from the listening ability measured? In other words, would pupils get higher scores if they were tested by a good reader rather than by a poor one?

It seems obvious that an extremely poor reading, such as one spoken so softly that it could not be heard, would greatly lower student scores on a listening test. However, the question is, given normal variation in teacher reading ability, would there be enough difference between "good" and "poor" readers so as to result in significant differences in test scores?

The object of the experiment, then, was to find out whether or not in a typical school situation there is enough variation in reading abilities among teachers so as to have a significant effect on test results. Furthermore, it was hoped to try out some methods other than the usual teacher-reader type administration to determine whether or not undue variation in scores could be decreased.

The Testing Instrument

The Listening Comprehension Tests of the Sequential Tests of Educational Progress were used in this experiment. These tests are available in four levels designed for grades four through fourteen. For this experiment, the tests were used at three levels, grades four through twelve.

Administration of an entire test takes 70 minutes with two 35- minute sections, each section paralleling the other in content and difficulty. For this experiment, the first 35-minute sections of the tests were used at all three levels.

In these tests, the student answers questions about a series of passages read to him. The questions for each passage are read immediately after the passage. The answer options, not the entire questions, are available to the student in a test booklet during the test. The selections represent typical listening situations which the student may encounter in school. They include directions, explanations, stories, arguments, poems, etc. The questions require the student to select the important facts and think critically about them.

Methods of Test Administration

How great are the effects on listening test scores caused by differences among readers? One way to approach this problem is to compare variations in test scores obtained from administrations under typical classroom conditions with teacher- readers, as contrasted with test administrations where differences among readers are presumably eliminated or at least minimized. Accordingly, it was decided to administer the test under four conditions, the first with teacher- readers in typical classroom situations. The other three methods were planned to help eliminate differences among readers as much as possible. It was thought that one of these three methods might provide more stable test results.

These methods of administration are described as follows:

1. REGULAR. The regular classroom teacher reads the test following the directions which are published with the test. Directions require the teacher to practice reading the selections and questions before administering the test.

2. TRAINED. The classroom teacher reads the test after receiving a special two- hour training session including supervised practice in reading the test. Basically, the purpose of the training is to make sure that the teachers actually do follow publisher's directions for giving the test, which include studying the test manual and practicing the selections at the suggested rate. The training does not in-

volve any attempt to change basic speech patterns.

3. MOVIE. The classroom teacher administers the test using a prepared sound motion picture where the test is given by a professional reader. The film is shown in a number of different classrooms using different projectors consistent with normal variations.

4. AUDIO. The classroom teacher administers the test using a prepared tape recording which duplicates the audio portion (sound track) of the motion picture.

The Sample Population
Substantially all the pupils in grades four through twelve of the Fargo Public Schools in Fargo, North Dakota, served as the population.

Results of the experiment were reported to the teachers and community through a half-hour television program and through an article in the North Dakota Teacher, the magazine of the state education association.

TESTING THE STUDENTS

It is believed that the problems encountered in the test administration are typical of those which might be expected in many school systems. In most classes, the administrations went smoothly and standardized procedures were followed.

The results will be discussed separately for high school, junior high school, and elementary school. A different level of the test was used for each of these groups.

Results: High School
The summary of the results of testing at the high school are given in Table 1.

The data in Table 1 were analyzed to determine (1) if the observed differences in variances were greater than that expected by sampling differences and (2) if the differences in means were beyond chance expectations.

TABLE 1

MEANS AND VARIANCES OF LISTENING TEST SCORES BY
METHOD OF PRESENTATION FOR GRADES 12, 11, AND 10

Grade			Regular	Trained	Movie	Audio	Totals
12	$\overline{X}$	(mean)	23.9	24.1	26.9	24.9	25.0
	s^2	(variance)	.81	4.68	1.78	1.84	
	$\underline{n}$		5	5	5	5	20.0
11	$\overline{X}$		24.4	23.0	24.4	24.4	24.0
	s^2		1.85	1.42	.91	1.28	
	$\underline{n}$		5	5	5	5	20.0
10	$\overline{X}$		21.7	23.0	24.4	22.6	22.9
	s^2		.57	3.44	.92	.60	
	$\underline{n}$		5	5	4	5	19.0
TOTALS	$\overline{X}$		23.3	23.3	25.2	23.9	23.9
	$\underline{n}$		15	15	14	15	59.0

Note: $\underline{n}$ refers to number of classes of about 25 pupils each.

It should be noted, from Table 1, that two of the cell
variances are considerably larger than the other ten.   These
two extremes occurred with the trained teachers at the tenth-
grade level and at the twelfth-grade level.   Further inspection indicates that the increased variance in each case is
produced by one class unit.   In the case of the tenth grade,
the score for one class unit is considerably higher than for
the other four.   At the twelfth grade, the score for one class
unit is considerably lower than for the others.

In a sense then, after examining carefully the 59
classes in the twelve groups, only two scores were identified as varying markedly from the others in their group,
possibly because of the method of administration.   Since
there were a relatively large number of classes, the two
"unusual" classes may be explained on the basis of chance
factors quite apart from the way the tests were administered.
It may be simply a matter of chance in the sense that an in-
ordinately large number of poor listeners were assigned to
the low group in the twelfth grade; and conversely by chance
a large number of good listeners may have been assigned to
the class which did better than expected at the tenth grade.
Thus, summing up the evidence, there does not seem to be

much reason to believe that the regular teacher-reader
method of administration leads to any more variability in
test scores than do the other three methods.

The second question--possible variation in means of
the subgroups--was tested by use of a four- by three-way
analysis of variance. This question relates to whether or
not any one of the four methods resulted in generally higher
test scores than did the others. The results of this analysis
are shown in Table 2.

TABLE 2

ANALYSIS OF VARIANCE BY METHODS OF ADMINISTRATION
AND GRADE LEVELS, GRADES 10 - 12

Source of Variation	df	SS	MS	F
Methods of Administration	3	35.72	11.91	6.96**
Grade Levels	2	41.40	20.70	12.11**
Methods X Grade Levels	6	18.68	3.11	1.82
Within Cells	47	80.42	1.71	

**Significant at .01 level.

As indicated in Table 2, the differences among
methods of test administration were significant beyond the
.01 level. As might be expected, highly significant differences among grade levels were also obtained. No interaction effects were noted between methods of administration
and grade level.

The mean score for the movie groups is significantly
higher than for the other three methods at the .05 level and
there are no significant differences among the mean scores
of the other three methods. It would appear then that comprehension of the movie version of the test is better than
other methods.

The fact that students made higher scores with the
movie method should not be interpreted to mean that the
movie is a better testing instrument for measuring listening
ability. From the point of view of statistical reliability,
the less difficult test is not necessarily the best.

Results: Junior High School
        The summary of the results of testing at the junior
high schools are given in Table 3.   The data in Table 3 were
analyzed in a manner similar to the high school group to determine (1) if the observed differences in variance were
greater than that expected by sampling differences and (2) if
the differences in means were beyond chance expectations.

        Using the same procedure as with the high school,
possible variation in means of the subgroups was tested by
use of a four by three analysis of variance.   The results of
this analysis are shown in Table 4.

TABLE 3

MEANS AND VARIANCES OF LISTENING TEST SCORES BY
METHOD OF PRESENTATION FOR GRADES 9, 8, AND 7

Grade		Regular	Trained	Movie	Audio	Totals
9	$\overline{X}$ (mean)	31.2	31.0	31.2	30.3	30.9
	s^2 (variance)	2.23	.87	.94	.70	
	n	5	5	5	5	20
8	$\overline{X}$	30.0	29.7	30.4	29.5	29.9
	s^2	1.32	1.64	2.09	.51	
	n	5	5	5 ·	5	20
7	$\overline{X}$	27.4	27.6	27.0	27.8	27.5
	s^2	1.05	1.05	.97	1.91	
	n	5	5	5	5	20
TOTALS $\overline{X}$		29.5	29.4	29.5	29.2	29.4
	n	15	15	15	15	60

TABLE 4

ANALYSIS OF VARIANCE BY METHODS OF ADMINISTRATION
AND GRADE LEVELS, GRADES 7 - 9

Source of Variation	df	SS	MS	F
Methods of Administration	3	1.01	63.37	.27
Grade Levels	2	127.94	63.97	50.27**
Methods X Grade Levels	6	5.23	.87	.69
Within Cells	48	61.07	1.27	

**Significant at .01 level.

As indicated in Table 4, differences among methods of test administration were not significant. Nor were there any interaction effects between method of administration and grade level. As expected, differences in scores among grade levels were significant beyond the .01 level.

Thus, to sum up results for the junior high school, with this particular test, the method of administration does not appear to affect the variability of scores among class units nor the comprehension level.

Results: Elementary School

No elementary school in the system was large enough to permit replication of each treatment condition at each grade level. Nor (with the exception of one school at grade six) was it possible to administer each treatment condition at least once at any grade level.

This problem was obviously not encountered at the senior high school level where only one school was involved and all the students in the sample were available at one time and location. Nor was it a problem at the junior high school level where there were two schools, but these did not differ significantly in listening test scores.

In the analysis of the listening test scores in the elementary schools, possible differences in the methods of test administration and also difference in grade level are partially confounded by possible differences among schools.

The summary of results of testing at the elementary schools is shown in Table 5.

Following the approach used at the senior and junior high school levels, analysis of variance of test scores was made according to method of administration by grade levels as indicated in Table 6.

Differences among methods were significant at the .05 level and, as expected, differences among grade levels were highly significant. An interaction effect significant at the .05 level casts some doubt on the direct interpretation of the effects of grade level and of methods of administration.

TABLE 5

MEANS AND VARIANCES OF LISTENING TEST SCORES BY
METHOD OF PRESENTATION FOR GRADES 6, 5, AND 4

Grade			Regular	Trained	Movie	Audio	Totals
6	$\overline{X}$	(mean)	34.5	34.3	33.4	32.4	33.7
	$\underline{s}^2$	(variance)	1.31	1.42	1.79	1.49	
	$\underline{n}$		5	5	5	5	20.0
5	$\overline{X}$		31.5	30.6	32.3	32.0	31.6
	$\underline{s}^2$		1.66	1.21	2.66	1.37	
	$\underline{n}$		5	5	5	5	20.0
4	$\overline{X}$		30.4	28.6	31.0	28.8	29.7
	$\underline{s}^2$		1.46	.85	3.07	4.03	
	$\underline{n}$		5	5	5	5	20.0
TOTALS	$\overline{X}$		32.1	31.1	32.2	31.0	31.3
	$\underline{n}$		15	15	15	15	60.0

TABLE 6

ANALYSIS OF VARIANCE BY METHODS OF ADMINISTRATION
AND GRADE LEVELS, GRADES 4 - 6

Source of Variation	df	SS	MS	F
Methods of Administration	3	17.05	5.68	3.05*
Grade Levels	2	155.72	77.86	41.86**
Methods X Grade Levels	6	26.14	4.36	2.34*
Within Cells	48	89.22	1.86	

*Significant at .05 level.
**Significant at .01 level.

At the fourth-grade level, although both the trained
teacher and movie groups have the same rank on the Iowa
Tests of Basic Skills, there is considerable spread between
mean scores of the two groups with the movie being higher.
On the other hand, at the sixth-grade level, the mean scores
for the different methods of administration are consistent

with scores made by the schools on the Iowa Tests of Basic Skills.

It would appear foolhardy to offer with much confidence any explanation for these interaction effects. Interpretation is complicated by the probability that differences among schools are affecting some of the mean scores obtained with the different methods of administration.

However, this hypothesis is tentatively suggested: At the fourth-grade level, teachers speak to their pupils quite slowly and precisely. By the time the sixth-grade level is reached the teachers speak to pupils in a manner more consistent with ordinary patterns of speech. In the testing situation, it may be that the trained teachers, in attempting to follow directions, spoke at a more rapid pace than usual for these pupils. On the other hand, observation indicated that, despite test directions, those administering the test under regular conditions tended to speak more slowly than the others. This may explain why the regular teachers were comprehended better than the trained teachers and the audio at the fourth-grade level.

Of·course, in the fourth grade movie where scores were relatively high, the presentation was consistent in rate with the audio where scores were low. However, the filmed visualization may have compensated for the rapid delivery.

The factors just mentioned may not have been operating at the sixth grade level where the students are accustomed to a more normal speed of delivery of speech. Again, to say the least, this hypothesis for some of the interaction effects between method and grade is offered in a tentative manner.

Actually the differences are not very great among the scores for the various methods of test administration by grade level. At the fifth-grade level, results of the Duncan Multiple Range Test reveal no significant differences at the .05 level of confidence as can be seen in Table 7. At the fourth and sixth grade levels, differences which are significant are also indicated in Table 7.

TABLE 7

DIFFERENCES IN MEAN SCORES AMONG THE
METHODS OF ADMINISTRATION FOR GRADES 6, 5, AND 4*

Grade 6	AUDIO	MOVIE	TRAINED	REGULAR
X̄ (Mean Score)	32.4	33.4	34.3	34.5
Grade 5	TRAINED	REGULAR	AUDIO	MOVIE
X̄ (Mean Score)	30.6	31.5	32.0	32.3
Grade 4	TRAINED	AUDIO	REGULAR	MOVIE
X̄ (Mean Score	28.6	28.8	30.4	31.0

Any two treatment means not underscored by the same line
are significantly different (.05 level of confidence).

Any two treatment means underscored by the same line are
not significantly different (.05 level of confidence).

*Based on Duncan's Multiple Range Test.

Summing up the results for the elementary school
level, there was no evidence of undue variation among scores
for class units using the same methods of test administration.
Nor was the variability of scores among class units using
different methods of test administration especially high. Interaction effects between methods of administration and grade
level were noted.

Discussion of Results
        For reasons of interest, a brief discussion follows
concerning some of the advantages and disadvantages of the
various methods of administering the test apart from the
question of variability of scores.

        1. REGULAR. Possibly the greatest advantage of
this method is that it is more natural than either the
MOVIE or AUDIO methods. The pupil listens to his own
teacher. Neither the pattern of speech nor the mode of presentation is unnatural.

        This method also has the advantage of involving the
teacher directly in the testing process. Since the teacher
has to practice reading the test and questions, she becomes
more aware of exactly what the test is attempting to measure
and she can probably interpret test results better.

This method also permits a certain flexibility. That is, if there is some unusual happening, such as a student having a coughing spell, the teacher can stop, and if necessary, repeat part of a selection or question.

The obvious disadvantage to this method is that it does require considerable time and effort on the teacher's part to prepare for the test. Another disadvantage is that some teachers read the selections in a dull manner, causing pupils to become bored.

2. TRAINED. The purpose of this method was to make sure that the teachers actually followed the publisher's directions in getting ready for the test. Results of the experiment seemed to indicate that this special training was not necessary, that probably in fact the REGULAR teachers who prepared on their own were essentially as well prepared as the TRAINED teachers. Using this method would seem to constitute an extra and unnecessary burden for whoever might be in charge of the special training--probably the school principal or members of his staff. Thus there does not seem to be any special reason for using this method of administration.

3. MOVIE. The greatest advantage of the MOVIE method from the experimenters' point of view was the pleasure that the students seem to get from hearing the selections read by a professional reader. Very few of the teachers, indeed, approached the skill of the professional in the readings they gave.

Another advantage of the MOVIE version of the test is the fact that it is easier for the teacher since she does not have to practice the readings nor give them in the test situation.

With the MOVIE version there is no need to provide test booklets with answer options since these are shown on the screen.

An obvious disadvantage in giving the test by MOVIE is the problem of providing sufficient light for the pupils to mark the answer sheets and still have the room dark enough to view the picture. However, it is felt that this problem was not a serious one in the tests given in Fargo. Generally speaking, if most or all the lights in a room were turned off and the blinds at the front side of the room were pulled, a

kind of half-light was provided that seemed optimal for the
purpose.

Another disadvantage of the MOVIE method is the possibility of mechanical problems caused either by faulty pro-
jection equipment or by teachers inexperienced in projector
operation.

The fact that the MOVIE version of the test seemed
to be better comprehended and scores were higher is not
cited as either an advantage or a disadvantage. It cannot be
said that in this case a slightly easier test made a better
measuring instrument.

The experimenters do not feel competent to attempt
to compare costs of the MOVIE and REGULAR methods of
administration. Obviously, it costs money to make and distribute film. It also costs money to print and distribute test
booklets. Perhaps the extra time required by the teacher to
practice and give the test should also be figured in a cost
estimate comparing the REGULAR and MOVIE methods.

4. AUDIO. Of all the methods for giving the tests,
using the tape recorder was probably easiest for the teacher.
No practice in reading was needed beforehand, and tape recorders are simpler to set up and use than motion picture
projectors. The fidelity of the sound is better than that of
the MOVIE. The cost of making the tape is much less than
the cost of a motion picture.

The absence of visual presentation seemed to make
this method somewhat less stimulating and interesting to the
pupils.

As indicated by the foregoing discussion, there are
advantages and disadvantages to all of the methods of administration. No recommendation is made in favor of any
one of these methods.

INTERRELATIONSHIPS OF READING ABILITY, LISTENING SKILL, INTELLIGENCE, AND SCHOLASTIC ACHIEVEMENT

Edwin E. Vineyard and Robert B. Bailey

Previous research has frequently revealed that various linguistic skills such as reading and listening are positively related and that each is related to scholastic achievement; it has also demonstrated that each of these linguistic skills is positively related to intelligence of the symbolic type as measured by the usual group intelligence test. But only a little research has been done concerning the degree of relationship remaining between these linguistic skills or between each of them and scholastic achievement when the intelligence factor with which each appears to have some degree of saturation is ruled constant, experimentally or statistically. Furthermore, little research has appeared relating either of these linguistic skills to scholastic achievement when the influence of the other is ruled constant, or when both the other and intelligence are ruled constant. Likewise, little is known about the relationship remaining between intelligence and scholastic achievement when either reading or listening skills, or both reading and listening skills, are ruled constant. These are the problems investigated by the present research.

Specifically, the present study seeks to identify the following relationships:

(1) The coefficients of correlation between measures of reading ability, listening skill, intelligence, and scholastic achievement.

(2) First order partial coefficients of correlation between the following: reading ability and scholastic achievement with intelligence constant; listening skill and scholastic achievement with intelligence constant; reading and achievement with listening constant; listening and achievement with reading constant; intelligence and achievement with reading constant; intelligence and achievement with listening constant; listening and reading with intelligence constant; listening and intelligence with reading constant; and reading and intelligence with listening constant.

(3) Second order partial coefficients of correlation

between the following: listening and achievement
with intelligence and listening ruled constant;
reading and achievement with intelligence and listening ruled constant; and intelligence and achievement with listening and reading constant.

Measurement of Variables

Scores from the reading section of the Cooperative
English Test were used as measures of reading ability,
scores from the Listening Test of the Sequential Tests of
Educational Progress as measures of listening skill, total
scores from the American Council on Education Psychological Examination as measures of intelligence, and one year
grade point averages as measures of scholastic achievement.
Subjects for the study were 114 freshmen students of Southwestern State College.

Results of the Study

In attacking the problem outlined previously, the first
step was the derivation of the intercorrelation matrix of the
four variables involved. This is shown in Table 1.

TABLE 1

INTERCORRELATIONS OF READING, LISTENING, INTELLIGENCE AND ACHIEVEMENT

	Listening	Intelligence	Achievement
Reading	.708	.758	.531
Listening		.671	.560
Intelligence			.546

The relationship found between intelligence and achievement is fairly typical as is that between reading and achievement. Too little has been done as yet with listening relationships to judge adequately the typicality of the r's obtained
between this variable and the others, but it would appear that
these are stronger than might have been expected. It can
also be noted that the three symbolic abilities are closely
intercorrelated indicating a great deal of relatedness of those
traits, a high degree of communality in measurement devices,
or both.

Using the zero order r's in Table 1, meaningful first order partial r's between pairs of variables with one other variable ruled constant were calculated. These appear in Table 2. Unmeaningful calculations such as the relationships between mental test scores with achievement ruled constant were avoided.

TABLE 2

PARTIAL INTERCORRELATIONS OF READING, LISTENING, INTELLIGENCE, AND ACHIEVEMENT

Pairs of Variables	Constant	Partial r	Decrements
Listening and Achievement	Intelligence	.313**	.247
Reading and Achievement	Intelligence	.214*	.317
Listening and Reading	Intelligence	.411**	.297
Intelligence and Achievement	Reading	.261**	.285
Intelligence and Achievement	Listening	.277**	.269
Listening and Achievement	Reading	.308**	.252
Reading and Achievement	Listening	.231*	.300
Intelligence and Reading	Listening	.531**	.227
Intelligence and Listening	Reading	.291**	.380

*Significant at the .05 level.
**Significant at the .01 level.

In interpreting the above partial r's, some note should be taken both of their present strength and of the decrement in degree of relationship between the relationship of each pair of variables as a result of the removal of the third. The fact that each of the partial r's is still large enough after the removal of the influence of the third to be statistically significant and that some remain moderately high would indicate that no relationships between any of the studied variables are completely accountable to the influence of a third studied variable. Decrements in general run near the .300 figure in correlational points, reflecting further the high degree of interrelatedness of the variables noted in the interpretation of Table 1.

From the first order partial r's in Table 2 second order partial coefficients were calculated. These are shown in Table 3. Again, unmeaningful partial r's involving ruling achievement constant were avoided.

TABLE 3

SECOND ORDER PARTIAL CORRELATION COEFFICIENTS OF
READING, LISTENING, AND INTELLIGENCE
WITH ACHIEVEMENT

Variable	Constants 1	2	Partial r	Decrements from Partial r's 1	2	Decrements from zero Order r's
Listening	Intelligence,	Reading	.253**	.060	.055	.307
Reading	Intelligence,	Listening	.098	.116	.133	.433
Intelligence	Listening,	Reading	.187*	.090	.074	.359

*Significant at the .05 level.
**Significant at the .01 level.

From data in Table 3, it will be noted that relationship between reading skill and achievement has been reduced below the level of significance. Significant but substantially reduced relationships remain between both Listening and Intelligence with Achievement. All relationships have been considerably reduced from their original size as the partialing out process continued.

Summary
1. Reading ability, listening skill, and intelligence are highly related to one another and each is substantially related to scholastic achievement.

2. Upon the partialing out of the influence of any one variable each pair of other variables still remain significantly correlated although such correlations are substantially reduced in strength.

3. Upon the partialing out of the influence of both intelligence and reading, listening skill remains significantly correlated with achievement as does intelligence when both reading and listening are partialed out. However, upon the partialing out of both intelligence and listening, the relationship between reading and achievement falls below the level of significance.

AGE TRENDS IN SELECTIVE LISTENING

Eleanor E. Maccoby and Karl W. Konrad

The study reported here is concerned with the development of one aspect of skill in focusing attention: namely, the selection of one auditory message when two are simultaneously present. Selective listening has been fairly extensively studied in adults, but little has been done to trace the development of this process through childhood, nor to explore the conditions which may underly progressive changes with age in selective performance. The present study compares age levels (kindergarten through fourth grade) with respect to the effects of (1) practice, (2) binaural versus dichotic presentation of stimulus words, and (3) number of syllables in stimulus words, on the accuracy of selective listening.

Since this research takes the work of Broadbent as a point of departure, we will first present a few of the major elements of his theory, and then consider how these may be applied to developmental processes. Broadbent holds that the human organism has limited, though great, capacity for handling information in a given time. Up to the point where his capacity is reached, an individual can "divide" attention. Broadbent's studies have shown that the ability to handle more than one message at a time is a function of the amount of information in both. Whenever the amount of information exceeds the individual's capacity, he must select only part of the available information. Broadbent holds that this selection is accomplished, to a large degree, centrally, through coding of incoming information into fairly broad categories for initial acceptance or rejection, with only the accepted materials undergoing further processing and storage.

Broadbent did not deal with the developmental history of these selective processes. While it has not been demonstrated that children are less efficient than adults at selective listening, we will assume for the moment that they are, and consider the reasons, both those deriving from Broadbent's theory and others, why this might be so.

A first possibility is that children cannot easily maintain a selective set. Selective listening requires that the listener establish a set to listen for a restricted class of material. It has been demonstrated in reaction time experiments that young children cannot "hold" a set as readily as

adults or older children. It is reasonable to suppose that a
similar failure to maintain set would interfere with selective
listening--the child might simply forget what class of stimuli
he was attempting to listen for.

A second possibility is that the child has not yet discriminated some of the cues or established some of the coding classes that would be efficient for filtering information.
If a child has not yet learned to localize sound or to distinguish voice qualities, for example, then he could not use
directional source of sound or the identity of the speaker as
a basis for selection of a wanted message. Beyond this,
there is a third possibility that even when a set of stimuli
can be appropriately discriminated and grouped, the young
child cannot use this differentiation as a basis for filtering
out a set of sounds. There may be, in listening, a phenomenon analogous to the "mediational deficiency" that is
evident when a child does not use verbal labels to mediate
in learning, even though the appropriate words are present
in his repertoire of responses.

Fourthly, there is the possibility that there are age-
correlated differences in language redundancy, both between
words and within words (phonemes, syllables). This sup-
position is not unreasonable, since older children have presumably overlearned the language to a greater extent. Redundancy could favorably affect selective listening performance in the following way: having heard only part of the input, the S is more likely to reconstruct the correct response,
since his partial information restricts the range of possibilities.

Finally, there is the possibility that there is an increase with age in the total amount of information that can
be "processed" in a given time. Older children then are
less likely to undergo an information overload and will be
under less necessity to adopt a selective strategy.

In the study to be reported below, a simple selective
listening situation was used, in which two speakers simultaneously spoke single words, with the S being instructed to
listen for and report one of them. The study is intended to
provide information relevant to the following questions:

1.   Is there an improvement in selective listening
with age?
2.   Is there an improvement with age in the ability

to make use of a simple, already-discriminated filter-cue?

3. Assuming that multisyllable words provide more redundancy than monosyllabic words, is there an increase with age in the advantage this redundancy provides in selective listening?

4. Is there any indication of greater lapse of set among younger than other subjects?

METHOD

Subjects

Our Ss were 96 children from an upper-middle-class elementary school. Thirty-two were taken from each of three grades, kindergarten, second grade, and fourth grade. The mean age of these groups was respectively 5.8, 7.8, and 9.9 years. The Ss in each grade were equally divided as to sex. The Ss were selected randomly from the lists of children whose parents gave permission for their participation in the research. In the second and fourth grades, where scores on the California Test of Mental Maturity were available, the lists were first stratified by ability level before random selection, so that proportional representation of all the ability levels occurring in the original list was obtained. Neither children with hearing difficulties nor those with severe speech handicaps were included.

Design

All Ss listened twice to 23 pairs of words spoken simultaneously by two speakers. Monosyllabic words and multisyllabic words were alternated through the list. In one run through the list, the S was instructed to repeat the words spoken by the male voice; in the other, the words spoken by the female voice. In one run through the list, the voices of both speakers came to both ears--this will be called the "mixed" condition. In the other, the voices were separated, one coming to each ear through earphones designed for dichotic listening (the "split" condition). In the split condition, all of the male words came to one ear, and all the female words to the other ear. Which ear received which condition was randomized across Ss. The Ss were assigned at random to the following groups: (1) mixed presentation with set for male voice, followed by split presentation with set for female voice; (2) mixed with female voice followed by split with male voice; (3) split with male voice followed by mixed with female voice; and (4) split with female voice followed by mixed with male voice. In each grade, four boys and four girls were assigned to each of these conditions.

Procedure
   The Ss were tested in a research trailer equipped with
acoustic tile and located in such a way as to provide a considerable degree of shielding from normal school noises.
The S was seated at a table opposite to E and shown headphones and a tape recorder, with the explanation that the
tape recorder would play words through the earphones. The
earphones were adjusted to the S's head. The E said, "Now
you're going to hear a woman's voice saying some words.
I want you to tell me, after every word, what she says."
The S heard a woman saying a list of five words at 3-second
intervals. The S repeated the words back. The E said,
"Now you're going to hear a man's voice saying some words.
I want you to tell me, after every word, what he says."
After S repeated them back correctly, E said, "Now you're
going to hear something different--a man and a woman's
voice together, each saying different words. Now I want
you to tell me what the man (woman) says, and if you're
not sure, I want you to guess, O.K.?" The E then set the
apparatus for split (mixed) presentation, repeated the instructions and commenced the first run.

   Then S heard 23 pairs of words, one of the words in
each pair spoken by the woman's voice and the other spoken
simultaneously by the man's voice, with the stimulus pairs
being presented at three-second intervals. The voices were
the same as those used during the practice session. As the
S gave his responses, it was not indicated to him whether or
not he was correct. Instead, E interjected at random intervals, "That's fine," "Good," "O.K." The E recorded the
S's responses on a prepared sheet. In the case of nonsense
responses (i.e., nonwords), E attempted to record the phonetic spelling of the response.

   The words the Ss heard were selected from first
grade readers. Pre-testing indicated that the words were
familiar to children of the age levels included in the experiment. There were eleven pairs of one-syllable words, ten
pairs of two-syllable words and two pairs of three-syllable
words. Within a pair, the words were matched for number
of syllables (and thus roughly for time of articulation). The
two voices were equated for loudness on the basis of judgments by a group of adult judges.

After the first run, the S̲ was told, "Good, you did well.   Now we're going to listen to the same words again, but this time I want you to tell me what the woman (man) says.   And if you're not sure, I want you to guess.   O. K. ?" The E̲ adjusted the apparatus for mixed (split) presentation, repeated the instructions and began the second run.   The second presentation of the stimulus was identical in every respect other than method of delivery (split- mixed) and instructional set (man- woman).

RESULTS

Figure 1 shows the mean number of words correctly reported, by age and method of presentation.   A response was scored correct when the S̲ repeated the word spoken by the voice he had been instructed to listen for.   Correct second guesses were permitted as correct- - although this situation rarely or never occurred for most S̲s.

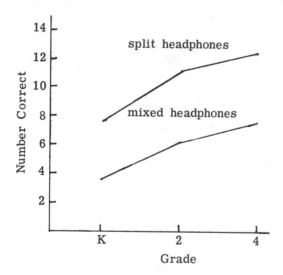

Fig. 1.   Selective listening with split and mixed headphones, by grade level, mean number correct.

The task was fairly difficult: taking all ages and ex- perimental conditions together, the S̲s reported correctly only about one- third of the words they were instructed to listen for.   Variances were quite homogeneous among the different age groups and experimental conditions, and it was therefore not considered necessary to transform scores. A three-way analysis of variance (split-mix X grade X sex of $\underline{S}$) shows that there is a clear improvement of performance with age ($\underline{F}$ = 19.96; $\underline{df}$ = 2, 90; $\underline{p}$ < .001), and for all ages combined the performance was significantly better under the split condition of presentation ($\underline{F}$ = 61.97; $\underline{df}$ = 1, 90; $\underline{p}$ < .001).

That this improvement was selective in some sense is indicated by the fact that while correct reports of the word which the $\underline{S}$ was instructed to repeat increased with age, the number of "intrusive errors" (reports of words spoken by the other voice) decreased with age. Mean intrusive errors for split and mixed conditions combined were 2.80, 2.25 and 1.00 for the kindergarten, second, and fourth grades, respectively. A three-way analysis of variance of intrusive errors (mix-split X grade X sex of $\underline{S}$) yields an $\underline{F}$ of 12.3 for the grade effect ($\underline{df}$ = 2, 90; $\underline{p}$ < .001).

For all ages, performance (number correct) improved through a run and from the first to the second run. The 23 pairs of words were divided into three blocks--the first eight pairs, the second seven, and the last eight. Each $\underline{S}$ received a score for the proportion of items in each block correctly reported. (The scores were computed as proportions because of the difference in number of items from block to block.) Table 1 shows improvement through successive blocks of items in a single run, and from run 1 to run 2, at each of the three age levels studied. The $\underline{F}$ for blocks is 82 ($\underline{df}$ = 2, 186; $\underline{p}$ < .001), for runs is 4.7 ($\underline{df}$ = 1, 93; $\underline{p}$ < .05).

TABLE 1

MEAN PERCENTAGE CORRECT IN SUCCESSIVE BLOCKS OF ITEMS AND SUCCESSIVE RUNS, BY GRADE LEVEL. SPLIT AND MIXED PRESENTATIONS COMBINED
($\underline{N}$ = 32 FOR EACH MEAN)

	Block 1 (Items 1-8)	Block 2 (Items 9-15)	Block 3 (Items 16-23)
Kindergarten			
First run	12.8	23.6	29.6
Second run	21.0	26.5	34.3

TABLE 1 (cont'd.)

MEAN PERCENTAGE CORRECT IN SUCCESSIVE BLOCKS OF
ITEMS AND SUCCESSIVE RUNS, BY GRADE LEVEL. SPLIT
AND MIXED PRESENTATIONS COMBINED
($\underline{N}$ = 32 FOR EACH MEAN)

	Block 1 (Items 1-8)	Block 2 (Items 9-15)	Block 3 (Items 16-23)
Second grade			
First run	26.1	37.6	41.4
Second run	29.9	45.4	49.6
Fourth grade			
First run	26.8	45.1	52.8
Second run	34.7	50.6	53.9

A three-way analysis of variance (number of syllables X grade X sex of voice) shows that for all grades combined the Ss made more correct responses when listening to multi-syllabic than to monosyllabic words (see Table 2). The $\underline{F}$ ratio is 133, which for $\underline{df}$ of 1 and 93 yields a $\underline{p} < .001$. The older the child, the greater the advantage derived from increased length of words. There is a significant interaction of grade by number of syllables ($\underline{F}$ = 9.99, $\underline{df}$ 2, 93; $\underline{p} < .001$). The advantage of longer words was greater for one of the speakers than the other ($\underline{F}$ = 73; $\underline{df}$ = 1, 93; p < .001). But for both speakers, it was true that accuracy of reporting monosyllabic words improved from kindergarten to grade two and then levelled off, while performance on longer words continued to improve between the second and fourth grade.

TABLE 2

MEAN PERCENTAGE CORRECT, MONOSYLLABIC VERSUS
MULTISYLLABIC WORDS BY GRADE LEVELS. SPLIT
AND MIXED PRESENTATIONS COMBINED
($\underline{N}$ = 32 AT EACH GRADE LEVEL)

	Monosyllabic words	Multisyllabic words
Kindergarten	20.2	28.6
Second grade	32.9	43.1
Fourth grade	33.4	53.1

An analysis of errors (other than intrusive errors) revealed a qualitative change with age in the nature of the Ss'
misreports. Frequently, when unable to report correctly the
word spoken by either speaker, the S made no response.
But in other instances, the S responded with a nonsense word,
or with a word that occurs in English but which was not one
of the stimulus words. These error responses were sometimes composed of sound elements taken from the two stimulus words. These "composite errors" were scored as either
composite words or composite nonsense. For example, if
one stimulus word was down and the other wish, and the S
reported that he heard dish, the response was scored as a
composite word, while with the stimulus pair squirrel and
turtle, if the S reported squirtle the responses were scored
as composite nonsense. Table 3 shows that the absolute frequency of these types of errors was not very great at any of
the three age levels, but there are some significant age
trends.

TABLE 3

MEAN COMPOSITE WORD ERRORS AND COMPOSITE
NONSENSE ERRORS BY GRADE LEVEL. SPLIT AND MIXED
CONDITIONS OF PRESENTATION COMBINED
($\underline{N}$ = 32 AT EACH GRADE LEVEL)

	Composite word errors		Composite nonsense errors	
	Mean No.	Mean % of Total errors	Mean No.	Mean % of Total errors
Kindergarten	1.34	8.0	1.52	8.3
Second Grade	1.53	11.1	.72	4.8
Fourth Grade	1.56	12.6	.27	2.0

A three-way analysis of variance (grade X sex of subject X
split-mix) of the proportion of composite nonsense errors
shows that younger children are considerably more likely to
give a nonsense word ($\underline{F}$ = 15.7; $\underline{df}$ = 2, 90; $\underline{p}$ < .001).

DISCUSSION

Skill in selective listening in the situation employed
in this study does increase with age, at least through the
range of ages found in kindergarten through the fourth grade.

What processes underly this change?   One possibility is that
the younger children could not easily discriminate between
the male and female voices, and hence could not listen selectively on *he basis of sex of speaker's voice as a cue. A
sub-sample of the kindergarten children used for the main
study were given a discrimination test, and proved to be
able to distinguish the male from the female voice almost
without error when these were presented separately.   There
must be other factors, therefore, which produce the difficulty
of the younger children with selective listening.

        Did the younger children more often lapse in their
selective set, either as momentary fluctuations or as a progressive loss through the run?   As regards momentary fluctuations of set, we have no relevant evidence. With respect
to a progressive loss of set through a run: no such loss is
apparent in the data.   For all grades, the rate of correct
responses improved through any one run, and at about the
same rate for all grades.   And an analysis of intrusive errors over the course of a run (data not presented) does not
support the hypothesis that intrusive errors increased more
through a run for younger than older subjects.

        The improvement in performance that occurred through
the course of a run cannot be unequivocally labeled "practice
effects," since we have no independent information about the
homogeneity of item difficulty through the list, and item
order was not varied in the experiment.   By chance, the
more difficult items could have been placed toward the beginning of the list.   However, the improvement from run 1 to
run 2 may be called a practice effect, since the items are
the same for the two runs.   This practice effect may reflect
improvements in distinguishing the voice qualities of the two
voices in noise, or learning of some other aspect of the task
such as the range of the verbal stimuli being used.

        Are the younger children handicapped in selective lis-
tening because they cannot use a simple, available cue for
"filtering?"   In the split condition, we gave all Ss the opportunity to use "earedness" as a filtering cue for selecting the
correct input.   By earedness we mean that a given voice was
always associated with a single ear of stimulation.   In a preliminary test, we had determined that children of kindergarten
age can readily discriminate which ear is being stimulated
when a series of sounds is presented in random alteration to
the separate ears.   Hence earedness is available as a cue to
even the youngest Ss in this study.   We expected a grade by

split- mix interaction, but none was found; split presentation did improve performance, but about equally so at all age levels. This fact suggests either (a) that children at all the ages tested make the same use of the earedness cue, or (b) that the peripheral sound- masking inherent in our mixed condition tended to hurt performance uniformly across grade levels. Of course, some combination of these factors across ages may have produced the results.

If we assume that language becomes steadily more over- learned with age, there should be a steady improvement with age in word recognition under noisy listening conditions, until such time as a ceiling on over- learning is reached. In addition, it is reasonable to expect that words with fewer elements will reach a ceiling of over- learning before words with more elements. In the present study, performance on monosyllabic words levels off between the second and fourth grades, while performance on multisyllabic words continues to increase through the fourth grade. These findings suggest that older children's superior performance in selective listening arises at least in part from their greater familiarity with the redundancies in the material to be selected. The design of the present study does not yield information concerning whether knowledge of the linguistic probabilities in the material to be excluded makes an independent contribution to the accuracy of listening. This is an interesting problem for further research.

SELECTED BIBLIOGRAPHY

Note: This bibliography includes a small number of items useful to the student of elementary school listening as well as complete bibliographical entries for all the items from which material has been excerpted for use in this book.

Barbe, Walter M. and Robert M. Myers. "Developing Listening Ability in Children." Elementary English 31:82-84, 1954.

Beery, Althea. "Experiences in Listening." Elementary English 28:130-32, 1951.

Beery, Althea. "Listening Activities in the Elementary School." Elementary English Review 23:69-79, 1946.

Bower (see Fawcett)

Brassard, Mary Butler. Listening and Reading Comprehension in Intermediate Grades. Doctoral dissertation. Boston University, 1968. Abstract: Dissertation Abstracts 30:921A-22A, 1969.

Brown-Carlsen Listening Comprehension Test. New York: Harcourt, Brace & World, 1955.

Canfield, George Robert. "Approaches to Listening Improvement." Elementary English 35:525-28, 1958.

Canfield, George Robert. A Study of the Effects of Two Types of Instruction on the Listening Comprehension of Fifth Grade Children. Doctoral dissertation. Syracuse, N. Y.: Syracuse University, 1960. Abstract: Dissertation Abstracts 21:2622, 1961.

Cashman, Mildred Berwick. "Channel L-I-S-T-E-N." Education 82:50-52, 1961.

Crink, Cedric L. and Arline Buntley. "Learn to Listen."

Grade Teacher 72(3):51+, 1955.

Duker, Sam. "Goals of Teaching Listening Skills in the Elementary School." Elementary English 38:170-74, 1961.

Duker, Sam. "How Listening Can Be Taught." Instructor 64(9):35+, May 1955.

Duker, Sam. "Listening" in Encyclopedia of Educational Research, 4th ed. (Edited by Robert L. Ebel.) New York: Macmillan, 1969.

Duker, Sam. Listening Bibliography. 2d ed. Metuchen, N. J.: Scarecrow Press, 1968.

Duker, Sam. Listening: Readings. Metuchen, N. J.: Scarecrow Press, 1966.

Duker, Sam. "Teacher of Elementary Science and Listening." Science Education 42:341-44, 1958.

Durrell, Donald D. Durrell Listening-Reading Series, Advanced Level. New York: Harcourt, Brace & World, 1969.

Durrell, Donald D. and Mary B. Brassard. Durrell Listening-Reading Series, Intermediate Level. New York: Harcourt, Brace & World, 1969.

Durrell, Donald D. and Mary T. Hayes. Durrell Listening-Reading Series, Primary Level. New York: Harcourt, Brace & World, 1969.

Durrell, Donald D. "Listening Comprehension Versus Reading Comprehension." Journal of Reading 12:455-60, March 1969.

Early, Margaret J. "Developing Effective Listening Skills." in Frontiers of Elementary Education V. Syracuse, N. Y.: School of Education, Syracuse University, 1958, p. 78-88.

Educational Testing Service. Cooperative Primary Tests: Listening. Princeton, N. J.: E.T.S., 1965.

Educational Testing Service. Sequential Tests of Educational

Progress (STEP): Listening. Princeton, N. J.:
E. T. S., 1956.

Evertts, Eldonna L. An Investigation of the Structure of
Children's Oral Language Compared with Silent Reading, Oral Reading, and Listening Comprehension.
Doctoral dissertation. Bloomington: Indiana University, 1961. Abstract: Dissertation Abstracts 22:3038,
1962.

Farrow, Vern Leslie. An Experimental Study of Listening
Attention at the Fourth, Fifth, and Sixth Grade. Doctoral dissertation. Eugene: University of Oregon,
1963. Abstract: Dissertation Abstracts 24:3146,
1964.

Fawcett, Annabel Elizabeth. The Effect of Training in Listening upon the Listening Skills of Intermediate Grade
Children. Doctoral dissertation. Pittsburgh: University of Pittsburgh, 1963. Abstract: Dissertation
Abstracts 25:7108-09, 1965.

Furness, Edna Lue. "Proportion, Purpose, and Process in
Listening." Educational Administration and Supervision 44:237-42, 1958.

Graham, Justyn Lair. The Teaching of Listening Skills
Through Music Lessons in Fourth and Fifth Grade
Classrooms. Doctoral dissertation. Greeley:
Colorado State College, 1965. Abstract: Dissertation
Abstracts 26:7114-15, 1966.

Hall, Robert Oscar. An Exploratory Study of Listening of
Fifth Grade Pupils. Doctoral dissertation. Los
Angeles: University of Southern California, 1954.

Hampleman, Richard Samuel. Comparison of Listening and
Reading Comprehension Ability of Fourth and Sixth
Grade Pupils. Doctoral dissertation. Bloomington:
Indiana University, 1955. Abstract: Dissertation
Abstracts 15:1757-58, 1955.

Hancock, Jewell Hazel Thompson. The Effect of Listening
and Discussion on Social Values Held by Sixth-Grade
Children. Doctoral dissertation. Boulder: University of Colorado, 1960. Abstract: Dissertation Abstracts 21:3377, 1961.

Harvey, John C. Study of the Durrell-Sullivan Reading Capacity Test as a Measure of Intelligence. Master's thesis. Sacramento, Cal.: Sacramento State College, 1961.

Hayes, Mary Therese. Construction and Evaluation of Comparable Measures of English Language Comprehension in Reading and Listening. Doctoral dissertation. Boston: Boston University, 1958. Abstract: Dissertation Abstracts 18:1721-22, 1958.

Hollingsworth, Paul M. "So They Listened: The Effects of a Listening Program." Journal of Communication 15:14-16, 1965.

Hollow, Kevin, Sister M. An Experimental Study of Listening Comprehension at the Intermediate Grade Level. Doctoral dissertation. New York: Fordham University, 1955.

Jackson, Ann Elizabeth. An Investigation of the Relationship Between Listening and Selected Variables in Grade Four, Five, and Six. Doctoral dissertation. Tempe: Arizona State University, 1966. Abstract: Dissertation Abstracts 27:53A, 1966.

Kellogg, Ralph E. A Study of the Effect of a First Grade Listening Instructional Program Upon Achievement in Listening and Reading. Doctoral dissertation. Los Angeles: University of California, Los Angeles, 1967. Abstract: Dissertation Abstracts 28:395A, 1967.

Laurent, Marie-Jeanne. The Construction and Evaluation of a Listening Curriculum for Grades 5 and 6. Doctoral dissertation. Boston: Boston University, 1963. Abstract: Dissertation Abstracts 27:4167A-68A, 1967.

Lewis, Maurice S. The Construction of a Diagnostic Test of Listening Comprehension for Grades 4, 5, and 6. Doctoral field study. Greeley: Colorado State College of Education, 1954.

Lewis, Maurice S. The Effect of Training in Listening for Certain Purposes upon Reading for Those Same Purposes. Doctoral field study. Greeley: Colorado State College of Education, 1952.

Lewis, Thomas R. and Ralph G. Nichols. Speaking and Listening. Dubuque, Iowa: Wm. C. Brown, 1965.

Los Angeles City Schools, Division of Instructional Services, Curriculum Branch. Research Related to Development of Listening Skills. Instructional Bulletin No. EC-76. Los Angeles, 1964.

Lundsteen, Sara W. Teaching Ability in Critical Listening in the Fifth and Sixth Grades. Doctoral dissertation. Berkeley: University of California, 1963. Abstract: Dissertation Abstracts 24:5247, 1964.

Maccoby, Eleanor E. and Karl W. Konrad. "Age Trends in Selective Listening." Journal of Experimental Child Psychology 3:113-22, 1966.

Nichols, Ralph G. Factors Accounting for Difference in Comprehension of Materials Presented Orally in the Classroom. Doctoral dissertation. Iowa City: State University of Iowa, 1948.

Nichols, Ralph G. and Leonard A. Stevens. Are You Listening? New York: McGraw-Hill, 1957.

Niles, Doris. "Teaching Listening in the Fundamentals Course." Speech Teacher 6:300-04, 1957.

Pratt, Lloyd Edward. The Experimental Evaluation of a Program for the Improvement of Listening in the Elementary School. Doctoral dissertation. Iowa City: State University of Iowa, 1953. Abstract: Dissertation Abstracts 13:1118-19, 1953.

Rankin, Paul Tory. The Measurement of the Ability to Understand Spoken Language. Doctoral dissertation. Ann Arbor: University of Michigan, 1926. Abstract: Dissertation Abstracts 12:847, 1952.

Reasoner, Charles F. The Development of a Series of Television Scripts Dealing with the Language Arts Practices in Elementary School Classrooms. Doctoral dissertation. New York: Teachers College, Columbia

University, 1961.

Russell, David H. "A Conspectus of Recent Research on Listening Abilities." Elementary English 41:262- 67, 1964.

Russell, David H. and Elizabeth F. Russell. Listening Aids Through the Grades - One Hundred Ninety Listening Activities. New York: Teachers College, Columbia University, Bureau of Publications, 1959.

Smith, Thomas Wood. Auding and Reading Skills as Sources of Cultural Bias in the Davis- Eells Games and California Test of Mental Maturity. Doctoral dissertation. Los Angeles: University of Southern California, 1956.

Stodola, Quentin, Donald F. Schwartz, and Ralph H. Kolstoe. Administering a Listening Comprehension Test Through Use of Teacher- Readers, Sound Film and Tape Recorders. Fargo: North Dakota State University, 1962.

Vineyard, Edwin E. and Robert B. Bailey. "Interrelationships of Reading Ability, Listening Skill, Intelligence, and Scholastic Achievement." Journal of Developmental Reading 3:174- 78, 1960.

Wagner, Guy, Max Hosier, and Mildred Blackman. Listening Games -- Building Listening Skills with Instructional Games. Darien, Conn.: Teachers' Publishing Corporation, 1962.

Wilt, Miriam E. A Study of Teacher Awareness of Listening as a Factor in Elementary Education. Doctoral dissertation. State College: Pennsylvania State College, 1949.

Wynn, Dale Richard. "Children Should Be Seen and Not Heard." New York State Education 41:353- 56, 1954

NAME INDEX

Anderson, Harold A. 20, 314
Anderson, Harold M. 327

Bailey, Robert B. 355-358, 374
Baldauf, Robert J. 314, 327
Barbe, Walter B. 24, 31-33, 369
Bean, C. H. 320, 327
Beery, Althea 24, 44-46, 54, 60-65, 158, 319, 327, 369
Betts, Emmet A. 179, 180
Blackman, Mildred 374
Bowden, Florence 173, 180
Bower (See Fawcett)
Brassard, Mary B. 250, 251, 256, 257-292, 369, 370
Broadbent, Donald E. 342
Brown, James I. 260
Brown, Kenneth L. 21, 228, 229-246
Buntley, Arline 25, 46-50, 369
Buros, Oscar K. 259, 260, 261

Caffrey, John 320, 327
Canfield, G. Robert 86-95, 319, 327, 369
Carlsen, G. Robert 260
Cashman, Mildred B. 25, 50-53, 369
Chase, Stuart 213
Clark, Willis W. 327, 328
Cleland, Donald L. 327
Crabbs, Lelah M. 177, 180
Crink, Cedric L. 25, 46-50, 369

Dale, Edgar 265
Dawson, Mildred A. 55, 174, 175, 180
Dow, Clyde W. 55
Duker, Sam 58, 59, 66-71, 100-105, 370
Durrell, Donald D. 21, 25, 249, 251-257, 261, 293 370

Early, Margaret J. 24, 34-44, 370
Eicholz, Gerhard 265
Evertts, Eldonna L. 304, 308, 371

Farrow, Vern L. 97-99, 371
Fawcett, Annabel E. 158-159, 171-180, 371
Fitzgerald, James A. 265
Furness, Edna L. 25, 53-57, 371

Gates, Arthur W. 279
Graham, Justyn L. 305, 333-341, 371
Green, Gladys 265

Hall, Robert O. 371
Hampleman, Richard S. 304, 305-308, 327, 371
Hancock, Jewell H. 328-333, 371
Harvey, John C. 250, 293-303, 372
Hatfield, W. Wilbur 54
Hayes, Mary T. 256, 257, 260, 261, 370, 372

375

SUBJECT INDEX

Active process, L as 46

Bibliography on teaching L as 369-374

Climate of L 38, 61
Communication
   Reciprocal nature of 60
   Obstacles to 45
Concepts about L 24, 32, 57
Content analysis of language arts textbooks 229-246
Correlations between L and variables (See Relationship between L and variables.)

Definition of L 89

Evaluation of L 112, 167-168 (See also Tests, L)
   Diagnosis of L ability 33
   Existing L tests, review of 257-260
   Studies using measures of L, review of 314-322
   Test administration 343-354
      Advantages of various modes of 353-354
      Elementary school, in 349-351
      High school, in 345-347
      Junior high school, in 348-349
      Sound film, by 343-354
      Tape recording, by 343-354
      Teacher-reader, by 343-354
      Trained teacher-reader, by 343-354
   Test construction
      Listening and Reading Tests 257-293
         Answer form, developing 282-85
         Categories, selection of 266
         Criteria for 261-262
         Planning of 261-262
         Paragraph Comprehension measures 279-292
            Criteria for 280
            Sources of material for 280
         Review of previous literature 249-260

377